KU-539-493

LEEDS POl

To

38

ne

LEEDS BECKETT UNIVERSITY

DISCARDED

71 0147931

ALSO BY LEON TROTSKY
(Published in English)

THE YOUNG LENIN

THE YOUNG LENIN
by Leon Trotsky

Translated from the Russian by
MAX EASTMAN

Edited and Annotated by
MAURICE FRIEDBERG

David and Charles

ISBN 0 7153 5790 5

Translation and Foreword Copyright © 1972
by Doubleday & Company, Inc.
Introduction Copyright © 1972
by Yvette Szekely Eastman as Executrix
of the Estate of Max Eastman
All Rights Reserved

LEEDS POLYTECHNIC

189238

S V

32699

12 JUN 1973

947.0841092 LEN

First published in Great Britain
by David & Charles (Publishers) Limited
Newton Abbot Devon
Printed by Lewis Reprints Tonbridge Kent

INTRODUCTION

THE MANUSCRIPT of this book disappeared from my files some-
time in the 1930s. As there had been raids and rumors of raids
by the Stalinists on Trotsky's files and archives in Europe, I assumed that this was part of the same operation, and after a
gloomy search, I said good-by to Trotsky's *Lenin* for good. By
what odd circumstance it came back into my possession thirty
years later and is here presented, I will explain.

First I want to tell how I came to be chosen for the task of
translating this extraordinary document. I spent the two years—
or rather the year and nine months—from September 1922 to
June 1924 in Soviet Russia, and, sustained by a feeling that I was
traveling hand in hand with history, I learned the Russian language. I had defended the Bolsheviks as a socialist editor in
America, and these two facts gave me a good introduction to the
leaders of the party in Moscow. I became well enough acquainted with Trotsky to suggest that he tell me his life story in
leisure moments and let me write his biography.

His leisure moments and my patience both gave out when the
book was half done, and it was published as *Leon Trotsky—
The Portrait of a Youth*. One of its results was to establish a personal friendship between Trotsky and me, notwithstanding my
heretical and sinful opinion that Marx's philosophy of dialectical
materialism is nothing but a grandiose exercise in wishful thinking. We got along in spite of this obstacle, and I became Trotsky's chief English translator. I translated the three volumes of
his *History of the Russian Revolution*, a book called *The Revolution Betrayed*, and a number of articles for the American press
that were his chief source of income after his expulsion from
Stalin's Russia in 1929.

Indeed, from 1929 to 1933 I functioned unofficially as Trotsky's
literary agent, selling his current articles to American publications
that paid him some very handsome prices. Our correspondence

during that period amounts to almost a hundred letters back and forth. There was no contract between us, but I was armed with an authorization to make without consulting him any editorial changes demanded by "the technique of American journalism" or by "the digestion of the American brain."

Trotsky had in mind a book about Lenin for a long time. Indeed, in a letter of January 1929 telling me of the contract he had signed for his famous history of the revolution, he added:

"By next fall I hope to finish another book: *Lenin and the Epigones*. This will be a sort of prolongation of the *History*. I am going to square accounts with a number of people. A little polemic with you about Marxism will be necessary. There will be theoretical chapters in the book, historical, psychological, personal characterizations, plenty of polemic. . . ."

After his world-famous career as a warrior and political leader was so rudely smashed and erased from Russian history, Trotsky turned to the job of earning his living as a writer with unquenched zeal and energy. Plans for books and articles flowed out of him, enough to fill a dozen young lives. Here is an example:

"In a few words I want to let you know about a new book I am writing in the interval between two volumes of *The History of the Russian Revolution*. The book will perhaps be called 'They or We' or 'We and They' and will include a whole series of political portraits: representatives of bourgeois and petit-bourgeois conservatism on the one hand, proletarian revolutionaries on the other. For instance: Hoover and Wilson from the Americans; Clemenceau, Poincaré, Barthou, and certain other Frenchmen. From the English: Baldwin, Lloyd-George, Churchill, MacDonald, and the Labourites in general. From the Italians I would take Count Sforza, Giolitti, and the old man Cavour. Of the revolutionaries: Marx, Engels, Lenin, Luxemburg, Liebknecht, Vorovsky, Rakovsky. Probably Krassin as a transitional type. I've been working on this book throughout the past month. From that, you can see that it hasn't yet gotten very far forward, but its general physiognomy is already clear to me. . . . Its character will be determined by a most serious study of all these figures in the context of the political conditions surrounding them, etc. . . . When will this book be ready? That depends on how soon I must deliver the second volume of my history of the revolution. If the second volume is postponed for about eight months I might finish the book of portraits in the next four months."

It was well along in the thirties that this flood of projected miracles subsided enough to let him undertake the long-premeditated *Lenin*. I have a letter from him dated November 2, 1934, which says: "I haven't yet gone beyond Lenin's youth," and adds, "How about publishing two volumes: Volume I— Lenin's Youth—until, say 1905, and Volume II—from 1905 to 1924? This would give me an opportunity to do the theoretical part more thoroughly. I would deliver the first volume—about 350 pages—by next January 1. What is your opinion?"

My opinion on this question was soon outdated by financial pressure, which impelled Trotsky to postpone the second part of the Lenin and first write a brief life of Stalin.

I had finished translating the first twelve chapters of the Lenin and filed them in my little barn-study at Croton-on-Hudson; one day I went to make some small correction in the text and found it was missing. The place it had occupied was empty. There had been some question between Harper and Doubleday as to which one was to publish it, since Harper was publishing the Stalin. Perhaps a copy of the manuscript was in the hands of one publisher or the other—but neither one had it. Nor did Maxim Lieber, a professional agent who had for a couple of years taken my place in marketing Trotsky's writings.

To those who remember the diabolical intricacy and thoroughness of the efforts directed by Stalin to defeat the aims and frustrate the purposes and ultimately bring to a bloody end the life itself of Leon Trotsky, it will be no surprise that, after a glum search, I gave up hope of ever retrieving this unique work. It had been stolen and destroyed, I concluded, by Trotsky's ingenious and implacable enemies.

One evening twenty years later, I happened to appear on a national radio broadcast—a debate, I think, on some phase of the situation in Soviet Russia. In the course of my argument, as an illustration of the manner in which Trotsky's point of view had been falsified and misrepresented, I mentioned this mysterious disappearance of my translation of his *Lenin* and my suspicion about it. A day or two later I received from the Houghton Library of Harvard University a letter telling me that they had a copy of my translation of the story of Lenin's youth.

How it had got there no one seemed to know. Was it restored to posterity by some Stalinist with an uneasy conscience or a lingering relic of his youthful respect for history? (In response to a recent request for the latest information as to how and from where it came to Harvard, I received the following answer from Mr. W. H. Bond, the Curator of the Houghton Library: "The official record of the typescript is somewhat more mysterious than usual: it is recorded as a 'deposit' but the depositor is not named. . . .")

Again the project was set aside, but not forgotten, until February 1963, when, at my request, a copy was made of the typescript by the Houghton Library. This copy of my translation, having found its way home after twenty-five years, I was content to let rest. I was absorbed in writing my autobiography until January 1968, when I gave the twelve translated chapters to my friend and agent, Florence Crowther, and suggested that some publisher might be interested in it.

Without any help or clues from my hazy, skipping memory, Mrs. Crowther considered the list of top publishers and chose to submit it first to Samuel S. Vaughan of Doubleday for consideration. Mr. Vaughan, upon opening a manuscript to a title page that said simply

THE YOUNG LENIN
by
LEON TROTSKY
Translated by Max Eastman

immediately called Mrs. Crowther and asked where this manuscript had been. Mrs. Crowther said frankly that it had been in my desk. Sam Vaughan read the manuscript, liked what he read, and before leaving for Europe, asked Florence and a Doubleday editor, Walter Bradbury, if they would authenticate the manuscript and check into its background.

Bradbury wrote Vaughan in London and me in Barbados, saying that Doubleday not only had reason to be interested in the manuscript, they already had a contract for its publication: "A contract dated December 21, 1933, between Leon Trotsky and Doubleday & Company gave Doubleday world book rights in the English language to Trotsky's *Lenin*. . . . The book was to be published in the United States and Canada by Doubleday."

"The original contract," Bradbury noted, was "still in effect."

So, on a lovely spring morning in 1968, Florence Crowther, my wife Yvette, and I gathered with Ken McCormick, Editor-in-Chief at Doubleday, and other editors, on the eighth floor of their Park Avenue offices, each of us smiling, but for different reasons. The Doubleday people were smiling because they had been offered an unpublished Trotsky manuscript that they had owned for thirty-five years but had almost forgotten (well, for the past quarter of a century, anyway . . .), the three of us were smiling mock-rueful smiles—Florence because she hadn't sold a book, I because Doubleday had already paid me (a long time ago) for translating the twelve chapters, and my wife because she was reading a Charlie Brown card stuck on the wall over a secretary's desk that said: MY LATEST PHILOSOPHY IS I ONLY DREAD ONE DAY AT A TIME.

But Sam Vaughan had proposed that the company pay me an additional sum for translating the last three chapters—chapters 13, 14, and 15, which would complete the book—and for writing an introduction.

The original Russian typescript of the last three chapters was still missing, and Sam agreed to start a search for a French edition published during the 1930s in Paris, which had contained them. Since none of us had the vaguest idea where the Russian originals could be found, I planned to translate from French to English.

When Doubleday's new letter of agreement arrived to supplement the old contract, I signed and returned it but called attention to the fact that the date of my finally fulfilling the contract would depend on their finding the French edition. Sam wrote back, noting dryly: ". . . it is quite clear that we will have to provide you with the missing chapters before you can translate them—and that this will have some effect on the delivery date."

While waiting, I turned my attention to this introduction. When I reached a point where I needed to refer to some cor-

respondence, I asked my wife to find a folder in my files marked
"Letters 1957." It wasn't there, although folders for the year before and after were. She went up to an atticlike passageway we
have, one wall lined with bookshelves holding hundreds of bulg-
ing file folders lying on their sides. With some dismay, she
wondered where to begin looking—which folder to pick up first.
Sighing, she picked up one of the file guide-cards lying on the
nearest shelf. On the card was written in ink in my hand:
"TROTSKY'S LENIN—RUSSIAN TEXT (finished)." The folder,
containing thirty-three oversized pages in Russian, was lightly
marked in pencil: *Chapters XIII, XIV, XV.* Scribbled on the face
of the folder was "Untranslated."

MAX EASTMAN

Contents

EDITOR'S FOREWORD

ONE OF THE founders of the Soviet state, its first Commissar for Foreign Affairs, and the organizer of its army, Leon Trotsky became, only twelve years later, a homeless exile, banished from his homeland by a rival who, though intellectually indubitably his inferior, proved more skillful at political maneuvering.

Though once Lenin's political opponent, Trotsky later became one of his most trusted and certainly most effective associates. No doubt Trotsky felt deeply hurt by the savage attacks, both before and after his exile, of Stalin's propaganda, which spared no effort to portray Trotsky as an archvillain and hater of Lenin.

Trotsky's role as Lenin's biographer dates back many years; in fact, it antedates Lenin's death in 1924. Not surprisingly, many pages of Trotsky's writings in exile are devoted to Lenin, particularly of Trotsky's three-volume history of the Russian Revolution, which appeared in 1932–33. *The Young Lenin,* the long-lost account of Lenin's childhood, boyhood, and youth, written in the mid-1930s, is also, in a sense, a history of the Russian revolutionary movement. The thrust of Trotsky's portrayal of young Lenin and his family is to show Lenin's political evolution. The very cautious and moderate liberalism of the father is succeeded, in Trotsky's narrative, by the blind and suicidal revolutionary zeal of Lenin's brother Alexander. Gradually, Lenin evolves a "scientific," and therefore successful, blueprint for a revolution.

Trotsky's biography is not the work of a scholar; indeed, many pages of it are frankly nothing but conjecture and read like an old-fashioned *vie romanisée.* In relating his story, Trotsky is unswerving in his admiration for Lenin. Adulation for his hero is coupled with scorn and venom for his idol's critics. The book is often dogmatic and bristles with hatred for Lenin's ideological opponents, particularly those who seemed to doubt any of the basic premises of Marxism. Trotsky seems to me in places to despise objectivity and to ridicule those whose Marxist faith is so weak that it must be reinforced by reason. He is equally disdainful, in his own words, of "self-satisfied ignoramuses and well-read mediocrities." He has no patience for democratic "frills," which to him are a sham and an excuse for an unwillingness to serve the Communist cause honestly. None of this detracts at all from the value of the book. And, as if to compensate for what his biography fails to reveal about Lenin, Trotsky reveals much about himself and about the spirit of the movement they both created.

It is ironic and yet, in a way, fitting that Trotsky's biography of young Lenin, long presumed lost, should finally appear with the flood of Leniniana that gushed forth from the presses throughout the Soviet bloc in 1970, during the centennial observances of Lenin's birth. It is equally parodoxical, though perfectly consistent with the laws of Soviet censorship, that this book, an admiring account of Lenin's youth, will not be allowed to appear in the country where worship of Lenin is a state religion—only because its author was once excommunicated by the man who ultimately succeeded to Lenin's mantle. The fact that the myth of Stalin's goodness and infallibility was called into serious question by his heirs, particularly by Khrushchev, did not result in any basic reappraisal of Trotsky the man and revolutionary. Failure to lift, if only partly, the rigid anathema surrounding Trotsky's name is in itself a testimony to the superficiality of the much-heralded de-Stalinization of Soviet Russia in the nearly two decades since the dictator's death.

Born in Russia in 1879, Lev Davidovich Bronshtein, the man who became famous under the name of Leon Trotsky, died in 1940 in faraway Mexico, killed by an assassin. To orthodox Soviet Communists the death of Trotsky was a cause for none-too-concealed rejoicing: the Prince of Darkness, Stalin's archenemy, the central evildoer of Soviet history, had at long last met his end. That their glee was somewhat premature has been demonstrated in recent years. At a time when millions of volumes of Stalin's turgid prose were being removed from the shelves of Soviet libraries, many of Trotsky's ideas, long thought to have been—to use his own famous phrase—relegated to the dustbin of history, were somewhat incongruously resurrected by the West's radical New Left and, if one is to believe Soviet sources, in Communist China.

The late Max Eastman left behind his uncompleted draft of the English translation of Trotsky's manuscript. It was decided that a revision of the Eastman manuscript was preferable to a new translation. The revisions and notes are mine.

MAURICE FRIEDBERG

Indiana University
Bloomington, Indiana

THE YOUNG LENIN

1

HOMELAND

AMID so much else, the revolution upset also the old administrative structure of the country. The *gubernias*—created in the reign of Catherine II,[1] and in the course of a century and a half so closely woven in with the political establishment, the mores, and the literature of the country as to become almost subdivisions of nature itself—disappeared. Simbirsk *gubernia,* in which the future Lenin passed his childhood and early youth, was part of the vast region united and dominated by the Volga, queen of Russian rivers.

Whoever is born on the Volga carries her image through life. The uniqueness and beauty of the river lie in the contrast of its shores: the right a high, mountainous barrier against Asia, the left a level plain sloping away to the endless east. Five hundred feet above the motionless mirror of the river rises the hill upon which Simbirsk,[2] the most backward and provincial of all the Volga capitals, spreads its wandering streets and green orchards. This slight elevation forms the watershed between two rivers, between the Volga and its tributary the Sviyaga. Although parallel for seventy miles, these two rivers flow—such is the caprice of the topography —in opposite directions, the Volga to the south, the Sviyaga to the north. At Simbirsk, moreover, the Sviyaga comes so near to the Volga that the city actually stretches over the right banks of both rivers.

At the time our tale begins, with the moving of the Ulyanov family to Simbirsk in 1869, the city was about two hundred and twenty years old. The Great Russians were stubbornly penetrating the rich middle reaches of the Volga, already occupied by the Chuvash, the Mordva, and the Tatars. They were seizing lands, driving the nomads eastward, and building wooden forts. In the same year that England achieved her "great rebellion" (1648), by order of the Moscow tsar Simbirsk was founded on the right bank of the Volga as an administrative center of the colonized region and as a military bulwark against the natives. This wide ring of colonizers, frontiersmen, and Cossacks was not only a mobile guard, but also a threat to the tsardom. For out here to the frontier fled the landlords' serfs, the miscreant soldiers and clerks—in short, everybody who could not get along with Moscow, or later with Petersburg—schismatics and sectarians of all kinds and not a few ordinary criminals as well. Here in the spaces of the Volga ranged the dashing highwaymen, preying upon merchants, boyars, and local governors, forming into regular calvary detachments, raiding towns, holding up tax collectors—in gratitude for which an oppressed people, forgiving their own injuries at the bandits' hands, praised and glorified them in song.

A little more than twenty years after the founding of Simbirsk, there broke out here the famous rebellion of Stepan Razin, who assembled countless armed freemen "to wipe out the notables and the boyars," and for five years dreadfully triumphed along the Volga and the Caspian Sea, plunging Moscow into a fever fright. Tsaritsyn,[3] Saratov, Samara[4]—one after the other, the Volga towns surrendered to the rebels. Simbirsk held out. The nobles and scions of the boyars withstood the siege until regular troops came to the rescue from Kazan. Here, near Simbirsk, the rebel bands suffered a cruel defeat at the hands of the tsar's European-trained army. The shores of the Volga stood thick with gallows; eight hundred were executed. Razin himself, covered with wounds, was carried captive to Moscow, and as was the custom, was drawn and quartered. The memory of Razin lived, though, on the Volga—yes, and throughout all Russia. The hills near Kamyshin, where the rebels camped, retain his name today —the "mounds of Stenka Razin." In folk epics he remains one of the most beloved figures. With great fervor the radical intelligentsia used to sing romantic songs about Stenka composed by radical poets.

One hundred years or so later, under Catherine, when France was approaching her great revolution, a new thunderstorm swept over the Volga in the form of the Don Cossack Yemelyan Pugachev[5] heading a great army of the discontented and rebellious, seizing one city after another, not touching Simbirsk but moving as far south as Tsaritsyn. There he was shattered by the regular army, betrayed by his own comrades, and sent in an iron cage to Moscow, where he shared the fate of Razin.

These two Volga rebellions constitute the authentic peasant-revolutionary tradition of old Russia. In spite of their portentous scope, however, they brought no relief to the people. An iron law of history decrees that a *Jacquerie* left to itself cannot rise to the stature of a real revolution. Even when it is completely victorious, a peasant revolt is only able to set up a new dynasty and establish new feudal castes. Such is the whole history of old China. Only under the leadership of a revolutionary urban class can a peasant war become a tool of social transformation. But the old Russian cities, mere accumulations of the nobility, the bureaucrats, and their retainers, contained no progressive forces of any kind. That is why, after each of these grandiose movements of the seventeenth and eighteenth centuries, the Volga washed the bloodstains into the Caspian Sea, and the tsar's and landlords' oppressions weighed heavier than ever.

In both rebellions, Simbirsk held out. One of the reasons was undoubtedly its character as a strong nest of boyars and of gentlefolk. This middle-Volga city, where Lenin was to first see the light of day, kept its reactionary role to the end—both in the period of the October *coup d'état* and afterward during the Civil War.

Old Russia was almost completely rural, and Simbirsk *gubernia* was the quintessence of old Russia. Even toward the end of the last century, thirty years after the days just described, the urban population was still below 7 per cent of the *gubernia's* total, and even that small percentage differed little in quality from the rural. In the steppes and forests, social contradictions were even more apparent and brutal. The Simbirsk peasants were considerably poorer in land than were peasants elsewhere in the Volga region. A third of the peasant households were classified as horseless— that is, as truly poverty-stricken, real pauper farms. The most destitute group were the aborigines—the non-Russians—who endured a double yoke. The principal and better lands were in the hands of the landlords; 73 per cent belonged to the nobles. The forest map of the *gubernia* looked even more malignant: out of four million acres of forest, more than half belonged to the ap-

panage estates—that is, to the tsar's family—and about one third
to the landlords. One fiftieth was left to the peasants, who constituted 95 per cent of the population. Truly, anyone who wanted to
learn to hate feudal barbarity should have been born in Simbirsk.

Even to the casual observer, the town reflected with admirable
clarity the social structure of the *gubernia,* and indeed of the
whole country. Old Simbirsk consisted of three distinctly different
sections: that of the nobles, that of the merchants, and that of the
townfolk. The best section, that of the nobles, occupied the sum-
mit of the hill called "the Crown." Here were the cathedral, the
administrative institutions, the schools, the promenade. Signs
read not only "Noble Assembly Hall" and "Noble Tutelage,"
but also "Noble Rooming House," even "Noble Baths." On the
spacious streets with modern sidewalks, the landlords' houses
stood uncramped amid their surrounding orchards, rather like
rural estates. On the promenade above the river, a military band
played in the evenings for the well-to-do public.

The Volga herself, as seen from the promenade a score of miles
in either direction—the Volga with her poverty, her epidemics,
the slavery of her peasants and penal labor of her barge haulers—
was transformed into an incomparable panorama of gentle,
smooth waters, small wooded islands, and beyond the river,
plains stretching off into the distance.

The Simbirsk nobility gave the fatherland no small number of
high-ranking bureaucrats and military men, none of them, however, attained any distinction. The Crown prided itself most of all
on the historian Karamzin, who in the caustic words of Pushkin
demonstrated with elegant simplicity "the necessity of the
autocracy and the charms of the whip." A favorite during the life
of Nicholas I, this official historian was much pampered and
earned for himself after death an allegorical monument in his
home town. This antique Muse of History, harmonizing badly
with the climate and the flora and fauna of the Volga region, was
known among the people as the "Pig-Iron Woman." Peasant
women coming to Simbirsk for annual welcomings of the icon of
the Holy Virgin of Kazan, would pray fervently to the pagan
Clio, taking her in their simplicity of mind for the martyred Saint
Barbara.

The slopes of the hill were covered with orchards, many of

which were tilled by the Beloriztsy, then a persecuted religious sect. Beyond the little Simbirsk River, which cleft the town, lay the trading squares, where on market days, bark and tar, dry and salt Volga fish, wheat loaves, sunflower seeds, pastry, and other delicacies would be set out and piled up in the dust. Commercial activities centered around the square. In the sturdily built houses with heavy locks lived the merchants—drygoods, flour, vodka, grain, and lumber dealers. Some of them already handled rubles by the hundreds of thousands, and had their eye on the aristocratic upper parts of the hill. And finally, the townfolk, ignorant and downtrodden, inhabited the outskirts. Their little cabins and huts with cracks for windows, with dovecotes and birdhouses, were thrown about hit or miss, in pits or mounds, alone or in bunches, along narrow, winding streets and alleys, between tottering woven fences. Gaunt, dirty hogs and mongrel dogs with matted fur enlivened this unappealing town landscape. And a little farther on began the peasant village, equally poverty-stricken whether in the forest or the prairie section.

Cruel and ugly was this belated social gothic of old Russia—especially here on the Volga, where the forest, cradle of the great Russian state, met the nomad steppe in hostile confrontation. Social relations had neither finish nor stability; they were like those homely structures the Russian colonizers threw together for living quarters out of hastily felled forest trees. Russia's wooden cities, too, bore the mark of something temporary, burning down periodically and being hastily put up again. In 1864 an enormous fire, burning steadily for nine days, destroyed almost three quarters of Simbirsk; hundreds of people died in the flames. But in a few years the pinewood phoenix rose again from the ashes with twenty-nine churches. On the whole, though, Simbirsk grew slowly; in the 1870s its population was still below thirty thousand. This primitive and hungry *gubernia,* scraping the earth with its old wooden plow, had no need, and indeed no power, to sustain a big city.

As if to compensate for all this, in the spring Simbirsk would become quite beautiful. The old hill would grow into a flowering orchard. A fragrance of lilacs, cherries, and apple blossoms would hang above the city's lordly cupola. The Volga would twinkle at the street ends, overflowing its banks for two or three miles, and the nightingales would sing in the orchards at night. This town seemed a lost paradise to former inhabitants of the Crown. But nature's spring festival would pass; the sun would scorch the green orchards, and the neglected city would lie exposed in the dust of streets and alleys that in the rainy autumn would disappear completely in mud and in winter would slumber under a heavy carpet of snow. "It is not a town but a graveyard, like all those towns," says Goncharov of his own native Simbirsk.*

On the heights, life proceeded leisurely, with food and drink in abundance. There was, decidedly, nothing to hurry toward. It is no accident that it was Goncharov, a man born and brought up in Simbirsk, who created the character of Oblomov, that incarnation of lordly sloth, fear of effort, blissful inactivity—a genuine and authentic old Russian type, a product of serfdom that did not die with serfdom, in fact one that is not totally extinct even today. Fifteen hundred kilometers from Petersburg, nine hundred from Moscow, Simbirsk had no railroad until the end of the 1880s. The official *Gubernia News*, which appeared twice a week, was its only political newspaper. To the very end of the last century the town did not know the use of the telephone. Truly an ideal capital of all-Russian Oblomovism!

Two allied and hostile hierarchies, the bureaucratic and the aristocratic, dividing the influence, dominated the town and the *gubernia*. First came the governor, the eye of St. Petersburg, repository of power, protector of the landlord's sleep against the ghost of Pugachev. Officially, of course, the church came first, but in reality the priests stood somewhere below the merchants. Only the archbishop was still an acknowledged figure on Olympus, something in the nature of a spiritual governor with a consultative vote. Officialdom had its unalterable Table of Ranks, which established, once and for all, thirteen degrees of recognizable human worth.[6] The nobles were also guided, over and above that, by delicate shades of aristocratic blue blood, and tried to look down on these upstart government officials. Questions as to who should occupy what place in the cathedral or what order should be followed in approaching to kiss the cross or the hand of the

* Ivan Goncharov (1814–91), author of *Oblomov* (1859), one of the great Russian novels. (Ed.)

governor's wife, stirred great passions and belligerent side-
takings, which ended invariably in grandiose drinking parties
and not infrequently in fistfights as well. To settle questions of
honor, the knights of Simbirsk, especially after a drink, would
spare neither their own nor others' jaws. Upon the landlords' estates, meanwhile, there bloomed those gentle maidens of Turgenev's novels, who would subsequently, as decreed by nature,
turn into avaricious mistresses of landed estates or into envious
wives of government officials.

In the very beginning of the 1860s, when our muckraking literature burst forth at full force, Minayev, a radical poet and himself a nobleman of Simbirsk *gubernia,* celebrated his homeland
at the capital in satiric verse: "Abode of dried fish, mud, and
gossip." The most blue-blooded among the nobles, with their
"impudent luxury," their jesters and snobbish pranks, and their
feudal harems, indulged in the sport of losing serfs at the gaming
table.[7] Some were liberals making speeches "in honor of the
whip," others were churchgoers breaking the jaws of their servants. There was also the archbishop roughing up the deacons
during mass, and there was the director of the high school, a
"bureaucratic scoundrel" cursed by the whole town. All these
were openly identified by name in Minayev's sufficiently sonorous iambics. And when, ten years later, the poet, a sick old man,
humble and subdued, returned to his home town—where by that
time a whole new generation had grown up—none of the nobles
would return his calls, and ultimately nobody went to his funeral.
Those people knew how to stand up for the honor of a family
tradition!

However, the hour struck. It was some ten years before the
one hundredth anniversary of Pugachev's rebellion and the bi-
centennial of Razin's, and serfdom, already deeply undermined
by the development of bourgeois relations, had to be abolished
from above. The tsar compelled the serfs to pay their landlords
not only for personal freedom, but also for the lands that had
been the serfs' own from time immemorial—filching the lands
from them, moreover, by means of reforms that benefited the
landlords. The act of "emancipation" was converted into a gigantic financial operation doubly ruinous to the peasantry. Moreover, the redemption payments contributed to the landlords'

economy the one thing that was always in short supply: ready cash. Those noble gentlemen held sumptuous wakes in memory of the Golden Age wherever they could—in Paris, on the Riviera, in Petersburg and Moscow, and less ostentatiously on their own estates or in Simbirsk, that common estate of the *gubernia's* nobility.

However, these redemption payments melted away like wax; a repetition was not in sight. The more-enterprising landlords, those capable of keeping step with the age, got hold of the *zemstvos*,[8] or a little later took to railroad construction. Others married their sons to merchants' daughters, or gave their daughters to the merchants' heirs. A far greater number entered into historic liquidation—mortgaged their lands, mortgaged them again, then sold their city houses and family estates, with all their wings and shady gardens and plaster-of-paris muses and croquet grounds. In their ruin they cursed the "reforms," which had pampered the people, depleted the lands, killed off the martens and ermine in the Simbirsk forests, and even caused the Volga to cease producing good fat sturgeon as of old. The reactionaries demanded the restitution of the lash, and sent formal memoranda to Petersburg about the timeliness of a restoration of serfdom. The liberals fumed at the slowness of progress and secretly contributed money to the revolutionary Red Cross. The partisans of the lash were incomparably the more numerous.

In the merchant section of Simbirsk, where the conservative stagnation took even cruder forms than among the nobles, the period of reform and dummy business ventures gave a hitherto unknown scope to the traditional greed. It was from this section that the buyers of the landlords' property and the nobles' city residences generally came. These bearded merchants moved up into the sacred precincts of the provincial Olympus, still shy about changing their padded caps for hats and their high boots for French shoes, but already free of the obsequiousness of their class. Thus there began to install itself even on the Simbirsk Crown that not very harmonious, but nevertheless enduring, symbiosis of nobility, merchantry, and bureaucracy, which in various incarnations determined the aspect of official Russia for more than half a century—the period, that is, between the abolition of serfdom in 1861 and the collapse of old Russia in 1917.

Economic progress moved from west to east and from the center to the circumference; political influences followed the same road. The Volga region, a backward section of a backward country, could not remain immune to those ideas and attempts at action which were clearing the path for a revolutionary transformation of the country. During the first quarter of the nineteenth century the cultivated Simbirsk nobleman and state counselor N. I. Turgenev,* an admirer of the French Encyclopedists and an enemy of serfdom, joined a Petersburg secret society, one of those which were preparing the famous semi-insurrection of the guard regiments of December 14, 1825. That heroic and hopeless constitutional flare-up of progressive military youth, which no doubt included in its ranks the flower of Simbirsk's noble families, was routed with a shower of bullets. Escaping abroad, Turgenev was condemned to death *in absentia;* he was to win fame in Europe with a French book about Russia. The uprising of the Decembrists gained an enduring place in Russian history as the watershed separating eighteenth-century palace revolutions from the subsequent struggle for liberation to which it was a dramatic introduction.

It was the tradition of the Decembrists that nurtured the so-called generation of the forties, which, in the words of another Turgenev, the famous novelist, took a "Hannibal's oath" to struggle against serfdom. The most celebrated publicist of this generation was A. I. Herzen. On the extreme left wing rose the monumental figure of the democratic Slavophile and future father of world anarchism Bakunin, a Russian nobleman. Simbirsk, forming an exception, gave the generation of the forties, instead of a liberal landlord, a conservative merchant's son, Goncharov. His politics notwithstanding, it was Goncharov's good fortune to pronounce in his portrait of Oblomov what was, in effect, an irrevocable death sentence upon the culture of serf-owning Russia.

The Crimean War (1853–56) ended with a collapse of the alleged military power of tsarism: the screw propeller triumphed over the sailing vessel, and capitalism over the serf-owning economy. The system of starched-up braggadocio, established on

---

* A relative of the novelist. (Ed.)

the bones of the Decembrists and lasting for a good thirty years, was decomposing with a stench. The mysterious death of the tsar, whom Herzen had nicknamed Nicholas the Bludgeon, opened the sluices of social discontent. Suddenly the press began to speak up with unaccustomed candor. The usurious emancipation of the peasants inaugurated the epoch of the so-called "great reforms." Deceived in their hopes, the villages grew darkly agitated. Progressive social thought arrived at an open split, the radicals coming out against the moderates. This clash of political tendencies was consecrated by a touchy Turgenev in his novel *Fathers and Sons* as a decisive break between the men of the 1840s and those of the 1860s. Turgenev's reduction of the question to a generation gap was only a part of the truth, however, and that part disguised the whole. At its roots the struggle had a social character. The cultivated landlords, elegantly repenting of their noble privileges, were replaced by a new social stratum, without privileges and therefore without repentance, lacking in aesthetic upbringing and hereditary good manners, but more numerous, resolute, and self-sacrificing. These were the sons of priests, of lower-ranking officers, of petty functionaries, of merchants, of ruined nobles, sometimes of townfolk and peasants—students, seminarians, schoolteachers—in short, the so-called *raznochintsy*, the casteless intelligentsia, who just at that time got hold of the idea of guiding the destinies of the country. The front of the stage was immediately occupied by acts of protest from student youth, and the word *student* became for many years a popular synonym for the nickname "nihilist," coined by Turgenev.

At the same time, the abolition of feudal servitude freed the older generation from its "Hannibal's oath" and relegated them politically to the back benches. The liberal westernizers were of the opinion that Russia would now, step by step, draw near to European civilization. The *raznochintsy*, on the other hand, brusquely raised the question of a special destiny for the Russian people, the possibility of avoiding capitalist slavery, and of direct struggle with the oppressors. Although it contains a large admixture of utopianism, the gospel of the men of the sixties sounds immeasurably more courageous than the stale "oath" of their fathers. It was with a degree of defiance that Turgenev answered in 1863 some of his well-meaning advisers, "I have never written

for the people. I have written for that class of the public to which
I belong. . . ." Meanwhile, new men were fervently seeking
roads to the people. Instead of addressing humanitarian pleas
to the rulers, they decided to appeal to the hatred felt by the
oppressed. Turgenev, like Goncharov, turned away from these
"sons" as if they were unloved stepchildren. Turgenev did this
with a degree of coquetry that was so characteristic of him, while
Goncharov did so spitefully and slanderously. In his novel *The
Precipice*, set on a nobleman's estate near Simbirsk, Goncharov
publicly pilloried a nihilist, Mark Volokhov, who had dared to
replace God with the laws of chemistry, had borrowed money
from liberal nobles without paying it back, undermined respect
for authority among the young, and seduced the nobles' daughters. The real-life Volokhovs, however, proved not of the timid
sort; they were not intimidated by the disapproval of the
"fathers," but on the contrary took the offensive. The 1860s
opened a period of unceasing and ever-more-resolute revolutionary struggle.

That Simbirsk made early acquaintance with the nihilists is
confirmed not only by *belles lettres* but also by historical evidence. Some were exiled there from more-important cities by the
police. Others developed locally under the influence of the exiles.
It is worth noting in general that some of the sturdiest revolutionaries of that period often hailed from the dreamiest backwoods
parts of the country. For example, among the leftist students a
notable place was occupied by Don Cossacks and by Siberians—
people, that is, from an utterly conservative milieu of prosperous peasantry, or from such God-forsaken *gubernias* of the landed
gentry as that of Simbirsk. The sharp clash of new influences with
the inertia of these rural rustic backwaters created in the more
sensitive of the younger generation that bold and sometimes
frenzied break with old bonds and beliefs which would drive
them finally into selfless service to the revolution. In general,
backwardness is apt at a certain moment to swing over to progress
with a catastrophic determination. This is demonstrated by the
destinies of Russia.

The great Simbirsk fire of 1864, like a number of other fires that
during those years swept St. Petersburg and provincial cities, had
a mysterious political background. The government looked for

the culprits among the Poles and revolutionaries, but found nothing.[9] The serf owners accused the nihilists of arson and insisted, for that reason, that the peasant reforms be postponed. To make their case more convincing, they apparently went in for arson themselves. Baron Wrangel, who investigated the causes of the Simbirsk fire, found nothing. Nevertheless, as scapegoats, two soldiers were sentenced to death. Whether they were ever executed is not known. Senator Zhdanov, who replaced Wrangel, allegedly collected, in the course of two years of investigation, incontrovertible evidence of the guilt of a reactionary gang; but Zhdanov died suddenly while on his way to St. Petersburg and his briefcase was never found. The third investigator, General Den, set free all the suspects rounded up by his predecessor and discontinued the investigation itself as hopeless. Finally, in 1869, when the Ulyanovs moved to Simbirsk, the government senate resolved to "consign the matter to oblivion"; this was successfully accomplished.

At the edge of the noble section of Simbirsk—in a wing on the court of a two-storied wooden house at the spot where, as tradition has it, Razin's army was smashed—on quiet, deserted Streletsky Street, not far from the prison square, a third child was born, on April 10, 1870, to the inspector of public schools Ulyanov. The wing itself has long ceased to exist, and it is not even known exactly where it stood, but we may assume that it differed in no way from all other wings of wooden houses on the Volga. The boy was christened with the sonorous Slavonic name Vladimir, which means *lord* or *ruler of the earth*. The parents and the priest hardly suspected that the name contained a prophecy. This boy born on the Volga was destined to become the leader and ruler of a people. Simbirsk was to become Ulyanovsk. The Simbirsk Assembly Hall of Nobles was to become The Lenin Palace of Books. And Russia of the tsars was to be transformed into the Union of Soviet Socialist Republics.

2

THE FAMILY

MEMBERS of the inner circle and outsiders, even those who were to become bitter enemies, all speak in nearly the same terms of the friendly and industrious character of the Ulyanov family, of the purity and honesty of their domestic relations, of the cheerful mood in the family dining room. The absence of humiliating want or of flabby excess, the continual vivid examples of duty and industry in the father, the active and tender vigilance of the mother, a common interest in literature and music—all these conditions were very favorable to the bringing up of healthy and firm-hearted children.

Ilya Nikolayevich Ulyanov, the head of the family, was descended from Astrakhan commoners. All the squalor of old Russia's urban culture was incarnate in this townsman class. Its active and lucky elements soon escaped into the merchant class, or having made their way through the schools into the bureaucracy, gained admittance into the nobility by service to the state. Except for industrial workers—who on their passports continued to be classified as peasants and townfolk, being neither the one nor the other—there remained in the townfolk caste a motley crowd of social failures, unfortunate artisans, traders on the edge of pauperism, gardeners, petty saloonkeepers, people with indefinite occupations finding shelter in the suburbs and somehow earning a living off the gentry, the bureaucrats, and the merchants. The trade of the commoner Nikolai Ulyanov, grandfather of Lenin, is unknown; there is some indication, however, that he was a tailor and worked in some sort of commercial enterprise. In any case, he left his family without means. But obviously it was an uncommon family of commoners: its members were characterized by an overly powerful desire to study. Only the early death of the father, which cast the entire burden of supporting the family upon the eldest son, forced the son to take up employment. He transferred his own dreams of education to his brother Ilya, Lenin's father, who was then seven years old. The older boy's persistent labor and deprivation made it possible for the younger to graduate from the Astrakhan High School, and afterward supported him in the university until he got on his feet. All his life Ilya retained a feeling of devoted gratitude to his brother, who made these immeasurable sacrifices for him. Loyalty, a sense of duty, persistence in attaining a chosen goal— it is not by accident that we encounter these qualities first in the scant pages relating to Lenin's forebears.

Ilya studied stubbornly and with success, entering Kazan University in 1850 in the faculty of physics and mathematics. He completed his course "in general subjects satisfactorily, and in his special subjects with distinction." A supplementary examination earned him the title of "senior teacher of high school mathematics and physics." The course of the young man's life had been laid out. Upon leaving the university, he took up at once a position as teacher at the Penza Institute for Children of Noble Families; in 1863 he was transferred to a public high school in Nizhni Novgorod. While still in Penza, he met his future wife, Maria Aleksandrovna Blank, a sister of the wife of Veretennikov, a fellow teacher. The wedding took place in the summer of 1863, establishing a firm and happy union.

The student years of Ilya Nikolayevich coincided with the end of the reign of Nicholas I, the years of reckoning for this hated regime. Even moderate liberals rejoiced in the military defeats, and the radical intelligentsia rejoiced even more. That turning point in the internal affairs of the country proved a great education in citizenship for the younger generation. No thinking person in those days could simply overlook the peasant question. Programs of social transformation were debated openly for the first time. The destiny of Russia was compared with that of Western Europe or America. It was believed that progress would thenceforth be uninterrupted; that the people, once awakened, would move swiftly toward emancipation from ignorance and poverty; that the intelligentsia would fulfill with honor its mission as the people's leader. It was with such or similar high-minded, misty thoughts that the young teacher set out upon his life's journey.

In his social roots and in the date of his spiritual awakening, Ilya Nikolayevich was a typical *raznochinets* of the 1860s. However, the political coloring of this broad and variegated social stratum was far from uniform. Only a minority really tried to organize their ideas about the fate of the people into a finished system: only the left wing of the minority embarked on the road of revolutionary activity. The vast majority of the *raznochintsy* were satisfied, while young, with general ideas of love for the people, and quite prepared to forget them completely later in their careers. Otherwise, where would the government find its department heads and prosecuting attorneys, and the growing bourgeoisie its lawyers and engineers? There was much truth in the anonymous aphorism: "Le Russe est radical jusqu'à trente ans, et après—canaille."* Ilya Nikolayevich did not belong to the revolutionary wing; there is no reason to assume that he developed any consistent social views. But on the other hand he took seriously the elementary idea of duty to the people, which corresponded to his origin and cast of character, and he remained faithful to it throughout his life.

Two or three of his high-school students who subsequently attained eminence have written with respect about this young Nizhni Novgorod teacher of mathematics and physics, about his deep devotion to his work. He was demanding of his pupils, and still more of himself. He would meet the slower students in the schoolhouse on Sundays and tutor them free of charge, giving up his day of rest. He carried out his humble duties as a provincial schoolteacher with a warm and disinterested persistence that contained a grain of heroism.

He spent almost thirteen years at such work, a married man during six of them. His daughter Anna was five years old, and his son Alexander three and a half, when a change came in the life of the family, a change bound up with a turning point in the life of the country. The reforms of the new reign had extended into the sphere of education. A network of public schools was being

* The Russian is radical until he is thirty, and after that—not to be trusted.

established, partly by the ministry but chiefly by the *zemstvos*. These schools needed governmental control and guidance. Ilya Nikolayevich was offered the post of inspector of public schools of Simbirsk *gubernia*, with its population of about a million people. To accept the appointment meant forsaking the physical and mathematical sciences he loved, and tearing himself away from familiar surroundings and personal ties. The new work would be less pedagogical than administrative, and would be done in unfamiliar surroundings and difficult conditions. On the other hand, the scope was wider, and he would no longer be dealing just with select pupils, as in the high schools, but with the children of the true common people—i.e., the peasantry. It is possible, too, that the salary offered him was higher than a schoolteacher's. Without hesitation, Ilya Nikolayevich accepted the appointment. In September of 1869 the family moved down the Volga from Nizhni Novgorod to Simbirsk, where they were to settle for two decades.

In Simbirsk *gubernia*, the *zemstvo*, which had come into existence five years earlier, was taken over by cliques of the landed gentry—more so than anywhere else. In an impoverished and roadless *gubernia*, with a significant minority of Asiatic ethnic groups, it was not easy, even given the best of intentions, to get the oxcart of public education moving. The newly appointed inspector of public schools was to discover that his district was a desert. Radical newspapers of the period cited a district in Russia with a population of 180,000 that boasted sixteen schools and three hundred taverns. Educational statistics for the majority of other districts were not much better. It was with good reason that the young publicist Shelgunov, on the eve of the period of reforms, wrote to his wife from some provincial backwater: "Wilderness, wilderness, wilderness, stagnation and stupidity. By God, it frightens me."

The peasants learned to fear everything that came from the state: prisons, hospitals, and schools. The authorities needed literate persons to oppress the people. Some teachers took money from the peasants in return for a promise not to take the students away from their work at home. The inspector's first concern was to refute the official lie and to make known how things really were. He had to begin virtually from scratch: build new schools, transform the few schools that existed, and select, train, or retrain the teachers.

The *gubernia* had neither highways nor railroads. Still, one had to travel almost constantly, by cart or sleigh, making one's way over wagon trails through the steppes and forests, drowning in the mud or getting caught in snowstorms.

One had to negotiate endlessly with members of the *zemstvo*, with teachers, peasant societies, officials; one had to get excited, try to persuade, often compromise, sometimes threaten. After seventeen years of such work, some 450 schools were built in the *gubernia*, and the number of students doubled. These results, modest in themselves, were attained in large part because of Ilya Nikolayevich's unusual ability to get along with people of different social standing and education. He passed on this capacity to his son, although in different and unexpected dimensions.

The reminiscences that were written about the Ulyanov family in the years of the Soviet regime must, of course, be treated with some caution: as shall be demonstrated, even conscientious authors tend to discover in the parents traits that would correspond to the image of the son. Fortunately, we have convincing testimony, published while Lenin was still a boy, a very young man, a hunted revolutionary. The Simbirsk landowner Nazaryev, a member of the *zemstvo* and a contributor to liberal publications, a man given to enthusiasms, referred in print to Inspector Ulyanov as a "rare, extraordinary phenomenon," and with great inspiration described his untiring chase across the *gubernia*, in defiance of the elements and the indifference of men: "Such endurance and strength can come only from a boundless dedication to one's work, to the point of self-abnegation." (*Vestnik Yevropy*, 1876) The ministry itself recognized in writing that the initiative and perseverance of the Simbirsk inspector "merit complete attention." A history of public-school education published in 1906 notes that among leading figures in the field of education in the Simbirsk *gubernia*, "in the unanimous opinion of contemporaries, the first place belongs to Ilya Nikolayevich Ulyanov." There is no reason to doubt such disinterested testimony.

That charge of social idealism which had been implanted in Ilya Nikolayevich during his youth had found a peaceful and praiseworthy application. His moral equilibrium had been assured. He had nothing to repent of. On the contrary, even now, especially in summertime in the country, Ilya Nikolayevich loved to sing the song of his student years set to the words of Ryleyev, the Decembrist poet hanged by Nicholas I. It was an oath of hostility to the "scourges of our native land." The first scourge was serfdom—it had fallen. The second scourge was the people's ignorance—against it Ilya Nikolayevich was waging war with all his might. Of the third scourge, the autocracy, the inspector of public schools preferred not to talk, and apparently not even to think. Though a progressive-minded government official, he was no revolutionary.

In his personal makeup, his ways and manners, Ilya Nikolayevich was a far cry from the stereotype of the cut-and-dried bureaucrat. On the contrary, he was a very warm human being—sociable, alert, with a good sense of humor. During his endless journeys, when stopping at the estate of some liberal *zemstvo* member, he loved to open up his heart in conversations about the life of the *gubernia* and especially its educational affairs. He would bring home fresh tales of the teachers and schools of which his life was so full. He loved to tell these tales, with his gently guttural r's, at the family table, and he would laugh with great gusto, throwing his whole body back until tears came to those small brown eyes, slit like a Kalmuk's. Whoever saw Lenin and heard his speech and laughter can form a lively image, at least in boldest outline, of his father: the short, stocky figure, the agility of his body, the high cheekbones, high forehead, swarthy skin, and early baldness. Only the son's physique, it seems, was stronger and stockier than the father's.

In 1874 Ilya Nikolayevich was appointed director of the public schools. By now, several inspectors were his subordinates. He was recognized as an important personage in the *gubernia*. The order of St. Vladimir and the rank of civil councilor brought the former townsman hereditary nobility. In the innumerable police questionnaires right up to 1917, his sons and daughters had to write down in the proper space their noble rank. But there was nothing aristocratic in the physical molds of either himself or the members of his family. Wide noses, high cheekbones, and stubby fingers clearly revealed their plebeian origin. Ilya Nikolayevich was also in no way the typical bourgeois *gentilhomme*. The inborn democracy of his nature, his distaste for any snobbery, his unaffected way of dealing with people, were his best qualities. He passed them on in full to his children.

Generally speaking, his influence upon his children was profound and effective. To be sure, the father spent most of his time away on business, and the family would frequently not see him for weeks at a stretch, but his very absence acquired a special significance, as though continually suggesting to the children: duty above all! His never-slackening zeal for the cause—for its essence and not its form—his integrity and accessibility, purged the father's image of those traits of bureaucracy which were all too well known to the children from their high-school experiences. His tales at the family table of overcoming obstacles on the road of popular education were eagerly absorbed by the children's minds. Their father seemed the incarnation of a higher principle standing above the narrow interests of the family circle. "His authority in the family," writes the eldest daughter, "and his children's love for him, were very great."

Maria Alexandrovna came from a more affluent and cultivated family than her husband. Her father, a physician and owner of an estate in Kazan *gubernia,* was for those times, according to his granddaughter, a man of advanced views. He bore an obviously non-Russian name, Blank—as to his nationality, unfortunately we know nothing—and was married to a German woman who reared her children in German traditions.[1] The family lived always, it seems, in the country. The father gave careful attention to the physical education of his children. His daughter Maria enjoyed a healthy childhood and a tranquil youth, was never restless, and lover her native village of Kokushkino. Things were less favorable with matters educational. Pedagogical considerations, and perhaps certain prejudices, deterred the parents from sending their daughters away from the village to boarding schools. Tutors were brought in for the older ones. But by the time Maria was grown up, the family finances had become shaky, there was no money for a tutor, and the youngest daughter received the so-called "home education" common to many provincial young ladies of that time. Under the guidance of a German aunt, she received some training in foreign languages and music, and for the rest was left to her own devices. Later, observing the studies and progress of her own children, she grieved often over the fact that she had not in her time managed to obtain an education.

Maria married at twenty-eight; her husband was four years her senior. Ilya Nikolayevich had a modest but solid social position. The bride's dowry consisted of a fifth of her father's estate. The marriage was founded, most likely, upon mutual attraction, if not stronger feelings. The 1860s with their slogan of woman's emancipation, dealt a serious blow to parental control over their children's love lives. Moreover, Ilya Nikolayevich was independent, and the father of Maria Alexandrovna was inclined to progressive ideas.

The first years of their family life in Nizhni Novgorod were wholly auspicious. The apartment in the high-school building was sufficiently well appointed, according to the standards of Russian provinces of old. Other teachers' families lived nearby. The young wife made women friends with whom she could read and enjoy music and intimate conversation. They subscribed to Petersburg journals in which beat the pulse of the libertarian movement of the times. Ilya Nikolayevich spent his free hours with his family, sometimes reading aloud in the evening. It was just at that time that Tolstoy's epic, *War and Peace*, was being serialized.

With the move to Simbirsk, Maria Alexandrovna being pregnant at the time with the future Vladimir, the conditions of her life changed sharply. The town was far behind Nizhni Novgorod, which was no real gem of culture either. They had to settle on the outskirts of the Crown, apart from society, without friends, without "their own circle." An inspector, of townsman origin and married to a half-German wife, could not, of course, be received in noble society as one of their own. Furthermore, relations with the little world of the *gubernia* bureaucracy, which was sulkily adjusting to the consequences of the reforms, were not harmonious. The pedagogical circles of Simbirsk were possibly the most musty and rotten section of the bureaucracy. The mere fact that Ulyanov zealously attended to the business of establishing schools made him a stranger in that circle of bribetakers and sycophants. His approachability and unaffected manner earned him the malicious and partly ironical nickname "The Liberal." The merchant milieu was too crude, and moreover no less shut-in, after its own fashion, than the aristocracy.

On the other hand, a government official, paterfamilias, and loyal citizen could not, of course, form ties with the suspected circles of the radical intelligentsia.

This isolation was an especially heavy blow to Maria Alexandrovna, because her husband's new duties kept him away from home. The young woman pined and languished, until gradually she lost herself in her children and her housekeeping. The family was growing. Her husband's modest salary was the sole income. There was no actual want, but every kopek had to be accounted for. The rules of thrift instilled in her by her German mother came in very handy. Ilya Nikolayevich often told his older children in later years that only thanks to the frugality of their mother was the family able to make both ends meet.

The mother gave the older children their first lessons in letters. But this was inevitably interrupted by many other tasks. In 1873, when the fifth child was born, a tutor was employed, a teacher from the parish school, Kalashnikov, who long outlived his principal pupils, Alexander and Vladimir, and subsequently published vivid recollections of them. Ilya Nikolayevich, who had the last word in matters of education, considered it advisable to send his children off to high school as early as possible. As an official of the ministry of education, he did not have to pay tuition in the state schools, and moreover he feared the permissiveness of the family, preferring masculine guidance, a steady course of study, and school discipline.

In the recollections of Anna, which are full of filial piety, it becomes clear that the father did not always give sufficient attention to the individual peculiarities of his children, and was guilty perhaps of being somewhat overdemanding, especially toward his eldest son, who was already too demanding of himself. The authoritarian personality of the father was further reinforced by his religious beliefs. Ilya Nikolayevich, the mathematician and physicist who wrote a university thesis on computing the orbit of the comet Klinkerfüss by the Olbers method, kept inviolate the orthodox faith of an Astrakhan burgher: he attended vespers, confessed, and received the sacraments, not only as part of the duties of a tsarist official, but through inner conviction.

Undoubtedly the mother's influence upon the children was the greater. She bore seven children in fourteen years, one of them dying soon after birth, the rest surviving, and each demanding care and attention. This mother had, it seems, an inexhaustible life force—laboring and bearing, nursing, bringing up, and again bearing, always at work, always serene, happy, and cordial. She was the authentic model of a mother, the continuer and protector of the species. The two eldest children never had a nurse. But, for the others, too, the mother was the source of nourishment, the playmate, always there, always at hand, the author of all blessings, the source of all joys, the angel of justice in the nursery. The depth of her influence rested, however, not only on her constant closeness to her children, but on the exceptional richness of her personality.

What little we know of them both justifies the conclusion that the mother was of a higher spiritual quality than the father. From her issued those invisible rays which warm the heart of a child and give him a reserve of warmth throughout his life. She did not caress her children stormily and kiss them to death, but she also never pushed them away, never lit into them. From their first day, she surrounded them with self-sacrificing love—without pampering, but also without nagging. Years later, the daughter, by then an old woman herself, recalled with tenderness her mother's music, and their rides together on chairs that they converted by their creative imaginations into sleighs on snowy roads amid pines and fir trees.

The evenness of the mother's temper was not rooted in a self-preserving egotism, as it sometimes is, but on the contrary in a fervent self-sacrifice. A woman of deep feeling, she experienced with equal passion her rare moments of joy and more frequent ones of grief, and even her petty everyday vexations. But a special modesty of nature made any sharp outbursts of feeling impossible for her. She suffered the cruelty of life not only for herself but for others, for her husband, her children; and that alone saved her from irascibility, from flaring up and making scenes— that is, from trying to work off a share of her suffering upon those near to her. An inexhaustible spring of moral fortitude enabled her after each new blow of fate—and there was no lack of them— to recover her inner equilibrium and support those who needed support. A moral genius not armed with any second-rate gifts is unnoticeable to the outsider: its light shines only at close range.

But were there not in this world such generous women, life itself would not deserve the name. Maria Alexandrovna found an active external expression for her precious powers only through her children. She lived to almost within a year of her son's historic victory.

Born and reared in a family that was not of the Russian Orthodox faith, Maria Alexandrovna, although wholly Russified, nevertheless possessed, in contrast to her husband, no firm church traditions—except, indeed, for the German Christmas tree—and was not distinguished in the least by religious observance. In the words of her daughter, she "went as rarely to the Russian church as to the German church." It is not even clear whether she remained a Lutheran or went over at marriage to the Orthodox faith. But Maria Alexandrovna never broke with religion entirely; in the most trying moments, she resorted to it with all the hidden passion of her nature. Once, when the life of her four-year-old son hung by a thread, the mother, frantic with grief, whispered feverishly to her six-year-old daughter: "Pray for Sasha!" And she herself fell to her knees in despair before the icon. That time, the danger passed. Sasha was saved, and the bright-eyed mother again taught her convalescent boy to walk. Seventeen years later —after how many alarms and labors and hopes!—through the bars of a Petersburg prison the mother repeated to her daughter the same admonition: "Pray for Sasha!" But this time she spoke only of the saving of his soul, for the tsar's noose had already strangled her beloved eldest son, the pride and hope of the family.

3

THE REVOLUTIONARY PATH
OF THE INTELLIGENTSIA

AN INTELLECTUAL of plebeian origin, Ilya Nikolayevich Ulyanov had entered the ranks of the bureaucracy but had not blended indistinguishably into it. His children felt no ties whatever with the bureaucratic milieu; revolutionary struggle became their profession. The movement of liberation, before becoming a mass movement toward the end of the century, passed during its earlier decades through a rich experience on a laboratory scale. One cannot understand the destiny of the Ulyanov family without understanding the logic of this earlier independent revolutionary movement of the Russian intelligentsia, and therewith the logic of its collapse.

In one of the famous political trials of the 1870s, known as "the case of the 193," the principal defendant advanced the thesis that, after the peasant reform, there had arisen, outside the peasantry itself, "a whole faction . . . prepared to respond to the call of the people, and serving as the nucleus of a social revolutionary party. This faction was the intellectual proletariat." These words of Ippolit Myshkin correctly describe, though they do not evaluate, the essence of the phenomenon. The decomposition of the feudal society proceeded at a faster pace than the formation of the bourgeoisie. The intelligentsia, a product of the decay of the old classes, found neither an adequate demand for its skills nor a sphere for its political influence. It broke with the nobility, the bureaucracy, the clergy, with their stale culture and serf-owning traditions, but it did not effect a rapprochement with the bourgeoisie, which was still too primitive and crude. It felt itself to be socially independent, yet at the same time it was choking in the clutches of tsarism. Thus, after the fall of serfdom, the intelligentsia formed almost the sole nutritive medium for revolutionary ideas—especially its younger generation, the poorest of the intellectual youth, university students, seminarians, high-school boys, a majority of them not above the proletariat in their standard of living and many below it. The state, having need of an intelligentsia, reluctantly created one by means of its schools. The intelligentsia, having need of a reformed regime, became an enemy of the state. The political life of the country thus for a long time assumed the form of a dual between the intelligentsia and the police, with the fundamental classes of society almost entirely passive. With a malicious glee, but not without some reason, the prosecutor at Myshkin's trial pointed out that both the "more advanced circles" (that is, the propertied classes and the older generations of the intelligentsia itself) and the circles "deprived of education" (that is, the masses of the people) were immune to revolutionary propaganda. In such conditions the outcome of the conflict was predetermined. But since the struggle was forced upon the "intellectual proletariat" by its whole situation, it had to have some grand illusions.

Having just broken away in the realm of consciousness from medieval customs and relationships, the intelligentsia naturally regarded ideas as its chief power. In the 1860s it embraced a theory according to which the progress of humanity is the result of critical thought. And who could serve better as the representatives of critical thought than itself, the intelligentsia? Frightened, however, by its small numbers and isolation, the intelligentsia was compelled to resort to mimicry, that weapon of the weak. It renounced its own being, in order to gain a greater right to speak and act in the name of the people. Myshkin pursued this course in continuing his famous speech. But "the people" meant the peasants. The tiny industrial proletariat was only an accidental and unhealthy branch of the people. The Populists' worship of the peasant and his commune was but the mirror image of the grandiose pretensions of the "intellectual proletariat" to the role of chief, if not indeed sole, instrument of progress. The whole history of the Russian intelligentsia develops between these two poles of pride and self-abnegation—which are the short and the long shadows of its social weakness.

The revolutionary elements of the intelligentsia not only identified themselves theoretically with the people, but tried in actual fact to merge with them. They put on peasants' coats, ate watery soup, and learned to work with plow and ax. This was not a political masquerade, but a heroic exploit. Yet it was founded on a gigantic *quid pro quo*. The intelligentsia created a "people" in its own image, and that biblical act of creation prepared for it a tragic surprise when the time came for action.

The earliest revolutionary groups set themselves the task of preparing a peasant uprising. Had not the peasant's capacity for revolt been demonstrated, after all, by his entire past history? And now the "critically thinking personality" was to replace Stepan Razin and Yemelyan Pugachev. This hope was not, it seemed, a mere castle in the air. In the years of preparation and carrying out of the reforms, there was peasant unrest in various parts of the country. In some places the government was compelled to resort to military force, though in a majority of cases matters went only as far as a traditional, old-time horsewhipping. These peasant disturbances provided a stimulus for the formation, in 1860 in Petersburg, of a small underground organization known as "Young Russia." Its immediate aim was: "a bloody and implacable revolution, which shall radically change the whole foundation of contemporary society." But that revolution was slow in coming. Without altering its views, the intelligentsia decided that this meant a brief delay. New circles arose, preparing the insurrection. The government answered with repressive measures whose fury gives the measure of its fright. For attempting to issue a proclamation to the peasants, Chernyshevsky, the famous Russian political writer and genuine leader of the younger generation, was pilloried and condemned to hard labor.[1] By this blow the tsar had hoped, with some reason, to behead the revolutionary movement for some time to come.

On April 4, 1866, the twenty-five-year-old Dimitri Karakozov, a former student from the petty nobility, fired the first bullet at Alexander II as the tsar emerged from the Summer Garden. Karakozov missed the tsar, but ended the "liberal" chapter of Alexander's reign. Attacks on the press, and police invasions of peaceful homes, put fear in the hearts of the liberal circles—none too brave to begin with. The independent elements of the bureaucracy began to fall in line. From that time on, we may assume, Ilya Nikolayevich Ulyanov stopped singing the songs of his youth. With the help of a sterilized classicism, a system for crippling young brains, Count Dimitri Tolstoy, the minister of education, decided to strangle free thought in the very embryo. A monstrous system was developed. Alexander and Vladimir Ulyanov had to make their way through the tortures of this police classicism, in which Athens and Rome served merely as gateways to tsarist St. Petersburg.

Six years elapsed between the first proclamation and the first armed attack on the tsar. The intelligentsia thus completed, in the dawn of its revolutionary activity, its first small cycle: from the hope for an immediate peasant uprising, through the attempt at propaganda and agitation, to individual terror. Many similar mistakes, experiments, and disappointments lay ahead. But, from that moment, from the abolition of serfdom, begins a unique phenomenon in world history: six decades of underground exploits by a body of revolutionary pioneers leading to the explosions of 1905 and 1917.

Two years after the Karakozov affair, an obscure provincial teacher, Nechayev, instructor in theology in a parish school, one of the mightiest figures in the gallery of Russian revolutionaries, attempted to create a conspiratorial society called "The People's Revenge," or "The Ax." Nechayev arranged for a peasant uprising to occur on the tenth anniversary of the reform, February 19, 1870, when the transitional relations in the villages were, according to the law, to be replaced by permanent ones. The preparatory revolutionary work was to proceed in accordance with a strict timetable: until May 1869, in the capital and the university centers; from May to September, in the *gubernias* and county seats; from October, "in the very thick of the people"; in the spring of 1870, a ruthless popular reckoning with the exploiters was to begin. But again no insurrection followed. The affair ended with the murder of a student suspected of betrayal. Having escaped abroad, Nechayev was turned over to the tsar by the Swiss Government and ended his days in the Peter and Paul Fortress. In revolutionary circles the word Nechayevism was long to be a term of harsh condemnation, a synonym for risky and reprehensible methods of attaining revolutionary goals. Lenin was to hear himself accused hundreds of times of "Nechayevist" methods[2] by his political opponents.

The 1870s opened a second cycle in the revolutionary movement, considerably wider in scope and intensity but reproducing
in its development the sequence of stages already familiar to us:
from the hope for a popular uprising and the attempt to prepare
it, through clashes with the political police with the people looking on indifferently, to individual terror. Nechayev's conspiracy,
built wholly upon the dictatorship of a single person, evoked in
revolutionary circles a sharp reaction against centralism and
blind discipline. Reborn in 1873, after a short calm, the movement took on the character of a chaotic mass pilgrimage of the
intelligentsia to the people. Young men and women, most of
them former students, numbering about a thousand in all, carried
socialist propaganda to all corners of the country, especially to
the lower reaches of the Volga, where they sought the legacy
of Pugachev and Razin. This movement, remarkable in scope and
youthful idealism, the true cradle of the Russian revolution, was
distinguished—as is proper to a cradle—by extreme naïveté. The
propagandists had neither a guiding organization nor a clear
program; they had no conspiratorial experience. And why should
they have? These young people, having broken with their families
and schools, without profession, personal ties, or obligations,
and without fear either of earthly or heavenly powers, seemed
to themselves the living crystalization of a popular uprising. A
constitution? Parliamentarism? Political liberty? No, they would
not be swerved from the path by these Western decoys. What
they wanted was a complete revolution, without abridgements
or intermediate stages.

The theoretical sympathies of the youth were divided between
Lavrov and Bakunin. Both these captains of thought had come
from the nobility, and they had been educated in the same military schools in Petersburg, Mikhail Bakunin ten years earlier
than Pyotr Lavrov. Both ended their lives as émigrés—Bakunin
in 1876, when Vladimir Ulyanov was still in baby shoes. Lavrov
lived till 1900, when Ulyanov was becoming Lenin. The former
artillery officer, Bakunin, had already emigrated for the second
time and progressed from democratic pan-Slavism to pure
anarchism, when the artillery-school teacher, Colonel Lavrov, an
eclectic with an encyclopedic education, began to develop
in legal journals his theory of "the critically thinking personality,"

a kind of philosophic passport for the Russian "nihilist." His doctrine of duty to the people fitted to perfection the Messianism of the intelligentsia, whose theoretical haughtiness was combined with a constant practical readiness for self-sacrifice. The weakness of Lavrovism lay in its failure to indicate any course of action aside from the abstract propaganda of revealed gospel. Even such wholly peaceful educators as Ilya Nikolayevich Ulyanov might sincerely consider themselves followers of Lavrov. But for this very reason it did not satisfy the more resolute and active among the young. Bakunin's doctrine seemed incomparably more clear, and better still, more resolute. It declared the Russian peasants to be "socialist by instinct and revolutionary by nature." It saw the task of the intelligentsia as a summoning of the peasants to an immediate "universal destruction," out of which Russia would emerge a federation of free communes. Patient propagandism could only fall back under this assault from integral rebellion. In the full armor of Bakuninism, which became the ruling doctrine, the intelligentsia of the 1870s considered it self-evident that they need only scatter the sparks of "critical thought," and both steppe and forest would burst into a sheet of flame.

"The movement of the intelligentsia," Myshkin later testified at his trial, "was not artificially created, but was the echo of popular unrest." Although in a broad historical sense true, this idea could in no way establish a direct political connection between popular discontent and the revolutionary designs of the rebels. By a fatal combination of circumstances, the rural districts, which had been restless throughout almost the whole of Russian history, quieted down just at the moment when the cities became interested in them, and quieted down for a long time. The peasant reform had become an accomplished fact. The naked, slave-like dependence of the peasant upon the lord was gone. Thanks also to the high price of grain prevailing ever since the 1860s, the standard of living of the upper and more enterprising layers of the peasantry, controllers of its social opinion, was on the rise. The peasants were inclined to attribute the plundering character of the reform to a resistance on the part of the landlords to the will of the tsar. Their hopes for a better future rested with that same tsar. He was called upon to set right that which the landlords and functionaries had ruined. These moods not only rendered the peasants inhospitable to revolutionary propaganda, but inclined them to see in the enemies of the tsar their own enemies. The intelligentsia's impassioned, impatient, and powerful attraction toward the peasantry clashed with the peasants' embittered distrust for everything that issued from the gentry, from city folk, from educated people, from students. The villages not only did not open their arms to the propagandists, but repelled them with hostility. This fact decided the dramatic course of the revolutionary movement of the 1870s, and its tragic end. Only a new generation of peasants, growing up after the reform, was to gain an acute new awareness of its land hunger, its burden of taxation, its oppression as a class, and undertake—this time under the guiding influence of the working class—to smoke out the landlords from their settled nests. But it took a quarter of a century to bring this about.

In any case, the movement "to the people" during the 1870s suffered a complete defeat. Neither the Volga nor the Don, nor yet the Dnieper region responded to the call. Moreover, carelessness in the precautions necessary for illegal work soon betrayed the propagandists. An overwhelming majority of them—more than seven hundred persons—had been arrested by 1874. The public prosecutor conducted two great trials, which are remembered in the history of the revolution as "the case of the 50" and "the case of the 193." The challenge thrown in the face of tsarism by the condemned over the heads of the court stirred the hearts of several generations of the young.

This costly experience demonstrated the fact that short raids on the villages would not suffice. The propagandists decided to try a system of genuine settlement among the people, moving to the country and living there as craftsmen, traders, clerks, medics, teachers, etc. In its scope, this movement, which began in 1876, was considerably less chaotic than the first wave, that of 1873. Disappointment and repression had given rise to a selective process. In going over to a settled mode of life, the propagandists found themselves obliged to dilute the strong wine of Bakuninism with Lavrovian water. Rebellion was crowded out by educational work, work in which individual socialist preaching occurred only as an exception.

In accord with the Populist doctrine, which denied a future to

Russian capitalism, the proletariat was assigned no independent role at all in the revolution. It happened accidentally, however, that propaganda, designed in its content for the villages, found a sympathetic response only in the cities. The school of history is rich in pedagogical resources. The movement of the 1870s was perhaps most instructive in the fact that a program carefully cut to the pattern of a peasant revolution succeeded in assembling only the intelligentsia and some individual industrial workers. This exposed the bankruptcy of Populism and prepared the first critical elements of its revision. But before arriving at a realistic doctrine grounded upon the actual trends within society, the revolutionary intelligentsia had to experience the Golgotha of the terrorist struggle.

The overly remote and completely uncertain day of the eventual mass awakening of the people did not correspond at all to the passionate expectations of the revolutionary circles in the cities. Here the fierce governmental assault on the propagandists of the first line—years of pretrial detention, decades at hard labor, physical violence, insanity, and suicide—awakened a burning desire to pass from words to action. But how else could the immediate "work" of small circles express itself than in isolated blows at the most hated representatives of the regime? Terrorist moods began to make their way more and more insistently. On January 24, 1878, a solitary young girl shot the Petersburg chief of police, Trepov, who had recently ordered a prisoner, Bogolyubov, subjected to corporal punishment. This pistol shot of Vera Zasulich—twenty years later Lenin was to work on the same editorial staff with this remarkable woman—was merely the instinctive expression of a passionate indignation. Yet in this gesture lay the seed of a whole political system. A half year later on the streets of Petersburg, Kravchinsky, a man equally skilled with pen and dagger, killed the all-powerful chief of gendarmes, Mezentsev. Here, too, it was a matter of avenging slaughtered comrades in arms. But Kravchinsky was no longer a loner; he acted as a member of a revolutionary organization.

The "colonies" scattered among the people had need of leadership. A little experience of the actual struggle overcame their prejudices against centralism and discipline, which had seemed somewhat tinged with "Nechayevism." The provincial groups

readily adhered to the newly formed center, and thus from selected elements was formed the organization called Land and
Freedom, a body of revolutionary Populists truly admirable in the
composition and solidarity of its cadres. But alas, the attitude
of these Populists toward the people, who were proving so un-
sympathetic to the bloody sacrifices of the revolutionaries, became more and more touched with skepticism. Zasulich and
Kravchinsky seemed by their example to be summoning their
followers to seize weapons and, without awaiting the masses, rise
immediately in defense of themselves and their own. Half a year
later, after the murder of Mezentsev, a young aristocrat, Mirsky
—this time on the direct decision of the party—shot at Drenteln,
the new chief, but missed!

At about the same time, in the spring of 1879, a prominent
provincial member of the party arrived at the capital with a pro-
posal to kill the tsar. The son of a minor government official, educated at government expense and afterward a district teacher,
Alexander Solovyov had passed through the serious schooling of
revolutionary settlements in the villages of the Volga before de-
spairing of the success of propaganda. The leaders of Land and
Freedom hesitated. This terrorist leap into the unknown frightened them. The party refused its sanction, but this did not stop
Solovyov. On April 2, in Winter Palace Square, he fired three shots
from a revolver at Alexander II. This attempt was also unsuccessful; the tsar escaped unharmed. The government, of course,
came down with a new hail of reprisals upon the press and the
youth of the country: Solovyov's attempt bears the same relation
to the movement "to the people" of the 1870s as Karakozov's does
to the first attempt at propaganda in the preceding decade. The
symmetry is all too obvious! But the second revolutionary cycle
was incomparably more important than the first, not only in the
number of people drawn into the movement, but in their temper and experience and in the bitterness of the struggle. The attempt of Solovyov, which Land and Freedom found it impossible
to disavow, did not remain, like the shot of Karakozov, an isolated
act. Systematic terror became the order of the day. The war with
Turkey, disturbing the national economy and leading to the
capitulation of Russian diplomacy at the Congress of Berlin
(1879), shook Russian society deeply, lowered the prestige of

the government, and gave rise to exaggerated hopes among the revolutionaries, impelling them upon the road of direct political struggle.

In June 1879, breaking with the group of orthodox Populists who refused to forsake the villages, Land and Freedom shed its skin, and entered the political arena as the People's Will. To be sure, in its manifesto the new party did not renounce propaganda among the masses. On the contrary, it decided to devote two thirds of the party funds to it, and only one third to terror. But this decision remained a symbolic tribute to the past. The revolutionary chemists had no difficulty in explaining in those days that dynamite and nitroglycerine, widely popularized by the Russo-Turkish War, could be easily prepared at home. The die was cast. At the same moment, propaganda, having disappointed all expectations, was once and for all replaced by terror, and the revolver, having revealed its inadequacy, was replaced by dynamite. The whole organization was reconstructed to answer the needs of terrorist struggle. All forces and all funds were devoted to the preparation of assassinations. The "villagers" among the revolutionaries felt utterly forgotten in their faraway corners. They tried in vain to create an independent organization, the Black Redistribution (*Chorny Peredel*), which was, however, destined to become a bridge to Marxism and had no independent political significance. The turn to terror was irreversible. The programmatic announcements of the revolutionaries were revised to correspond with the demands of the new method of struggle. Land and Freedom had spread the doctrine that a constitution was in itself harmful to the people, that political freedom ought to be one of the by-products of a social revolution. The People's Will acknowledged that the achievement of political liberty is a necessary precondition for social revolution. Land and Freedom had tried to see in terror a mere signal for action given to the oppressed masses from above. The People's Will set itself the task of achieving a revolution by terrorist "disorganization" of the government. What had been at first a semi-instinctive act of revenge for victimized comrades, was converted by the course of events into a self-contained system of political struggle. Thus the intelligentsia, isolated from the people and at the same time pushed forward into the historic vanguard by the whole course of events, tried to offset its social weakness by multiplying it with the explosive force of dynamite. It converted the chemistry of destruction into a political alchemy.

Together with the change of tasks and methods, the center of gravity of the work was abruptly shifted from village to city, from the cities to the capital. The headquarters of the revolution must henceforth directly oppose the headquarters of the government. At the same time, the psychological makeup of the revolutionary was altered and even his external appearance. With the disappearance of his naïve faith in the people, his carelessness with regard to conspiracy became a thing of the past, too. The revolutionary pulled himself together, became more cautious, more attentive, more resolute. Each day he was faced anew with mortal dangers. For self-defense he carried a dagger in his belt, a revolver in his pocket. People who two or three years before had been learning the shoemaker's or carpenter's trade in order to merge with the people, were now studying the art of assembling and throwing bombs and shooting on the run. The warrior replaced the apostle. While the rural propagandist had dressed almost in rags in order to resemble "the people" more closely, this urban revolutionary tried to be outwardly indistinguishable from the well-to-do, educated city dweller. Yet striking as was the change that took place in these few short years, it was easy enough, under both disguises, to recognize the same old "nihilist." Dressed in a worn-out coat, he had not been one of the people; in the costume of a gentleman, he was not a bourgeois. A social apostate seeking to explode the old society, he was compelled to adopt the protective coloration now of one and now of the other of its two poles.

The revolutionary path of the intelligentsia thus gradually becomes clear to us. Having begun with a theoretical self-deification under the name of "critical thought," it then renounced itself in the name of a merger with the people, in order, after that failed, once more to arrive at a practical self-deification personified by the terrorist Executive Committee. Critical thought implanted itself in bombs, whose mission was to turn over the destinies of the country to a handful of socialists. So it was written, at least, in the official program of the People's Will. In fact, the renunciation of the mass struggle converted socialist aims into a subjective illusion. The only reality remaining was the tactic of frightening the monarchy by bombs, with the sole prospect of winning constitutional liberties. In their objective role, yesterday's anarchist rebels, who would not hear of bourgeois democracy, had become today's armed squadron in the service of liberalism. History has ways of putting the obstreperous in their place. Her agenda called not for anarchism, but political liberty.

The revolutionary struggle turned into a contest between the Executive Committee and the police. The Land and Freedom group, and after them the People's Will, carried out their first actions in isolation from each other, in the majority of cases unsuccessfully. The police caught them and hanged them unfailingly. From August 1878 to December 1879, seventeen revolutionaries were hanged for two governmental victims. There remained nothing to do but give up striking at individual state dignitaries, and concentrate the entire strength of the party on the tsar. It is impossible even now, at a half century's distance, not to be struck by the energy, courage, and organizational talent of this handful of fighters. The political leader and orator Zhelyabov, the scientist and inventor Kibalchich, women such as Perovskaya and Figner, peerless in their moral fortitude, were the cream of the intelligentsia, the flower of a generation. They knew how, and taught others how, to subordinate themselves completely to a freely chosen goal. Insurmountable obstacles seemed not to exist for these heroes who had signed a pact with death. Before destroying them, the terror gave them a superhuman endurance. They would dig tunnels under a railroad track down which the tsar's train was to roll; and then under a street that his carriage was to pass through; they would climb into the tsar's palace with a load of dynamite—as did the worker Khalturin—and set it off. Failure after failure! "The Almighty protects the liberator," cried the liberal press. But in the long run the energy of the Executive Committee proved stronger than the Almighty's vigilance.

On March 1, 1881, on a street of the capital, after the young man Rysakov had missed his aim, another young man, Grinevitsky, throwing a second bomb of the Kibalchich make, killed himself and Alexander II simultaneously. This time a blow was struck at the very heart of the regime. But it soon appeared that the People's Will itself was to burn up in the fire of that successful terror. The strength of the party was concentrated almost entirely in its Executive Committee. Outside this were auxiliary groups only, having no significance of their own. The terrorist struggle, at least, including the work of technical preparation, was carried on exclusively by members of the central staff. How many of these fighters were there? The numbers are now known beyond a doubt. The first Executive Committee consisted of twenty-eight persons. Up to the first of March, 1881, the general membership, never all active at once, comprised thirty-seven persons. Completely illegal—that is, cut off from all social and even family ties—these people not only kept the whole political police force in a state of tension, but at one time even converted the new tsar into the "hermit of Gatchina."[3] The whole world was shaken by the thunder of this titanic attack on Petersburg despotism. It seemed as though the mysterious party had legions of fighters at its command. The Executive Committee carefully cultivated this hypnotic belief in its omnipotence. But one cannot hold out long on hypnosis alone. Moreover, the reserves dried up with unexpected swiftness.

According to the idea of People's Will, every successful blow at the enemy was to raise the authority of the party, recruit new fighters, widen the circle of sympathizers, and, if not immediately arouse the popular masses, at least encourage the liberal opposition. Not every element of these hopes was fantastic. Their heroism undoubtedly did evoke emulation. Very likely, there was no shortage of young men and women ready to blow themselves up along with their bombs. But there was now no one to unite and guide them. The party was disintegrating. By its very nature, the terror expended the forces supplied to it during the propaganda period long before it could create new ones. "We are using up our capital," said the leader of the People's Will, Zhelyabov. To be sure, the trial of the assassins of the tsar evoked a passionate response in the hearts of individual young people. Although Petersburg was soon swept all too clean by the police, People's Will groups continued to spring up in various provinces until 1885. However, this did not go to the point of a new wave of terror. Having burned their fingers, the great majority of the intelligentsia recoiled from the revolutionary fire.

It was no better with the liberals, to whom the terrorists, after turning from the peasantry, were looking with more and more hope. To be sure, due to the diplomatic failures of the government and economic disorders, members of the *zemstvos* did attempt a trial mobilization of their forces. It proved to be a mobilization of impotence. Frightened by the growing bitterness between the warring camps, the liberals hastened to discover in the People's Will not an ally, but the chief obstacle on the road to constitutional reforms. In the words of the most leftist of the *zemstvo* men, I. I. Petrunkevich, the acts of the terrorists only "frightened society and infuriated the government."

Thus, the more deafeningly the dynamite exploded, the more complete became the vacuum that surrounded the Executive Committee, which had once arisen out of a relatively broad movement of the intelligentsia. No guerrilla detachment can long hold out amid a hostile population. No underground group can function without a screen of sympathizers. Political isolation finally exposed the terrorists to the police, who with growing success mopped up both the remnants of the old groups and the germs of the new. The liquidation of People's Will by a series of arrests and trials proceeded rapidly, against the background of the reactionary backlash of the 1880s. We shall make better acquaintance of that bleak period in connection with the terrorist attempt of Alexander Ulyanov.

4

THE ELDER BROTHER

ALEXANDER, especially in childhood, was like his mother both in looks and character. "The same rare combination," writes the elder sister, "of extraordinary firmness and serenity, with wonderful sensitivity, tenderness, and fairness: but he was more austere and single-minded, and even more courageous." The children's tutor, Kalashnikov, asserts that behind the milk-white face of Alexander, his quiet voice and calm demeanor, even in his childhood a great inner force shone out. The isolation of the family in Simbirsk during the early period, the absence of playmates, and in part also the strictness of the father, could only increase the natural introversion and single-mindedness of the boy.

There was no lack of painful and coarse impressions. To begin with, the house in which the Ulyanovs lived on the Old Crown was situated not far from the prison square. The mother was busy with the younger children; there was no nurse for the older ones, and they wandered in the square alone. On holidays "plain folk" would assemble on the Old Crown—so different from the New Crown, where "society" took its walks. The square would be thoroughly sprinkled over with sunflower shucks, relics of dried fish, and other foods. At Easter they would roll colored eggs. Bright dresses and red shirts would cling to the merry-go-round, and accordians compete with each other. Toward evening, drunken songs and fierce fights would be heard on the square. On holidays, to be sure, children were not admitted to the Crown, but on weekdays, when digging in the dust, admiring the Volga, or listening to the birds singing in the orchards, they would often be distracted from their games by the clanking of chains, by a coarse shout, or by torrents of abuse. With pained curiosity Sasha would catch glances from behind the bars, experiencing a surge of fear and pity.

It was very fine in Kokushkino, on the estate of their maternal uncle in the Kazan *gubernia*, where the married daughters came with innumerable children for the holidays. Here there were lively games, walks, boat rides—and later, hunting parties—into which Sasha threw himself with enthusiasm. But the poverty of the peasants was all around them; the whole environment was still imbued with the mores of serfdom. A neighboring peasant, Karpei, a hunter and fisherman, told Anna and Sasha how with his own eyes he had seen them marching "little Yids" through Kazan *gubernia* on the way to Siberia—ten-year-old boys torn forcibly from their parents' homes for conversion to Eastern Orthodoxy and induction into the tsar's service. Karpei's tale was more painful and burned more deeply than had the poems of Nekrasov.[1] Later, in the university, Alexander read in an underground book of Herzen's how the author on his way to exile had come across a convoy of Jewish boys being driven to Siberia.[2] Among them were eight-year-olds who fell in their tracks from weariness and died on the road. Herzen tells how he shrank back into his carriage, wept bitterly, and impotently cursed Nicholas and his regime. Did Sasha weep? According to his sister he almost never shed a tear, even in childhood. But he felt injustice the more sharply, and knew the bitterness of inward grief.

To the question "What are the worst vices?" Sasha answered as a child: "Lying and cowardice." He always had opinions of his own, usually unspoken, but based on experience, and therefore firm. This taciturn boy spoke to no one in the family about his loss of religious faith. But when the believing father, suspecting something, questioned him: "Are you going to Mass today?" Sasha answered, "No," with such conviction that his father had not the courage to insist.

Sasha entered high school in 1874, in the preparatory class. Notwithstanding the preceding epoch of reform, the high schools of that time were still a kind of penal battalion for boys. The chief implement of torture was the classics. "The study of the ancient languages," explained the creators of the educational system, "because of the very difficulty of mastering them, inculcates modesty, and modesty is the foremost attribute, and the foremost requirement of a genuine education." The classics were called on to play the role of ball and chain fastened onto the child's intellect.

Church attendance was rigorously enforced, and poisoned all holidays. When not touching his forehead to the ground, the principal would be glancing around sharply at upper-grade students to see if anybody was impudent enough to remain standing, while he, the principal, went down on his knees before his God. Card playing, drunkenness, and other similar diversions were considered innocent trespasses in comparison with joining a study circle, reading liberal journals, visiting the theater, or not getting a sufficiently military-looking crew cut. Reticence or a proud walking posture were, in the eyes of the authorities—and not always unjustifiably—regarded as external signs of secret protest. These everlastingly tense relations led to stormy explosions in several high schools, and even to conspiracies against particularly hated teachers. It went so far that in 1880 Count Loris-Melikov, who had at one time played the role of liberal police dictator for the frightened Alexander II, reported to the tsar that the Department of Education had succeeded in arraying against itself "high dignitaries, the clergy, the nobility, the professorial caste, the *zemstvos*, and the towns." The authorities hastily dismissed Count Dimitri Tolstoy, the hated creator of the "classical system," replacing him with a "liberal" minister, Saburov. But this breath of air was temporary. With fluctuations now this way, now that—and most often in the direction of reaction—the school system lasted for a quarter of a century, and with some liberalization right up to the last days of the monarchy. Hatred for high schools became a sort of national tradition. It is no accident that the satiric poetry of Polezhayev, already quoted by us, devotes its bitterest stanza to the director of the Simbirsk High School.[3] Another poet, Nadson,[4] of the same generation as Alexander Ulyanov, wrote of the school period of his life:

"Curses upon you, boyhood years!
You passed without love, without friendship or freedom."

The crudeness and cruelty of the school regime was felt more deeply by Alexander than by the majority of his schoolmates. But he gritted his teeth and studied. On his visits home Ilya Nikolayevich would attentively supervise his son's studies, demanding that his homework be completed flawlessly. The father's insistence coincided with the inborn qualities of the boy, who, while very able, was also a hard worker. In that family, everybody worked hard.

Sasha entered fifth grade just as Vishnevsky, the prereform principal, was replaced by Kerensky, father of the future hero of the February revolution. The new director slightly freshened up the stagnant police-barracks atmosphere in the high school, but the basic principles of the school regime remained, of course, unchanged. On March 1, 1881, when Alexander was in the sixth - grade, stupefying news arrived from St. Petersburg. The revolutionaries had killed the tsar. The town was full of rumors and speculations. The principal, Kerensky, made a speech about this evil deed perpetrated against the tsar/liberator. The school priest described the martyr death of the anointed of God, calling the revolutionaries "outcasts of the human race." But the authority of the priest, like that of the high-school administration, already stood low in Alexander's estimation. At home the father spoke against the terrorists with the alarm of a citizen, a state functionary, and the head of a family. Ilya Nikolayevich had returned deeply shaken from the church, where masses had been said for the murdered tsar. His student days had chanced to fall in that darkest of periods which followed the suppression of the revolution of 1848. The coronation of Alexander II had entered his consciousness forever as the beginning of an era of freedom. For the educator, at least, there *had* opened a field of action not to be dreamed of under Nicholas I. In years to come he spoke with passion on more than one occasion of the reaction that began after March 1, extending banefully even into school affairs. In his father's criticisms Alexander could not have failed to detect the voice of the liberal government functionary frightened by this gloomy drama. But the event was so unusual, the pressure of philistine indignation so overwhelming, that Sasha found no words for his confused thoughts. His sympathies, at any rate, were on the side of the executed revolutionaries. He did not speak them aloud, because of inadequate self-confidence, a fear of influencing the younger children, the dread of a sharp comment from his elders. He was like that always.

During nine years of school work there was never a complaint against Alexander. He was an excellent student, was promoted from one grade to the next with first honors, was never impudent or rude to anybody—not through lack of courage, but through self-restraint. The high school was for him only a bridge to the university, and he passed over the bridge without joy but with brilliance, graduating at the head of his class with a gold medal, a year, and even two years, ahead of his peers.

Alexander's high-school years coincided exactly with the main cycle in the revolutionary movement among the intelligentsia. He entered the preparatory class in 1874 at the height of the movement "to the people," and finished high school in 1883, when the People's Will seemed still at the peak of its powers. Simbirsk did not remain completely untouched by that movement. Persons under suspicion were exiled here from larger cities, and exiles returning from Siberia would stay here for a time. Mysterious travelers were from time to time driven through Simbirsk in troikas or on horseback by mustachioed gendarmes. In 1877 and 1878 the Simbirsk High-School teacher Muratov, an active member of *Chorny Peredel,* implanted Populist ideas here, and under his influence groups of schoolboys and military youth were formed, which even included some teachers. Although after a year and a half in the schools Muratov himself was exiled from Simbirsk, the youth circles continued to exist for some years. But Alexander had no contact with them. The atmosphere of his own family, with its interest in education and its love of Nekrasov and Shchedrin,[5] evidently provided, for the time being, sufficient satisfaction to the ideological needs of the boy, the adolescent, and the young man. Even in the first three years of his university life, however, Alexander continued to shy away from revolutionary circles. We must seek the cause in Alexander's character, in his special, self-contained quality and a certain aversion to haste. All forms of intellectual and moral dilettantism were alien to him —the easy acceptance and easy abandonment of people and ideas. He did not make up his mind lightly. Having made it up, he knew neither fear nor hesitation.

The summer of 1882, the vacation preceding his final year, Alexander spent principally in the unused kitchen of a wing of the house, which he converted into a chemical laboratory. He was always the last to come down for tea, finding it difficult to tear himself away from his work; often he had to be called twice. Ilya Nikolayevich made jokes about his son's preoccupation with chemistry. Alexander remained silent and smiled "indulgently." "In a general conversation he would take little part." Hardly waiting to finish his tea, he would hasten back to his room. According to Anna, Alexander's preoccupation with chemistry began to come between them at the end of his high-school years. In reality the cause of this growing estrangement was not only, and not even primarily, the natural sciences. Alexander had come into that period of the re-evaluation of values, when boys and young men appraise those who were only recently closest to them, and not infrequently find them wanting. Alexander was taking less and less part in family diversions, preferring the hunt, or conversations with a girl cousin for whom his affection had grown into a timid early love.

In a novel by Chirikov dedicated to the life of his native Simbirsk, Alexander's preoccupation with chemistry is depicted as a conscious preparation for the activities of a terrorist—one of the many liberties with facts taken by this author, who began with a sympathy for Bolshevism and ended up among the White émigrés.[6] Alexander loved chemistry for chemistry's sake. His eyes, thoughtful, serious, somewhat lingering, were the eyes of a born experimental scientist. In 1883, Alexander left Simbirsk. In sending his son off to Petersburg, Ilya Nikolayevich urged him to be careful of himself—the dying rumble of the terror was still fresh in the memory of all. The son was able quite sincerely to say a few reassuring words to his father: his thoughts were still far from the revolutionary struggle. Alexander was excited about science; his head was full of Mendeleyev's formulas.[7] The capital meant to him, above all, the university.

It was still the old Petersburg, not yet having reached its first million in population. From a venerable old woman Alexander rented a room, equipped, according to his sister, with "silence, coziness, and the smell of an oil lamp." That vague feeling of dissatisfaction with the social system which Alexander brought with him was not strengthened or sharpened during his first university years. If it did not grow weaker, at least it withdrew into the depths of his consciousness. The university opened new horizons to his youthful mind. Alexander was possessed by the demon of knowledge. He plunged deep into the natural sciences, and soon

attracted the attention both of his fellow students and of professors.

The father had set aside forty rubles a month each for the living expenses of his son and daughter. This sum, we must suppose,
was twice if not three times more than the average budget of students of that time. In spite of assurances from Alexander that
thirty rubles was enough, his father continued to send his son as
much as he sent his daughter. Alexander made no protest, but on
his arrival in Simbirsk for the holidays he turned over eighty rubles for the eight months past. The most significant item in this
little story is the fact that during the whole winter Alexander had
not spoken a word to his sister of what he was doing. He did not
want to exert pressure upon her or to prejudice his own freedom
of action. Besides which, he no longer felt close to his sister. The
father, knowing there was no lack of temptation in the capital,
admired his son's self-restraint. This same episode shows, on the
other hand, how far Alexander stood, in the first period of his student days, not only from revolutionary organizations but from all
kinds of young men's associations. Otherwise, he would surely
have found something to do with those ten extra rubles a month.

According to the student Govorukhin, whose testimony may be
wholly relied upon, even at the end of 1885, when he was in the
third year of his studies, Ulyanov refused to join any student
circles, saying: "They jabber a lot, but study little." Just as a lay-
man ought not to practice medicine, so in his pedantic opinion it
was criminal for one ignorant of social conditions to embark on
the revolutionary road. Other observers describe Alexander during
this period in the same terms—particularly, except for certain con-
ventional phrases, his elder sister.

There is, however, other testimony, which may perhaps go
better with the abstract image of the born revolutionary, though
it does not correspond to the facts. In a book dedicated to the
memory of Ilya Nikolayevich Ulyanov, the younger daughter,
Maria, writes that her father "knew, and could not help knowing
of the revolutionary intentions of his eldest son." In reality the
father could not have known anything about these intentions because they did not exist. They began to take form only in the
autumn of 1886, when the father was no longer among the living.
At the time of Ilya Nikolayevich's death, Maria was not yet eight,

and there can be no question of independent political observations on her part. She herself does not refer to personal memories, but to general psychological considerations. "Their love for each other was too great. Their friendship was much too close. . . ." That filial love was just what compelled many a revolutionary son to conceal from his parents up to the last moment the dangers hanging over him. It happens in this particular case, however, that the son had nothing to conceal; this much may be considered firmly established. But besides this, the words "close friendship" hardly correspond to the actual relationship between Ilya Nikolayevich and Alexander. The elder sister often refers to the reticence Alexander displayed toward other members of the family even in early childhood, and notes the effect upon this trait of the excessive demands made by the father. From her, too, we know that Alexander did not confide his religious doubts to his believing father. The son's first refusal to go to Mass startled Ilya Nikolayevich; and both sides, it seems, avoided a showdown on the question. Could it have been otherwise in the sphere of politics, where a collision, had it ripened during the life of the father, would have been infinitely more sharp? Maria adduces the testimony of the brother Dimitri, who at the age of eleven was present during a long conversation between the father and Alexander in a garden path. This happened half a year before the father died, and a year and a half before the death of the son. The child did not understand the subject of the conversation, but throughout his life there remained with him the impression of something extremely weighty and important. "At present I am absolutely convinced," says Dimitri, "that the conversation I describe dealt with politics, and doubtless it was not accidental and not the only one." This guess of Dimitri's—and it is a guess made forty years after the event—must be interpreted in the light of the farewell advice sent through Anna, who was already living in Petersburg: "Tell Sasha that he must be careful of himself if only for our sake." At the time of his last meeting with his father, in the summer of 1885, Alexander was in that transitional state when in talks with revolutionaries a young man is inclined to defend his right to devote himself to science and in clashes with advisers wisened by life's experiences he feels compelled to defend revolutionary activities. Here too, however, we must add that Alexander could not feel the need of opening his mind to his father, who was the last man from whom he could expect ideological support in revolutionary questions.

But entirely apart from any confession on the part of Alexander, the father could not help feeling alarmed. The threat of the gallows and of hard labor stood inexorably before the eyes of many a father and mother. Ilya Nikolayevich must often have asked himself: Will not my beloved son be lured into some kind of irremediable disaster? The last conversations of the vacation might, and indeed must, have traveled along this line—especially on the eve of the son's departure. How many such words of counsel must have been spoken in all the remote corners of Russia by conservative and liberal parents to their more radical children! One side was seeking a way out of the cruelty and lies of the regime; the other was threatening them with the consequences. The final fatherly adjuration, "Have pity at least on your mother and me," caused pain, but was rarely persuasive.

During his first three and a half years at the university, Alexander did nothing but study. It seemed as though he were storing up knowledge enough for a long life. But he could not elude his destiny. . . . The resistance that Alexander at first put up against revolutionary influences, as well as the form taken by his brief revolutionary work thereafter, were determined by profound changes that had been going on in the political atmosphere of the country, and especially in the moods of the intelligentsia. This is where we must seek the key to Alexander Ulyanov's fate.

5

THE 1880'S

IMMEDIATELY after the first of March, 1881, in an open letter to Alexander III, the Executive Committee of the People's Will offered to cease the terrorist struggle if the new tsar would summon the representatives of the people. The expression "course of things" is not a metaphor, but a reality; it knows how to disavow those who do not understand it. It had seemed that only the other day the Populists were denouncing any constitution as a doorway to capitalism. Now they were promising to renounce revolutionary struggle in exchange for a constitution. The frightened tsar wept on the shoulder of his tutor, Pobedonostsev.[1] However, this weakness among the ruling groups did not last long. The terrorist acts had evoked no response in the country. The peasants saw in the murder of the tsar an act of revenge on the part of the nobles.[2] The workers joined the revolutionary movement only in isolated cases. The liberals were in hiding. Nobody supported the demand for a national assembly. The government, convinced that the terrorists represented nothing except their own heroism, took courage. On April 29, the tsar issued a manifesto proclaiming autocratic rule inviolate. At the same time, pogroms were set in motion. Henceforth a firm course was steered. The Procurator of the Holy Synod of the Russian Orthodox Church, Pobedonostsev, the minister, Count Dimitri Tolstoy, and the Moscow publicist, Katkov,[3] became the inspirers of the new regime. A popular assembly? Why, it suffices to cast a glance at those provisional "talk fests," the *zemstvos!* Who is running them? "Worthless people, immoral, living outside their families, debauched philanderers. . . ." Thus Pobedonostsev instructed the young tsar, who was known to be a good family man.

There was nothing for the terrorists to do but declare an open season on the new tsar. To this effect, one of the prominent members of the People's Will formulated a program of action: "Sashka after Sashka!"* But this formula hung impotent in the air. The capital of the People's Will was spent. It was a long way to a new change. In 1883 Degayev, an agent of the police, betrayed Vera Figner, one of the most admirable figures in the Executive Committee. In 1884 G. A. Lopatin, who had been in close contact abroad with Marx and Engels, returned to Petersburg to renew centrally directed terror. But there were no further successes. With the arrest of Lopatin, numerous addresses fell into the hands of the police, making it possible for them to liquidate all that still remained of the People's Will. There was a fatal logic in this chain of failures. The political movement of an isolated intelligentsia had been narrowed down to the purely technical effort to assassinate tsars, which isolated the terrorists even from the intelligentsia. The element of surprise had played a big role in the initial effectiveness of terrorism. But as soon as the police made their preparations and resorted to provocation, the little band of terrorists was caught in a noose. The continuity of the organization was completely broken, and there remained only a tradition, more and more preyed upon by doubts. The new attempts at revolutionary activity under the old banner had a disjointed, almost accidental character, and not even an occasional success. Nevertheless the inertia of fear did not soon disappear from the tsar's palace. Alexander III never left Gatchina. Through fear of assassination, the coronation was postponed to May 1883. But there were no attempts. At his coronation the tsar unfolded before the township leaders a clear program: "Obey the marshals of the nobility, and do not believe in these absurd and foolish rumors about a division of land. . . ."

That sharp turn toward aristocratic reaction which characterized the 1880s was promoted by disturbances in the world market. The incipient agrarian crisis brought great changes in the domain of ideas and programs. It was not accidental that the abolition of serfdom coincided with a period of high prices for grain. Capitalist agriculture, having increased exports, was bringing high profits to landowners. In the first years after the reform, only the more parasitical landlord estates went to ruin. These

---

* *Sashka* is a diminutive for *Alexander*. (Trans.)

could not even be saved by the peasants' redemption payments. The sympathy of progressive landowners for those liberal measures which converted Russia from a serf-owning into an aristocratic-bourgeois country, held out only as long as the prices of grain remained high. The world agrarian crisis of the 1880s struck a cruel blow at aristocratic liberalism. The landlords could now hold out only with direct financial subsidies from the state, and with a partial restoration of slave conditions in peasant work. As early as 1882 a Peasant Bank was founded, which helped the peasant bourgeoisie pay the discontented nobility immoderately high prices for their land. Three years later, the tsar, in a special manifesto, confirmed the dominant role of the nobility in the state, and established this time a Nobility Bank to make direct subsidies to aristocracy.

The decline of grain exports made possible, on the other hand, a sharp rise in import duties on industrial commodities from Western Europe. This was what the young and greedy Russian industries were trying to get. The ideas of free labor in agriculture and freedom in foreign trade had lost currency simultaneously. Alexander III revived semi-serf-owning relations in the interest of the landlords, and introduced semi-preventive tariffs in the interest of the industrialists. The official slogan of the reign, "Russia for the Russians," meant: no Western, and especially no constitutional, ideas; state positions—for the Russian nobility; the domestic market—for Russian industry; the ghetto for the Jews; enslavement of Poland and Finland in the interest of Russian officialdom and the Russian merchants. The semi-restoration of serfdom and the forced growth of capitalism, two processes working in opposite directions, together constituted the economic policy of Alexander III. And the landlords and industrialists received all that could be received at the expense of the people: cheap labor, high rentals, high prices for industrial products, and in addition to that, subsidies, bonuses, government contracts. The nobility had ceased—and the merchants had not yet begun—to play the liberal. The bureaucracy was taking revenge for the epoch of great reforms. Governmental reaction developed without hindrance throughout the whole reign. Such transformations as had been preserved from the spring days of the previous reign underwent a consistent revision in the spirit of aristocratic privileges, discrimination against national minorities, and police controls. As against the decade of the "great reforms" (1861 to 1870), there arose a decade of counterreforms (1884 to 1894).

The extremely conservative liberal Kavelin,[4] who had connections in the highest circles, wrote secretly in 1882 to a dignitary then in disfavor: "Everywhere there is dull-wittedness and idiocy, stupid routine and demoralization. Nothing useful can be made from this rot and dirt." The course of things, after its fashion, refuted Kavelin. From that rot and dirt was created a reign in the monumental style. After the first years of quietude, Alexander III finally came to believe in himself and his mission. Gigantic, fat, ignorant, inclined to vodka, greasy foods, and crude jokes, he did not admit even the thought of his subjects' having any rights. Thanks to the mortal antagonism between France and Germany, Russia's international position at that time seemed doubly secure. The Petersburg court lived hand in glove with the court in Berlin. At the same time, friendship with France opened to tsarism inexhaustible financial perspectives. The Western world, with its parliamentary "circuses," Alexander treated like an abomination. One summer, when he left unanswered an urgent diplomatic dispatch, he explained to his minister, "Europe can wait while the Russian tsar goes fishing." Of his crowned colleagues the tsar spoke with much candor: Queen Victoria he called an "old gossip"; Wilhelm II, "crazy"; the Serbian King Milan, "a beast"; the Turkish Sultan, "an old fool." Not all these designations were incorrect.

The tsar did not lack common sense. Kavelin wrote of him: "Great caution, shrewdness, great distrust, maybe a certain amount of slyness." The loyal liberal grieved only that the tsar lacked "knowledge and manners." Alexander III, moreover, was firmly convinced that his corpulent physique was of divine origin, and in all its functions served the welfare of Russia and the aims of Providence. There was character in this narrowness: the tsar was feared. Gray and bald-headed grand dukes, drunkenly scrapping with French actors, hid their capers like scared schoolboys. When the chief of the state police, Durnovo, was incautious enough to become involved in some shady affair, the tsar wrote: "Get rid of this pig"—which, by the way, did not prevent Durnovo from becoming, under Nicholas II, an all-powerful minister. To justify the official kowtowing to the roughneck on the throne, the war minister, Vannovsky, said: This is a new Peter I with a big stick. The minister of foreign affairs, Lamsdorf, wrote in his diary: Only a big stick without Peter I. The police system dominated everything without effort, by the mere motion of a finger. The patrolmen on their beats with their mustaches and medals, the famous burgomaster Gresser riding through "his" city behind a span of dappled grays, the state council, the Most Holy Synod, Pobedonostsev, the unbending spire of the Peter and Paul Fortress, the old cannon announcing the noon hour—what an ensemble! Without batting an eye, Gresser ordered the opera orchestra not to play so loud lest they disturb the most exalted listeners. And the orchestra obeyed, notwithstanding the notations of Wagner himself. Noise was strictly forbidden in literature, on the street, and even in music.

The spirit of the reign was subsequently incarnated, perhaps partly subconsciously, by the Russo-Italian sculptor Paolo Trubetskoy in his famous statue of Alexander III, where glorification is combined with satire. That obese giant, with his mighty pig-iron behind, holds down a horse that looks more like a well-fattened hog. All official Russia conformed to this style of insuperable hoggishness. The quarter-century experiment, opening with the liberation of the serfs and closing with the murder of Alexander II, had, so to speak, newly revealed the solidity of the national foundations: Autocracy, Orthodoxy, Nationality. Indeed, had it not been proved by experience that even dynamite cannot move the granite rock of tsarism? Everything seemed cut and sewn on the measure of eternity.

The old master of Russian satire Saltykov-Shchedrin, as he approached the end of his life, complained bitterly in his diary: "It becomes wearisome and hard to live. . . . A man feels as though he were in a dungeon and getting a blow on the head besides." It is hard now even to imagine the adoration among the circles of the leftist intelligentsia for the journal *Notes of the Fatherland,* an outspoken monthly closest in spirit to the revolutionary Populists. "We awaited the magazine," relates one of its contemporaries, "as a beloved guest who knew everything, and would tell about and explain everything. . . ." It was not only a

literary publication, but an ideological headquarters. The groupings and tendencies in educated Russian society had for many
years, and particularly since the peasant reforms, formed themselves around the so-called thick journals. But the pious trinity
that had declared war on "the demon of the sixties"—Pobedonostsev, Dimitri Tolstoy, and Katkov—were vigilant to good effect. "The blow on the head" did not delay. In 1884 *Notes of the
Fatherland* was suppressed. The world of the radical intelligentsia was left without a center of gravity. At the same time, the
works of Mill, Buckle, and Spencer, to say nothing of Marx and
Chernyshevsky, were removed from the libraries.

The last issue of the journal *People's Will*, which came out on
October 1, 1885, when the party itself no longer existed, painted
in bleak colors the morale of educated society: "Complete intellectual disintegration, a chaos of the most contradictory opinions
on the most elementary questions of social life . . . ; on the one
hand, pessimism both personal and social, on the other hand,
socioreligious mysticism." Those second-ranking men of the 1870s
who had survived and remained at liberty, looked around with
astonishment. The whole scene had become unrecognizable to
them. Advocates of terror, to be sure, were still to be found here
and there. "You can silence everything," they were repeating,
"but you can't silence the explosion of a bomb." However, even
the terrorists were not what they had used to be. Having renounced their utopian idea of a seizure of power, they were hoping to use their bombs only to extract liberal concessions. But only
a great idea, or at least a great illusion, can inspire the young to
go out to death. That great illusion was lost. Having become, in
essence, constitutionalists, the prophets of terror were looking
hopefully toward the liberals. But the property-holding opposition made no answer. Thus, terror was undermined from two
sides. There were prophets and defenders of the terror, but no
terrorists. In the revolutionary circles that did appear here and
there, the reigning mood was one of doom. The favorite song of
these times offered only one consolation: "From our bones an
austere avenger will arise." One of the last members of the People's Will, Yakubovich, branded his own generation in emotional
stanzas as "a generation accursed of God."[5]

The Populism of the 1870s consisted of a revolutionary hatred for class society and of a utopian program. During the 1880s the revolutionary implacability died out, leaving only utopianism. But, deprived of wings, this, too, was replaced by a program of reform in the interest of the small proprietor. To realize this program, latter-day Populists had only one hope—the good-will of the ruling classes. "Our times are not times for big tasks," said the humbled Populists, echoing the liberals. But it was only for a small minority that the process stopped even at this stage. The broad circles of the intelligentsia, in the eloquent words of a reactionary writer, wholly "renounced the heritage" of the 1860s and 1870s. In philosophy this meant a break with materialism and atheism, in politics abandonment of revolution. There was a flood of renegades of every kind. The more established strata of the intelligentsia frankly announced that they were sick and tired of peasants. Time to live for ourselves! The fading radical and liberal journals revealed the decline of social interest. Gleb Uspensky, the ablest of the Populist writers, complained that in the passenger trains general conversations on political subjects, which had recently been so loud, were no longer to be heard.[6] There was nothing left to talk about. But "life for ourselves" turned out to have an extremely meager content. Petersburg, complained the progressive press, was never so colorless as now: stagnation in trade, and complete intellectual stagnation reaching the point of prostration. It was still worse in the provinces. The provincial capitals were distinguished one from another by the fact that in one they drank more than they gambled, in another they gambled more than they drank. Any art that turned its eyes upon the people was condemned as tendentious. The intelligentsia put forward a demand for "pure art," which would not disturb it with reminders of unsolved problems and unfulfilled obligations.

The bard of the leftist circles at this time was the young Nadson, a poet with broken wings, a cracked lyre, and tubercular lungs. In his wistful verses, which ran through several editions in a short time, the principal note sounded is doubt. "We know no way out," wept this poet over his generation, which had lost faith in its former heroes and prophets. The star of Anton Chekhov was slowly rising in literature. Chekhov tried to laugh, but in the atmosphere of discouragement and melancholy, his laughter soon broke off. Chekhov found himself, and his times, in the "twilight tales" and "dreary stories," where a complaint against the cruelty and meaninglessness of life joins hands with an impotent hope for a better world "in three hundred years." Chekhov was supplemented, in painting, by Levitan, who depicted rural pastures inhabited by crows, and country roads washing away with rain in the melancholy rays of autumn twilights.[7] These gray colors became the basic hue of an entire epoch.

Especially significant for the 1880s was the influence of Count Leo Tolstoy—not the artist, long and deservedly famous, but the preacher and teacher of life. Tolstoy's curve of evolution more than once intersected the orbit of the Russian intelligentsia, but never coincided with it. Bound by all his roots to the aristocratic culture and frightened by its decay, Tolstoy was seeking a new moral axis. Bourgeois liberalism was hateful to him in its narrowness, hypocrisy, and *parvenu* manners, and the radical intelligentsia in its lack of roots, its nihilism, and its tendency to eat without a fork. Tolstoy sought peace and harmony, and wanted to hide from social alarms and also from the piercing and inexorable fear of death. At the very time when the radical intelligentsia was trying to impart life to the rural commune with its "critical thinking," Tolstoy found the peasants attractive in their lack of critical thought and of individual thought in general. In the final analysis Tolstoy was a repentant Russian nobleman— a frequently encountered species since the times of the Decembrists—only his repentance looked into the past and not the future. He thought of resurrecting the lost paradise of patriarchal harmony—but this time without compulsion and violence. The artist became a moralist. The moralist immediately sought the assistance of a sterilized religion. This most red-blooded of realists suddenly began to teach that the true goal of life is a preparation for death. Not permitting anyone to criticize his own revelation, he mocked science and art, boxed the ears of their priests, and preached meekness with an admirable fury. If you free his philosophic thought from the temptations provided by the still-unreconciled artist, there remains nothing but a depressing quietism. Every struggle against evil only increases it. The oppressed ought not to prevent the oppressor from voluntarily renouncing his oppression. The entire teaching of Tolstoy has necessarily a negative character. "Thou shalt not be angry, thou shalt not lust, thou shalt not take oaths, thou shalt not wage war." And to this was added other, more-practical advice: do not smoke, and do not eat meat. Christianity in its essence is not a doctrine about improving the world, but a prophylaxis of personal salvation, and an art for avoiding sin. Its extreme ideal is monasticism, just as the extreme of monasticism is found in the anchorites. It is no accident that Tolstoyanism leaned upon Buddhism.

This gospel of non-resistance fell most appropriately upon the soil prepared by the collapse of the plans and hopes of the People's Will. The quintessence of revolutionary violence having gone bankrupt, what could better replace it than a harmless solvent of Christian "love." If it had proven impossible to overthrow tsarism, tsarism could still be morally condemned. "The Kingdom of God is within you." The idea of moral self-perfection replaced the program of social transformation. In the circles of the intelligentsia, Tolstoyanism made devastating conquests. Some would try, in the steps of the master, to make bad boots or put up worthless stoves. Others would renounce tobacco and carnal love —most of them not for long. Still others created agricultural colonies, in which the evangelical wine of love soon turned into the vinegar of mutual recrimination. Five young ladies from Tiflis questioned Tolstoy, and the entire press repeated their question: How shall we live a holy life? But the holy life did not appear. On the contrary, the higher they looked for the rules of personal morality, the deeper they sank in the slime of actual existence. The idealistic philosopher Vladimir Solovyov tried ten years later to express the attitude of the Russian Enlightenment in this formula: "Man is only a species of ape, and therefore we ought to . . . give our souls for our lesser brethren."[8] This paradox was designed to be a mockery of materialistic narrowness; in reality, the bite of its satire was directed at idealistic hypocrisy. It was no accident that an epoch of crude and godless materialism, when people gave their lifeblood to pave a road to a better future, was replaced by a decade of idealism and mysticism when each man turned his rear to the rest in order to make sure of saving his own soul.

The political meaning of these ideological metamorphoses presents, especially in retrospect, no enigma. Having originated in

the main among circles where prebourgeois mores still prevailed,
and having passed with its left flank through a period of heroic
self-sacrifice in the name of the people, the intelligentsia, after
cruel defeats, had taken the road of bourgeois revivalism. In yesterday's saint, began to speak the self-centered man. His first need
was to free himself from the idea of a "duty to the people." Literature and philosophy hastened, of course, to welcome and
adorn these sickly awakenings of bourgeois individualism. The
propertied classes did what they could to tame that intelligentsia
which had caused them so much trouble. The rapprochement
and reconciliation of the bourgeoisie in the process of becoming
civilized, with the intelligentsia in the process of becoming
bourgeois, was, generally speaking, inevitable. Barbaric political
conditions, however, made impossible its smooth and uninterrupted development. The Russian intelligentsia was destined to
make more than one new departure in years to come.

Our narrative required this closer look at the 1880s, a period
during which Alexander Ulyanov, the university student, entered
the arena of struggle, and his younger brother Vladimir was pur-
suing his studies in the Simbirsk High School.

6

THE FIRST OF MARCH, 1887

ALTHOUGH the new university regulations introduced in 1884 had forbidden all student organizations whatever, there continued to exist at the capital as many as twenty home-town clubs, embracing about fifteen hundred students. This club movement was perfectly innocuous in character, centering around questions of cuisine and mutual-aid funds. In view of the poverty of the overwhelming mass of students, such organizations were a vital necessity. However, the government was not wrong in fearing them. The revolutionaries would make use of any kind of association to recruit followers, and in a moment of political awakening the most peaceable of home-town clubs would mobilize the youth for the struggle. But after the shattering of the People's Will, Petersburg had been considered entirely purged of revolutionaries; the few who survived were hiding in the provinces. The mood of the students seemed to the authorities so quiet that they closed their eyes to the home-town clubs. The vast majority of the students really had withdrawn from politics. More noticeable, against the gray university background, was a layer of young careerists, future government functionaries, who embodied, even in dress and haircut, the exact opposite of the nihilist type. The half-starving youth, stifled by the police regime, remained discontented, but did not go beyond surly inaction.

On the general tide of discouragement, however, there were still small ebbs and flows, and chiefly among these same students. Only in his third year at the university did Alexander become active in the student circles—biological, economic, and literary. But even here it was merely a question of elaborating scientific views, not of active politics. It was on this basis that he established closer ties with the radical elements of the home-town clubs. He began to devote more time to the study of social problems. In these circles the idea arose of marking the twenty-fifth anniversary of the Peasant Reform—February 19, 1861—by a mass in the Volkovo Cemetery for the heroes of the "peasant liberation." What a reappraisal of reputations! The great publicist Chernyshevsky had despised the peasant reform as robbery and deceit, and had paid cruelly for this bold and sober judgment, which lay at the basis of the revolutionary movement for the next twenty years. To the question of Alexander II: "Why did you shoot at me?" Karakozov, by then in the hands of the police, had answered: "Because you promised the peasants freedom and land and you deceived them." The "nineteenth of February" was appraised in the same way by Ippolit Myshkin and his comrades and by the adherents of People's Will. But as the clouds of reaction grew darker, the "great reform" of the preceding reign, celebrated by the liberal press, began to appear in a more favorable light even to the students. From behind the heavy back of Alexander III, the figure of Alexander II acquired an almost liberal outline.

To celebrate the peasant reform became gradually an act of opposition, and incurred police persecution. On this occasion the press was directed in advance to refrain from anniversary articles. Saying a mass over the official executors of the reform thus became an act of protest. The cemetery priest agreed, not without fear and trembling, to conduct the rites for the repose of the souls of the liberators—among them, of course, Alexander II, killed six years before by the elder brothers of those who were saying the mass. In this political move we see more clearly than in all the police persecutions the depth of social reaction that prevailed. To be sure, a number of the demonstrators thought of the mass as dedicated not to the bureaucrats, but to those writers who had fought for the liberation of the peasants. Nothing was clear; all dividing lines were blurred.

The Volkovo Cemetery figures as the setting for Alexander Ulyanov's first public activity. He participated actively in preparing for this mass. The liberal circles, to whom the initiators appealed, responded as usual: not at all. Only the students came —about four hundred of them. The police could not make up their minds, it seems, to disturb an oppositional religious service— or perhaps they simply failed to notice it. The young people dispersed, at any rate, almost with a feeling of having won a victory. The more resolute decided that it was possible to go farther along the same path.

From then on, the leaders of the students drew closer together, and in the following months created a union of home-town clubs. Ulyanov took a place in the directing center. But the activities of the union, extremely modest activities, were soon interrupted by the holidays, the last that Alexander was to spend on the Volga with his already fatherless family. In the autumn the activities of the circles and of the home-town clubs were revived. Their leaders, the same ones as before, hit upon the thought of using the approaching twenty-fifth anniversary of the death of the famous critic Dobrolyubov, pupil and comrade in arms of Chernyshevsky, to celebrate a new mass.[1] This time six hundred assembled—or, according to other sources, up to a thousand. But they found the gates of the cemetery closed; the police were not to be taken unawares. The request for a permit for a mass was refused by the burgomaster, Gresser. On their way back to the city, the student crowd was surrounded by the Cossacks and kept standing for two hours in the rain. Forty of them were subsequently exiled from Petersburg. This event, though insignificant in itself, nevertheless shook the initiators of the manifestation to the depths and transformed them, especially Ulyanov. It was a personal experience, his own, and it brought his whole store of previous observations and reflections to a quick focus in a burning demand for action.

How shall we answer the oppressors? There was no end of discussion, and of bold plans, for which only the strength was lacking. They drew up a proclamation addressed to "society"— that is, to professors, *zemstvo* members, lawyers, and writers. Most of the envelopes containing the proclamation were taken from the mailboxes by the police and did not disturb the peaceful doze of the liberals. The excitement among the students gradually subsided. But these days of hot feeling served to sift out a group of the more resolute, who drew from their own indignation and political impotence a conclusion already sanctified by the past: *Terror!*

Ulyanov still tried for a time to cling to his old position: One ought not to take up revolutionary activities without having

worked out correct views. They answered him: While you sit
with your books, violence triumphs and grows stronger. The argument was convincing because Alexander no longer wanted to
resist it. For him there was no more retreat. One of the chief initiators of a demonstration for which others were suffering, author
of a proclamation to "society" that had met no response,
Alexander already stood under the sign of the terrorist imperative. After brief dispute in a narrow circle, he finally joined a
small group with terrorist aims. Two or three of the conspirators
had a bit of experience and a few, modest contacts. Thus originated the affair of March 1, 1887.

The last period of his life Alexander divided between the
university laboratory, where he was investigating *Idothea en-
tonon,* a species of marine isopod, and a conspiratorial laboratory,
where he was manufacturing dynamite bombs. Intending to give
his life for the future of humanity, he nevertheless continued to
investigate with passionate curiosity the visual capacity of worms.
Science had a firm grip on him. He tore himself from science with
pain, like a warrior from his beloved on the eve of his first and
last battle. No less characteristic of this youth is the fact that on
the very last days before the attempt, when all the fibers of his
being must have been tensed with superhuman anxiety, he
found the strength of spirit to set in type, with his inexperienced
hands, the program of the "Terrorist Faction," of which he was
also the author.

From saying a mass over the men of the peasant reform to saying a mass for a radical writer who had died young, and from this
unsaid mass to a plan to assassinate the tsar—such was the road
traveled in a few brief months by those who made this attempt.
Subsequently, in court, the chief counsel for the defense described. quite accurately the genesis of the plot: "Why, these
people," he said, "were not always terrorists; in August 1886 they
were merely 'malcontents'; in November, after the unsuccessful
attempt to celebrate a mass at the grave of Dobrolyubov, they
were 'protesters'; and it was only in January that the terrorist
tendency had ripened among them. . . ." The liberal lawyer did
not add that the leap from saying masses to throwing bombs had
been possible only because under the heavy lid of the new reign
no small amount of mute discontent had accumulated among the

more-democratic layers of the intelligentsia, to say nothing of the people. But that did not make any difference. This bold undertaking of an isolated circle was condemned in advance to failure. If the revolutionary offensive of the years 1860 to 1866 (from the first proclamation to the shot fired by Karakozov) had been, in the inner consistency of its stages, a kind of rough draft of the great movement of the intelligentsia from 1873 to 1881, the episode of 1886–87 was its belated and declining echo.

In the afternoon of March 1, on the Nevsky Prospect,* six young men were detained by police officers. One of them carried a thick book with raised letters on the cover reading "Medical Dictionary." What was really involved, was the political medicine of the terror. The supposed dictionary contained dynamite and bullets poisoned with strychnine. Two of the others carried bombs of cylindrical form. The bombs were intended for Alexander III. An unprecedented series of searches and arrests followed. The participants in this bold attempt on the all-powerful ruler of Russia were nothing more than young students. Only one of the intended bomb throwers had reached his twenty-sixth year; one of the organizers was twenty-three. The other five most closely involved were only twenty or twenty-one. The preparation of the bombs had been entrusted chiefly to a natural-science student who was still three months under age. The name of this technician was Alexander Ulyanov. His amateur preoccupation with chemistry in the kitchen in a wing of the house in Simbirsk, had come in handy. The initiator of the whole undertaking was a sickly twenty-three-year-old student named Shevyryov. He had selected his men and divided the work among them. His own revolutionary experience was not, and could not have been, very significant. Between this Shevyryov, hasty and sanguine, and the more thoughtful Ulyanov, quarrels had arisen more than once about the question of bringing in relatively inexperienced people. However, there had been little to choose from. Two students accidentally involved in the plot subsequently betrayed Ulyanov. The organization had negligible technical and financial resources. In order to get nitric acid and 150 rubles for expenses, it had been

* St. Petersburg's main thoroughfare. (Ed.)

necessary to go to Vilna; but the acid proved too weak and the money did not arrive immediately. In order to enable one of the organizers to escape abroad, Ulyanov pawned his high-school gold medal for one hundred rubles. A pistol supplied to the bomb thrower Generalov to enable him to cover his escape, proved useless. Such was the level of their conspiratorial methods. The whole enterprise had hung by a thread.

Even in the preparations for March 1, 1881, an attempt made by incomparably more-hardened revolutionaries, the dreadful tension as the fatal hour approached turned into weariness and apathy. Could Ulyanov and the other youthful conspirators have helped but feel doubt tugging at their hearts? Rumors had arisen that the government already knew of the proposed attempt. Some member of the group proposed that they postpone the whole thing until autumn. But that meant new dangers. According to some reports, Alexander foresaw the failure of the attempt. More likely, the mood of the condemned handful wavered sharply between optimism and despair. But will overcame doubts. The preparations were not postponed; the bombs were made ready, the roles divided, the posts assigned. It remained only to kill and, whatever came, to die.

In reality, the government suspected nothing. After several years of calm, the police had ceased to think about terror. Without provocateurs, a police force is, in general, powerless to discover plots. There was no provocateur among the conspirators. But they managed to give themselves away—through their youth, naïveté, and the carelessness of one of them. Only after 1917, when the police archives were examined, did it become possible to discover the cause of their failure. The student Andreyushkin, designated as a bomb thrower, wrote a friendly letter to another student in Kharkov a month and a half before the event. In it was included a sort of hymn to Terror. The letter, which had an illegible signature, was intercepted by the police. The Kharkov addressee, summoned to the police station, betrayed his Petersburg correspondent. A correspondence between the two police departments dragged along for some time, the Kharkov people seeing no special reason for haste. Finally the Petersburg police secured the name and address of the writer, and put him under surveillance. This happened on February 28, the eve of the proposed attempt. Andreyushkin and others were seen on the Nevsky Prospect between noon and 5 o'clock in the afternoon with some heavy objects in their hands. It never occurred to the police that these might be bombs. They were seeking the author of the suspicious letter and nothing else. The next day, "the same persons, numbering six, were again seen on the Nevsky in the same circumstances." Only then were they arrested.

The surprise of the police when they stumbled upon a group of terrorists was unbounded. Alexander III was, of course, immediately informed of the discovery. The tsar wrote upon the report: "This time God saved us, but for how long?" Not fully confident of God's help, the tsar added a word of encouragement to his earthly guards: "Thanks to all officers and agents of the police that they do not slumber, but act with expedition." In reality the officers and agents hardly deserved his gratitude; a happy accident had come to his assistance. It is uncertain, however, how the attempt would have ended, without the interference of accident and the police. The question of the quality of the bombs remained unexplored to the end. The bomb hurler, Osipanov—when he was arrested, it never occurred to the police to take away his bomb—threw it in Police Headquarters, hoping to kill himself together with his police escort, but the bomb did not explode. There is no reason to think that the other bombs were any better. An artillery general, called in as an expert, testified that the "construction of the bombs was imperfect." Everything in this tragic undertaking was imperfect: ideas, personnel, conspiracy, and manufacturing technique.

The social position of the culprits was described by the prosecutor as follows: nine university students, one candidate for the Theological Seminary, one student of pharmacy, one townsman, two midwives, one elementary-school teacher. The defendants reflected the lowest, most democratic layer of the intelligentsia, and only its younger generation at that. "Not all of the defendants were of age," the prosecutor was compelled to acknowledge—which did not prevent him from considering them old enough for the gallows. The liberal lawyers did not differ much from the attorney general in the tone of their speeches. Being "one hundred per cent Russian," they could not believe that such evildoings had originated among Russian youth. They sought behind the backs of the defendants for "some foreign disrespect for Russia's sacred institutions."

The majority of the defendants did not know how to conduct themselves at the inquiry or the trial. Some were weakhearted and gave the plot away. But the courageous, too, told more than necessary and thus helped the prosecution—both against themselves and against others. Among the defendants was Bronislaw Pilsudski, son of a rich landowner, who had turned over his room to Ulyanov for the printing of the program. Bronislaw's brother, Jozef Pilsudski, was taken to the courtroom from prison to serve as a witness. Bronislaw demeaned himself, denied his sympathy with People's Will, and pleaded lack of character and naïveté. Jozef gave his testimony with great caution, but was compelled to admit sending telegrams from Vilna in the "agreed-upon revolutionary jargon." (Subsequently, as dictator of Poland, he managed to exchange "revolutionary jargon" for the fascist kind.)[2]

The trial exposed beyond a doubt the fact that, although Alexander Ulyanov was not the chief architect of the conspiracy, he was at any rate the most important figure in it. For in those trying days after the initiator and the organizer, in accordance with a previous plan, had fled from Petersburg, Ulyanov, in the correct testimony of the prosecutor, "took the place of both ringleaders of the conspiracy." Having had no role in the final act on the streets either as bomb thrower or as scout, Ulyanov was arrested in the room of a student, Kancher, where he walked into a police trap. Only through Kancher, who gave away everything that he knew, was the actual role of Ulyanov discovered by the authorities. From that moment, the defendant Lukashevich, who collaborated in preparing the bombs, read in the eyes of Ulyanov "an irrevocable determination to die." "If you have to, blame it on me!" whispered Ulyanov to Lukashevich in the courtroom. Another defendant, Ananyina, told her daughter many years later: "He was ready to be hanged twenty times over if that could ease the fate of the others."

The conduct of Ulyanov during the investigation and the trial gives us the full measure of this young man. He wants to take upon himself as much as possible in order to ease the fate of his comrades; at the same time, he is afraid of proclaiming his real role as leader in so many words lest he impinge on the dignity of the others. He claims sole responsibility, but not sole credit. "I fully believe," said the prosecutor, "the testimony of the defendant Ulyanov, whose confession, if at all distorted, is so only in the sense that he takes upon himself even that which he really did not do." This tribute of respect from the prosecutor made Ulyanov's execution all the more certain.

Those present at the trial, besides the judges, included the prosecutor, the lawyers for the defense, and the defendants. Plus one other participant, invisible but very real: the tsar. In a sense, the trial was a duel between two men: Alexander Romanov and Alexander Ulyanov. The tsar was at that time thirty-three years old. He was not accustomed to staring into a microscope or racking his brains over Karl Marx. He believed in icons and relics, and considered himself a "truly Russian" tsar, although he was unable to compose a single literate sentence in Russian (or, for that matter, in any other language). On the program written by Ulyanov the tsar wrote with his own hand: "This is the writing not even of a madman, but of a pure idiot." Beneath the program's assertion that under the existing political regime any attempt to raise the level of the people was almost impossible, Romanov wrote: "That is reassuring." In the margin of the practical part of the program, which included demands not only for democracy, but also for nationalization of the land, the factories, and all the means of production, the tsar made the notation: "A regular commune." And finally, the following words, spoken by Ulyanov on March 21, received the tsar's special attention: "As far as my moral and intellectual participation in this affair is concerned, it was complete —that is, all that my ability and the strength of my knowledge and convictions made possible." Opposite this the tsar wrote, "This frankness is quite touching!!!" The tsar was not too deeply touched, however, to hang five defendants whose ages totaled barely one hundred and ten years.

The terrorists of the 1870s had passed through a preliminary school of propaganda and revolutionary organization, which explains their more advanced age and experience. Before mounting the scaffold, Zhelyabov, Kibalchich, and Perovskaya had become politically mature and hardened revolutionaries. Having arisen out of the effort to create a mass movement, People's Will had set itself, at least on paper, the goal of mounting an insurrection, having first assured itself of the co-operation of the workers and the sympathy of a section of the armed forces. In reality, as we know, the Executive Committee found itself compelled to concentrate all of its forces on the assassination of the tsar.

The group of 1887 began straight off with the work upon which the Executive Committee of the seventies had broken its head. The disheartened mood of the intelligentsia had cut off in advance, so to speak, all roads leading to the masses. The plot of Shevyryov and Ulyanov did not even try to transcend the bounds of a small student circle. There was no attempt at propaganda, at the winning over of the workers, at the establishment of a press or the publication of journals. The initiators of this terrorist attempt counted neither on the help of the people nor the support of the liberals. They did not call themselves a party, but a faction —that is, a fragment of a no-longer-existing whole. They renounced centralization, having nothing and nobody to centralize. They chose to believe that there would be other groups in the country ready to act on their own initiative and that this would be sufficient to guarantee success.

In his speech in court, Ulyanov gave a very vivid explanation, if not of the terrorist struggle itself, then at least of the sources of his belief in its effectiveness: "We have not," he said, "any strongly united classes which might restrain the government. . . ." At the same time, "our intelligentsia is so weak physically and so little organized that at present we cannot enter into an open struggle. . . ." From this pessimistic appraisal of the social forces, the natural inference would be a political hopelessness of the kind prevailing in the 1880s, but it is well enough known that extreme despair often becomes the source of unrealistic dreams. "The weak intelligentsia, very weakly imbued with the interests of the masses . . . ," concluded Ulyanov, "can defend its right to think only with terrorism." Such were the psychological sources of the affair of March 1, 1887, that startling attempt by ten young men and women to give a new direction to the political life of society.

Six persons took part in the drawing up of the program of the group. Three of them, including Ulyanov, considered themselves adherents of People's Will; three others were inclined to call themselves Social Democrats. The distinction between the former and the latter, however, was not at all clear-cut. The so-called Social Democrats were willing to recognize the relevance of Marxism, not only for the West but also for Russia. On the question of "direct political struggle," however, they were adamantly in favor of terror. If a mass revolutionary movement—the argument went—can arise only in connection with the further development of capitalism, then the revolutionary intelligentsia has nothing to do at present but to pick up the weapon that fell from the hands of the People's Will. This thought united young people otherwise differing with each other. Terror as the central problem inevitably reduced all other questions to secondary importance. Little wonder that both these tendencies united under the name of "Terrorist Faction of People's Will." They were alike in looking not forward, but backward. Their thoughts were single-mindedly centered on the dazzling example of March 1, 1881. If the terror of the Executive Committee had not led to the desired goals, it was only because it had not been carried through to the end. "I do not believe in terror," said Alexander Ulyanov, who considered himself the adherent of a People's Will of a new type; "I believe in systematic terror."

Alexander had diligently read Marx and other books on economics and sociology. There are no reasons to doubt that with his great abilities and perseverance he had, during the last year of his life, amassed no small amount of knowledge in this sphere so new to him. But it was only knowledge. He had not worked out a total world view or a method for himself. He had established no real connection between the theory of Marxism and Russian reality, and he himself acknowledged in a narrow circle of intimates that he remained an ignoramus on questions of the peasant commune and the evolution of capitalism. He wrote his program to fit the already established fact of a terrorist plot. Hence his tendency to minimize the significance of disagreements that in the 1880s had already begun to split the revolutionary movement into what were to become two irreconcilable camps. The essence of that disagreement boiled down to the following alternatives: class struggle of the proletariat, or students with bombs. Ulyanov's program recognized, to be sure, the necessity of "organizing and educating the working class," but this task was deferred indefinitely. It declared revolutionary activity among the masses "under the existing political regime almost impossible." Such a formula simply evaded the essence of the dispute. Real Marxists, such as Plekhanov and his friends, saw in the development of the struggle of the working class the basic force for the overthrow of the autocracy. The terrorist faction, on the other hand, believed that the "physically weak" intelligentsia ought first to overthrow the autocracy by means of terror, so that the working class could enter the political arena. Hence the inevitable conclusion that the creation of Social Democratic organizations was, at the very least, premature.

As a basis for judging the subjective attitude of the participants in this plot toward the Marxist point of view, we have a human document of unusual psychological interest. The student Andreyushkin, one of those designated as a bomb thrower, no doubt also adhered "on the whole and generally" to the teachings of Marx; he wrote to his friend, in that same unfortunate letter which helped in the discovery of the whole plot: "I will not enumerate the merits and advantages of red terror, for I could not finish until the end of time, since that is my passion. And that is the source, I suppose, of my hatred for the Social Democrats." The expansive Andreyushkin was right, in his way. If the hope of an immediate transition from communal agriculture to socialism might still, somehow, be assigned to the misty domain of "theory," the dogma of "the independent importance of the intelligentsia" was of immediate practical relevance. A revolutionary about to convert himself into an explosive missile could not entertain either a denial, or even the slightest doubt, of the irreplaceable and redeeming importance of dynamite.

Attempts by official Soviet historians to portray the "terrorist faction" as something like a bridge between the old movement and the Social Democrats, in order to present Alexander Ulyanov as a link uniting Zhelyabov and Lenin, are wholly unjustified upon analysis of the facts and ideas involved. In the domain of theory, Ulyanov's group adhered to eclectic views characteristic of the 1880s as a period of decline. In effect, this group must be considered a latter-day version of People's Will, whose methods it reduced to the absurd. The undertaking of March 1, 1887, contained no seeds of the future; it represented, in essence, the last tragic convulsion of the already doomed claims of the "critically thinking personality" to an independent historic role. That, in the final analysis, is the lesson of this costly event.

7

CHILDHOOD AND SCHOOL YEARS

In the fourteen years from 1864 to 1878, the Ulyanovs had seven children. If you omit the fifth, Nikolai, who lived only a few days, the data we possess permit an instructive conclusion. The outstanding children in both character and ability—Alexander, Vladimir, and Olga—constitute the middle-age group, with Vladimir occupying the central place. The eldest daughter, Anna, and the two younger members of the family, Dimitri and Maria, although possessing many admirable qualities, hardly rose above the average level. At Vladimir's birth the father was thirty-nine and the mother thirty-five—the age of complete bloom of physical and spiritual forces. Moreover, the other children, except the youngest, Maria, were born only a year or two apart, but before the birth of Vladimir the mother's organism rested four years.

It would be most instructive, of course, to follow up the ancestry of Lenin for several generations. Up to this time, however, almost nothing has been done in that direction. Most likely it would be difficult and perhaps altogether impossible, in view of the plebeian origins of his grandfather, an unknown townsman of Astrakhan, to establish his ancestry on the father's side. Records of personal status among townsmen and peasants were kept haphazardly, and moreover, birth records and other books were incinerated from time to time in that kingdom of wooden structures. One genealogical fact, however, may be established with more certainty than the most irreproachable documents could provide: the features of Ilya Nikolayevich, and particularly the prominent cheekbones and the shape of the eye-slits, testify beyond a doubt to an admixture of Mongolian blood. Lenin's face tells the same story. This is not surprising, since a considerable part of the population of Astrakhan has long been Tatar, and according to the Mendelian school of genetics, Mongolian eyes are dominant over European. It is more difficult to explain why up to now almost nothing has been published about Lenin's ancestry on his mother's side. It is known that Maria Alexandrovna was the daughter of a physician named Blank who married a German woman. It is safe to infer that this grandmother derived from one of those German colonies on the Volga that produced no small number of prosperous and relatively cultivated families. But what of Blank himself? Maria Ulyanova says that her grandfather was a townsman by origin, but being a man of progressive and independent character he early resigned the position he held and took up agriculture. For some reason, nothing is said of his nationality. The name Blank, however, especially when borne by a townsman, testifies to non-Russian origins. Does that perhaps explain the strange silence upon this point? Official memoirists are, of course, capable of thinking that this or that detail of origin can diminish or aggrandize the figure of Lenin. But leaving aside the national origin of Blank, we can establish the fact that in Lenin's veins there flowed the blood of at least three "races": Great Russian, German, and Tatar. If anything suffers from this circumstance, it is only the cult of the "pure race."[1]

We know less, really, of Vladimir's childhood than of Alexander's. This is explained by the age structure of the family. But the children grew up in pairs. Anna, the most observant and prolific memoirist among them, who followed most closely the growth and maturing of Alexander, was a full six years older than Vladimir. Maria was almost eight years younger. The difference in either case was too great for close observation and accurate recollection. The closest companion of Vladimir's childhood, his sister Olga, died at nineteen. Vladimir's boyhood and youth are illustrated by individual events recalled by the elder sister; her sustained interest in Vladimir began only by the time he was already a young man. No childhood letters of Vladimir are preserved, and he probably wrote none, the family living constantly together. No diaries are preserved either, and again he probably wrote none. Even as a child he lived too intensely to record his experiences.

Volodya* learned to walk late—almost at the same time as his little sister Olya, who was a year and a half younger. Moreover, his first achievements in this activity were not altogether happy.

* Volodya is the diminutive of Vladimir and Olya of Olga. (Trans.)

He fell often and heavily, and moreover on his head, so that the neighbors could always accurately calculate his orbit. "Probably his head was too heavy," writes his sister. At every fall, Volodya would fill the entire house with his screaming. In general in those early years he never missed an opportunity to develop his vocal cords. "The passion for destruction," said Bakunin, who died in exile when the future Lenin was six years old, "is a creative passion."[2] Volodya was an unqualified adherent of this formula. He destroyed his toys before ever beginning to play with them. Upon receiving from his nurse the gift of a sleigh with three horses made out of cardboard, he hid behind the door in order to escape annoying interference by adults and twisted the horses' legs until they came off.

His independent and passionate character expressed itself, it seems, very early. Adults were often compelled to call this noisy and boisterous boy to order. Moreover, public places did not daunt him. "You mustn't yell so loud on a steamboat," said his mother as they sailed away for a summer in Kazan province. "But the steamboat is yelling loud himself," answered Volodya without lowering his voice. The mother controlled her children chiefly by persuasion and persistence. But when these pedagogical devices proved inadequate, Volodya would be removed to his father's empty study and seated in the "black chair." Volodya would quiet down then, and stop talking. Sometimes under the impact of the blow which had descended upon him, and perhaps because of the smell of the leather, he would even fall asleep.

Although he learned to walk late, the boy was very active. Because of his stocky and short build the family called him "Kubyshka."[*] Even though he remained rather indifferent to toys, he strove, with some success, to take first place in games that demanded liveliness, agility, and strength. Hide-and-seek, blindman's buff, sledding, and later on croquet and skating, captivated him.

Sasha was inventive in games, but restrained even in his favorites. Volodya was endlessly wanting to "catch up and overtake" everybody,[†] and did not mind using his elbows to this end. In

[*] Little wooden block. (Trans.)
[†] Trotsky is parodying a popular Stalinist slogan of the 1930s. (Ed.)

many other respects Volodya differed even in early childhood from his elder brother. Sasha was patient, loved to collect things and do scroll work with a saw, thus perfecting the attention and patience of the future biologist. Volodya had no use for finicky pastimes. At one time Sasha was sorting theatrical handbills and carefully spreading them out on the floor; little Volodya jumped on the precious colored sheets, stamping on them, messing them up, and tearing some. Sasha could not comprehend such barbarism. His eyes darkened. But he did not fight, nor even scold the mischief-maker: that was not in his nature. He carried his griefs, both great and small, within himself.

But no matter how he differed in temperament from Sasha, Volodya tried with all his power to imitate him. When the question was put to him whether cereal should be eaten with butter or milk, he answered: "Like Sasha." And just so later on—like Sasha—he had to shoot down a steep hill on skates. The moral force and integrity of Sasha were imposing to "Kubyshka." Yet, at the same time, the spirit of rivalry spurred him to equal his older brother. The formula "like Sasha," often laughed over by the family, had a twofold content: recognition of another's superiority, and aspiration to "catch up and overtake."

Sasha was organically and almost morbidly truthful. To trick people and to tell lies was as unthinkable to him as to mock and scold. In difficult situations he remained silent. In the healthy truthfulness of Volodya there was an element of slyness. With the overflowing expansive force of such a nature as his, it was impossible to get along without some defensive lies. One could not, for instance, enjoy an apple peel without picking it up on the sly when a vigilant mother had left the kitchen; one could not tear the legs off a paper horse without hiding behind the door. And could one think of confessing to an aunt, a relative stranger, that it was he, Volodya, who had broken the carafe while running through the rooms during a visit to her house? Three months later, however, before going to sleep, the boy would weep in his bed and confess to his mother that he had not only broken the carafe but had lied to his aunt. From which we see that the categorical moral imperative was not quite so alien to "Kubyshka" as it was asserted to be in the future by Lenin's many enemies.

Perhaps we should emphasize that Volodya was in no sense a

"child prodigy." That term is more applicable to his younger sister Olya. He grew up a normal healthy boy, perhaps even slightly retarded at a very early age. According to Yelizarova, Volodya learned to read from his mother at the age of five—again, simultaneously with his younger sister. This implies, to be sure, that it was the little girl who learned to read a bit too early. Maybe we ought to add six months or a year to the story. As a teacher, Ilya Nikolayevich received many children's books. Olya, however, had more interest than Volodya in reading and learning verses, being closer in character to Sasha, although linked to Volodya by the developmental process. Volodya read nimbly, but would eagerly drop his childish books to run and play. He loved life primarily as movement. In his father's study there would appear from time to time new equipment for experiments in physics and other subjects with the help of which the children in their free moments got acquainted with the mysteries of science. Volodya, we may be sure, would instantly grasp the most essential points. He rapidly matured, both physically and intellectually.

In contrast to Sasha, who was so considerate of the younger members of the family, Volodya loved on any pretext to demonstrate to them his superiority. When the children would sing to their mother's accompaniment the nursery rhyme about the little goat that was attacked by gray wolves, the sensitive Mitya would normally break into tears.* They tried to convince him that it was not necessary to be so concerned with the fate of an unknown little goat. Mitya tried to hold it in, to no avail. That gray wolf was watching for Mitya himself. When the song came to its critical moment, Volodya would intone the final stanza: "And left for grandma only the horns and feet" with such a mournful voice and gestures that poor Mitya would be convulsed with sobs.

Thanks to the mother, music played an important role in the life of the family. The children loved to sing—or, as the nurse said, "shout"—to her accompaniment. Legend testifies that Volodya was not only zealous in this pursuit, but had a good ear. Be that as it may, the musical talents of the boy, even if they did exist, were not in any way encouraged in the future; but he loved music all his life.

* Mitya is the diminutive of Dimitri. (Ed.)

The family tutor, Kalashnikov, and afterward the lady teacher Kashkadamova, prepared Volodya for high school. Kalashnikov remembers a boy of sturdy build with reddish hair curling above a high brow, little resembling the other children—more brisk, more quick-minded, and inclined to mockery. Having to do chiefly with the children of non-Russians in the city school, Kalashnikov grew accustomed to pronouncing his words with a slow drawl; the impatient Volodya, having no need of this system, thought nothing of mockingly imitating his tutor. This interesting little trait shows that the boy was not particularly respectful, and that he began early to test his claws not only on the young.

In 1878, when Volodya was eight years old, the Ulyanovs moved into a house of their own. It was made of wood, and modest, but it had an orchard, which became an object of care and concern to the entire family. Volodya was hardly less nimble and diligent than the others with the watering pot; nor was he the last, we may assume, in consuming the results of their labor. The family established an interesting regime in this matter. The children were accurately informed which bushes and trees were for them, and which for the winter storage or for their father's name day, and they all observed a strict discipline of enjoyment. A little girl visitor once playfully bit a piece out of an apple right on the tree, and then ran away. A half century later, Anna Yelizarova remembered this catastrophe: "Such hooliganism (!) was alien and incomprehensible to us." This judgment, astonishing in its pedantry, sheds pretty good light on the patriarchal ways of that family, where discipline was enforced in different ways, but with great success, by both father and mother. Thrift, orderliness, respect for labor and its fruits were learned early in life by the great destroyer of the future. Though he himself would not, of course, have called an innocent childish prank "hooliganism," in the future he strongly disliked slovenliness or extravagance among adults.

Thirteen-year-old Sasha conceived of the idea of publishing a weekly family journal. Not being inclined to writing himself, he undertook to be the editor, and published for the most part word-and-picture puzzles and charades, rebuses and illustrations. Nine-year-old Volodya became his first assistant, under the weighty pseudonym of Kubyshkin. Even seven-year-old Olya enriched the journal with her scribblings. The journal came out on Saturdays and was called *Subbotnik*. Fifteen-year-old Anna, who had already become acquainted with the works of the famous critic Belinsky,[3] cracked down in a sarcastic article on a story by the young litterateur Kubyshkin. Volodya listened avidly to this critical punishment, not taking the slightest personal offense; he learned from it and remembered. The father and mother would take part in these literary debates, their faces shining with joy in their children. "Those evenings," writes Yelizarova, "were the high point in the close relationship between us, the four older children, and our parents. Our memories of them are bright and joyous."

At the age of nine and a half, Volodya entered the first class at high school. Now he wore a uniform "like Sasha," and was subject to the authority of the same teachers, also uniformed, with double-headed eagles on their metal buttons. But Volodya's personality allowed him to endure far more easily than Alexander the high-school regime with its hypocrisy and coercion. Even classicism was no burden to him. The future writer and public speaker early developed a taste for the ancient authors. Vladimir learned with extraordinary ease. This active and noisy boy with his wide scope of emotions was also capable of truly astounding concentration. Sitting motionless behind his desk, he would seize and absorb every explanation made by his teachers, so that a lesson assigned was for him a lesson learned. At home, he would quickly finish the next day's assignment. While the two elder children had just spread out their books on the big table in the dining room, Volodya would already have begun his active life: noise-making, chattering, and teasing the younger children. The older sister and brother would protest. The mother's authority would not always be sufficient. Volodya would turn up everywhere. Sometimes the father, if at home, would take his jack-in-the-box to his study to find out whether he really had finished his lessons. But Volodya would give all the answers without hesitation. The father would then take his old notebooks and quiz him on the entire course. Volodya was still invulnerable. Latin words were firmly engraved in his memory. The father did not know whether to be happy or upset. The boy learned too fast, and would perhaps fail to develop systematic work habits.

On returning from high school Volodya would report to his parents the events of the day—chiefly what subjects he was called up on, and how he answered. Since his progress was rather monotonous, this report would take the form of a swift run past his father's office and a shout: "5 in Greek, 5 in German."* On the next day, and the day after: "5 in Latin, 5 in algebra." The father and mother would exchange secret smiles of satisfaction. Ilya Nikolayevich did not like to praise his children to their faces, and especially this self-confident boy to whom everything came so easy. But their children's success introduced, of course, a joyful note into the family life. In the evenings they would all gather happily round the big tea table. Ilya Nikolayevich never lost his taste for jokes and school anecdotes. There was much laughter, and the ringleader of it all was often the superintendent of schools. "You felt warm and cosy in that friendly family," related the tutor, Kashkadamova. "Keenest of all in conversation were Volodya and his second sister, Olya. How their happy voices and infectious laughter would ring out!"

Volodya's voice, it must be confessed, occasionally rang out overly loud. The boy held himself to such strict discipline within high-school walls that he inevitably brought home much unexpended nervous energy, which did not always enhance domestic tranquillity. His conduct within the bosom of the family, moreover, differed very much, depending on the presence or absence of the father. It seemed that Volodya was a little afraid of the father, who was capable not only of playing like a child with his children, but also at times of being quite stern. Yelizarova thinks that the overworked father did not take sufficient account of the peculiarities of individual children, especially of Alexander, but that his pedagogical system was nevertheless "quite correct" when applied to Vladimir. It served to counterbalance Vladimir's "great self-confidence and arrogance." We gratefully assemble these precious crumbs and only regret that they are so scant.

Did Ilya Nikolayevich's system, together with abstention from praise, comprise abstention from punishment? In 1872, while

* In the Russian system of grading, "five" is "excellent," "four"—"good," etc. (Ed.)

still an inspector of public schools, he wrote: "Teachers devoted to their work have no need to employ disciplinary measures with their pupils." Did he, as a father, follow his own pedagogical rules? There is no direct testimony on this score. Recollections by members of the family, without ever minimizing or holding back anything, emphasize in every way the even temper and restraint of the mother—which suggests that things were different with the father. The authoritarianism of Ilya Nikolayevich and his quick temper also serve to reinforce this assumption. Every family has its troubles. Can it indeed be otherwise when a family is burdened with obligations too heavy for it? A good family does not mean an impeccable one, but only one that is better than others in similar circumstances. The Ulyanov family was a good, conservative, provincial family, one with serious interests and wholesome relationships. The parents lived in harmony, and the children were completely free of the demoralizing influence of quarrels and conflicts between father and mother. The presence of older children, especially of Alexander, hastened the maturing of the younger child. Although Vladimir fell ill occasionally during his school years, he was of reasonably sturdy health and his body matured satisfactorily. With his abilities there could be no problem of an excessive expenditure of energy. He grew like a young oak, putting down deep roots and drinking in abundantly the air and moisture. What can one say but . . . "a happy childhood"?

The summers in his mother's home at Kokushkino were, as with all the more or less privileged children of the earth, the best time of the year. Here, many cousins would meet after a long separation. There would be endless games, long walks, and the friendships and "crushes" of childhood. Volodya was most venturesome in games, especially in competitive ones. In Kokushkino he came in contact with the world of the peasants, and once or twice even went out with peasant boys to watch horses through the night. The litterateur Kubyshkin could hardly suspect that these excursions among the people would fifty years later be interpreted as the source of the idea of a union of workers and peasants! But there is no doubt that in the roomy head of this boy even these casual vacation meetings laid up a precious store of impressions that would be of use in the future.

When Alexander II was killed, Valdimir was in the second class and not quite eleven years old. At that age Sasha, to be sure, had been reading Nekrasov and thinking after his fashion about the fate of the oppressed. But the father did not encourage his younger children to read radical literature. Reaction was already in the air, and its breath was felt not only at school but also in the family. We can confidently assert that political interests did not awaken in Vladimir until almost the end of his highschool years. The event of March 1, 1881, with the church services and speeches following, most likely merely excited him, as would a fire or a railroad crash. This son of a superintendent of public schools, brought up in a spirit of discipline and of Russian Orthodox faith, had not yet begun to doubt the correctness of the *status quo*. It is not without interest that his future close comrade in arms and subsequently leader of the Mensheviks and an implacable opponent, the then eight-year-old Yuli Tsederbaum (Martov), who grew up in a liberal Jewish family in Odessa, felt the events of March 1 more keenly than Vladimir.[4] In the kitchen, young Martov heard the servants talk about noblemen who had killed the "liberator," while in the parlor educated people spoke about madmen who dream of winning liberty with bombs. The pogroms of the Jews that marked the beginning of the new reign early determined the political road of the impressionable and gifted Yuli. The life-loving and active Vladimir, on the contrary, must have quickly shaken off the impression of this unusual event, which had taken place on unattainable heights and had no relation to him personally or to persons close to him. And so, back to the old routine: "5 in algebra, 5 in Latin. . . ."

The father's fears were unfounded. Volodya did not become overconfident; on the contrary, with time he acquired more self-control. At one time he was very much absorbed in skating, but found that after the exercise in the frosty air he would feel sleepy. He decided to give up skating in the interest of his studies. Relating this incident in the words of Lenin himself, Krupskaya adds: "From early youth Vladimir Ilyich knew how to push aside anything that stood in his way."[5] His wide-ranging attention, as we know, was also amenable to concentration, and ultimately moved in a utilitarian direction. He noted carefully not only weaknesses and comic features in others, but also the strengths that he himself lacked. Perhaps he did not always name these traits openly—Volodya learned early from his father not to be too quick with praise—but he tried all the harder to make these advantages his own. In his own family, others worked more assiduously and systematically than he—especially his brother Sasha.

The example of this elder brother never left his field of vision. Ever since Ilya Nikolayevich had bought his own house, the two brothers had lived in neighboring rooms in the attic, apart from the others. We may imagine that Sasha, buried in his own thoughts, often hastened past his overly noisy and boisterous brother without stopping. But Volodya was keenly watching Sasha, learning from Sasha, comparing himself to Sasha. So it continued until the elder brother went away to the university and the younger entered the fifth grade of high school. Living side by side with his brother undoubtedly had a beneficial effect on Volodya: his abilities were now enhanced by industry. But not only that. In contrast to Sasha, whose gentle reserve endeared him to all, Volodya had, like his father, a very quick temper, which must have caused him no little pain. As he grew up, he tried in this respect also to become like Sasha. It was not easy, for these explosions of irritation were a manifestation of a rather irrepressible temperament. When the older sister wrote: "In his more mature years we never noticed in him any, or hardly any, quick temper," she indubitably exaggerated somewhat. But Vladimir did, no doubt, succeed in pulling himself together.

There was a chess set in the house, whittled by the father in Nizhni Novgorod, which had gradually become a family heirloom of sorts. The male members of the family, beginning with the father, were devoted to the abstract intricacies of this ancient game —a game in which superiority in certain (to be sure, not very high) intellectual qualities finds a most direct expression and satisfaction. The sons always responded joyfully to a challenge from the father to play a game of chess. But the balance of power increasingly shifted to the younger generation. Alexander got hold of a textbook on chess, and with his usual calm persistence plunged into the theory of the game. After a while Vladimir followed him. The brothers evidently progressed alarmingly, for one evening, as he was going upstairs, Vladimir ran into his father filching the textbook from the attic with the obvious aim of arming himself for future battles.

But, as the proverb goes, an hour for fun, and time itself for work. Vladimir climbed the steps of his high-school curriculum without pause, and each year with prizes. Only in the seventh grade did he run into trouble with his teacher of French, an ignorant and shifty individual who then became a target for his mockery. His recklessness was punished: the Frenchman managed to get the prize pupil marked down one grade in conduct for the semester. Ilya Nikolayevich was ruffled, and Vladimir solemnly promised to put an end to these risky experiments. The incident had no consequences. Behind this insolence toward a disrespected teacher, the school authorities discovered no dangerous frame of mind. And they were not mistaken—for the time being.

In the chronicles of the Simbirsk High School Vladimir Ulyanov clearly outshone Alexander. In the sphere of intellectual tastes and preferences there were, moreover, sharp and interesting differences between the two brothers. Russian composition was not Alexander's forte; on the contrary, his essays were short and dry. That inward restraint which made his disposition so attractive, hindered him in expressing himself. He hated pretense and empty phrases, and everything in conversation that was not absolutely necessary embarrassed him. His thoughts, honest to the point of temerity, lacked flexibility. And since his keen critical sense was not complemented by literary gifts, he reduced his written work to a minimum that was truly ascetic.

Vladimir, by contrast, became famous in the class as a "literary man." He, too, had no love for rhetoric as such. On the contrary, he was as indifferent to embellishments in literature as in his own dress. His healthy intellectual appetite had no need of seasonings. But the verbal timidity of Alexander was also completely alien to him. That sturdy and aggressive self-confidence which alarmed his father, and must on occasion have been distasteful to the elder brother, remained with Vladimir in creative writing as well. When he sat down to write a composition—never at the last moment, but in good time—he knew in advance that he would say all that was necessary and say it right. Picking out a hard pencil and sharpening it well so that the letters might lie fine and compact on the paper, he would first of all sketch an outline, to make sure that his ideas would be expressed in full. Around this outline he would then group references and quotations—not only from school texts, but from other books as well. With this preparatory work finished, the references numbered, and the introduction and conclusions mapped out, the composition very nearly wrote itself. It remained only to carefully write out a clean copy. His language and literature teacher, Kerensky,[6] who was also the high school's principal, greatly favored this sturdy redheaded composition writer, and would set up his writings as an example to the others and reward him with the highest mark: 5 plus. When meeting his parents—and the relations between Kerensky and the Ulyanovs were friendly—the high-school principal never failed to praise this pupil.

In high school, Volodya remained indifferent to the natural sciences. Unlike his elder brother, he did not catch butterflies and fish, and did not set traps for birds, and he did not accompany Alexander on his summer boating excursions. A taste for the natural world developed in him, it seems, only in later years. His own disposition, with its continually unfolding gifts and potentials, claimed all of his attention in those years of spiritual awakening and early growth. He loved literature, history, the Latin classics—those areas of knowledge which directly relate to human beings and human concerns. Still, it would be wrong to define the general sphere of his interests as the *humanities*. That word smacks too much of dilettantism, of commonplaces and elegant quotations. From the earliest years, Vladimir's thinking was imbued with an organic realism. He knew how to observe, to note, almost to lie in wait for life in its various manifestations. He had a keen taste for fact in all its concreteness, and skeptically went after the essence concealed behind the deceptive appearance—just as in his early childhood he had tried his best to get at the hidden essence of those toy horses. His high-school predilections in the realm of knowledge illustrated not so much the fundamental bent of his intellect as they did a certain stage in his evolution. Neither literature nor history—and much less classical philology—remained in later years within the circle of his primary intellectual interests. Soon after finishing high school he stepped across all these studies to the anatomy of society—that is, to political economy.

So far we have said nothing of Vladimir's relation to religion. And purposely so. The question of Russian Orthodoxy and of the church became a major issue in his mind only in the final period of his high-school career. This circumstance, fully explained by environment, time, and personal disposition, seems—difficult though it is to believe—embarrassing to Lenin's official biographers. We can arrive at the truth now only by climbing over a veritable pile of obstacles. However, it is precisely the story of young Lenin's break with the myth of Christianity that enables us to see just how the Lenin myth is arising and expanding.

A well-known Soviet official, the engineer Krzhizhanovsky, writes: Lenin "told me that in the fifth class of high school he abruptly put an end to all religious questions: took off the cross he wore and threw it in the garbage."[7] Krzhizhanovsky wrote down his recollections of Lenin—with whom he was closely bound in youth by revolutionary work, prison, and exile—approximately thirty years after the conversation to which he refers. Is it true that the crisis of religious consciousness came upon Vladimir in the fifth grade? And is it believable that during this crisis his cross was thrown "into the garbage"? Or did Lenin merely spice his conversation with one of those pungent metaphors to which he was inclined? To resolve these questions, as will be seen, the belated testimony of Krzhizhanovsky requires serious revision. After so many years, not only others' experiences, but one's own, become deformed in memory. This makes all the more striking the further elaboration of Krzhizhanovsky's testimony by another old Bolshevik, a leading figure in Party historiography. Says Lepeshinsky: As soon as Lenin came to the conclusion that "there is no God, he impetuously tore the cross from his neck, spat scornfully on the 'sacred relic' and threw it on the ground."[8] We could cite other variants describing how Lenin not only threw the cross on the ground but "stamped on it" as well. The pedagogical reasons for these free elaborations on a basic text are most directly expressed by Lepeshinsky in a youth journal: Be it known to young Communists that young Lenin rid himself of religious prejudices "in his own way, strictly in the *Ilyich* way, in the revolutionary way. . . ." Other memoirists and commentators portray to us not so much Lenin in his youth as—alas—themselves in their declining years.

Krupskaya, who first met Lenin roughly when Krzhizhanovsky and Lepeshinsky did, recalls nothing relating to religion and the church. Only in passing does she refer to Krzhizhanovsky's story. "Ilyich understood the harmfulness of religion," she writes in her well-known *Recollections*, "as a fifteen-year-old boy. He threw away his cross and stopped going to church. In those days this was not as simple as now." As if justifying Lenin's overly late break with Eastern Orthodoxy, Krupskaya nevertheless makes a mistake about his age: if it happened, as she says, in the fifth grade, Vladimir was not fifteen, but only fourteen. All these not wholly consistent versions have been reproduced innumerable times. Yet there exists on this question not only incomparably more-convincing testimony, but a completely authentic document.

A. Yelizarova is the only living witness who can tell about the evolution of Vladimir, not on the basis of an accidental utterance or a conversation remembered from later years, but upon her own firsthand observations, against the background of the entire family, and consequently with immeasurably greater factual and psychological reliability. It would seem that she should be listened to first of all. In the winter of 1886, drawn together by the loss of their father, the sister and brother took many long walks together, and Anna noticed that Volodya's "mood was one of strong opposition to high-school authorities, high-school studies, and also to religion. . . ." Her brother said nothing to her about having thrown his cross into the garbage. We will return to Yelizarova's testimony later when we attempt to define Lenin's political evolution. Suffice it to note for the time being that only at the beginning of Vladimir's seventeenth year did his sister first come upon his adverse attitude to religion, and then as something new in him, supplementary, in her account, to his antagonism toward the high-school authorities. As though apologizing for this retarded development (if judged by later yardsticks), Yelizarova writes: "In those days young people, especially in the remote provinces, unacquainted with public life, did not define themselves politically so early." Besides this invaluable testimony of Yelizarova—whose recollections are the more reliable in the present case since after some months of separation any changes in the mood and opinions of her brother must have struck her attention—we have one more, and this time a completely authoritative, witness: Lenin himself. In a party questionnaire carefully filled out by him with his own hand, the question "When did you stop being religious?" is answered: "At the age of 16." Lenin knew how to be accurate. Yet his testimony, fully corresponding to that of his older sister, is disregarded because it is obviously insufficiently useful in the education of young Communists.

Yelizarova's reference to the retarded political maturing among young people in remote provinces is only partly true, and in any case inadequate as an explanation. According to her account, Sasha had turned his back on the church at an earlier age. There is nothing enigmatic in this disparity between the two boys. When Alexander was in high school, a militant atheism was universal among the progressive intellegentsia and was making headway even among high-school teachers. Conversely, in the 1880s an intellectual reaction among the best-educated strata eagerly welcomed the system of "ethical-religious education" fostered by Pobedonostsev. But we must not lose sight, either, of the differences between the two boys' personalities. Introverted and extremely sensitive to any hint of insincerity, Alexander could, indeed had to, succumb earlier to an attitude of criticism and discontent—before the cheerful extrovert Vladimir, who must have been held back for a time, by the furious pressure of his own emotions, from listening to the voices of doubt. In the religiosity of Vladimir, however, the last thing to look for would be any kind of mystic depth. Ties with the church were for him simply part and parcel of the milieu of family and school, where he was at home, as a fish in water, surrounded by games, jokes, and success upon success. One might say that he had no time to really examine his attitudes toward religious traditions. It took some strong external impulse to make that process of inner criticism, which had already accumulated a considerable fund of semiconscious observations, break suddenly to the surface. Such an impulse must have been provided by the death of his father. It was his first close encounter with death, the death of one near and dear to him.

8

THE STRICKEN FAMILY

"Happy families are all alike," says Tolstoy. "Each unhappy family is unhappy in its own way." The Ulyanov family had lived a happy life for almost twenty-three years, and been like other harmonious and fortunate families. In 1886 the first blow fell, the death of the father. But misfortunes never come singly. Others followed swiftly: the execution of Alexander, the arrest of Anna. And beyond these there were more, and still more, misfortunes to come. Henceforth everybody, both strangers and intimates, began to consider the Ulyanovs an unhappy family. And they had truly become unhappy, though in their own way. . . .

When Ilya Nikolayevich had completed twenty-five years of service, the ministry retained him for but one supplementary year, and not five as was usual with important government officials. Ilya Nikolayevich was pained by this failure of the authorities to recognize his services. Anna Yelizarova, in advancing the hypothesis that her father suffered—or, rather, came close to suffering—for his excessive interest in public education, makes a patent error in dates. The minister who refused to retain Ulyanov for the additional five years was that same "liberal," Saburov, who in 1880 was to represent the "dictatorship of the heart" in the domain of public education. It is even possible that, in order to bring in some new blood among his personnel, Saburov began by getting rid of some unimaginative old officials, and that through an oversight in the ministry Ilya Nikolayevich was listed in that category. Saburov was himself, however, very soon dismissed, together with his chief, Loris-Melikov; and his successor, after investigating the affair, retained Ulyanov for an additional five-year term. There is no doubt, at any rate, that these unexpected vicissitudes were very trying for Ilya Nikolayevich. Premature retirement threatened not only to tear him away from his accustomed work, but also to create financial difficulties for his family.

In fact, the change of governmental policy in educational affairs took place only after this incident concerning Ulyanov's retirement. The *zemstvos* then fell into disfavor, and together with them the *zemstvo* schools. In 1884, simultaneously with the new university constitution, new rules were issued for parish schools. Ilya Nikolayevich was opposed to this reform—not out of hostility to the church, of course, for he zealously saw to it that religion was regularly taught in *zemstvo* schools—but out of loyalty to the cause of education. As the winds of reaction grew strong, the Simbirsk superintendent of public schools, by the very fact that he felt concerned for the cause of literacy, willy-nilly found himself opposing the new course. What had formerly been considered his merit had now, it seemed, become a fault. He was compelled to retreat and adapt himself. His whole life's work was under attack. When an occasion presented itself, Ilya Nikolayevich was not averse to pointing out to his older children the disastrous consequences of revolutionary struggle, and how instead of progress it produced reaction. This was the mood of the majority of peaceful educators of the time.

A Simbirsk landowner, Nazaryev, in sending in his regular dispatch to the editor of the liberal journal *Vestnik Yevropy*, wrote to him confidentially about Ulyanov: "He is not in the good graces of the ministry, and is far from doing well." Ilya Nikolayevich took to heart the government's attack upon the elementary schools, although he obeyed the new policy. His former buoyancy had vanished. His last years were poisoned with uncertainty and anxiety. He fell sick suddenly in January 1886, while preparing his annual report. Alexander was in Petersburg, wholly immersed in his zoology term paper. Vladimir, only a year and a half away from high-school graduation, must have been thinking already about the university. Anna was at home for the Christmas holidays. Neither the family nor the physician took Ilya Nikolayevich's illness seriously. He continued to work on his report. His daughter sat reading some papers to him until she noticed that her father was becoming delirious. The next morning, the twelfth, the sick man did not come to the table, but only came to the dining room door, and looked in—"as though he had

come to say good-by," remembered Maria Alexandrovna. At five
o'clock the mother, in alarm, called Anna and Vladimir. Ilya
Nikolayevich lay dying on the sofa which served him for a bed.
The children saw their father shudder twice and go still forever.
He was not yet fifty-five years old. The physician described the
cause of his death—"hypothetically although with overwhelming
probability," to quote his own words—as a cerebral hemorrhage.
Thus the first heavy blow fell upon the Ulyanov family.

"Father's funeral," says Anna Yelizarova, "showed what great
popularity he had enjoyed in Simbirsk." The obituaries, as is the
custom, enumerated the services of Ulyanov to the cause of education. Most affectionate of all were the recollections of Simbirsk
teachers. The superintendent had been demanding, and sometimes even severe, but he had spared no effort to improve their
financial well-being. "There will never be another Ilya Nikolayevich," repeated the teachers as they returned from the funeral.

Anna remained in Simbirsk for a time in order to be near her
mother. It was at that time, as we have seen, that the elder sister
and Vladimir grew close to each other. The winter walks together date from that time, and the long conversations in which
her brother revealed himself to her as a rebel and nonconformist,
the embodiment of protest—so far, however, only in relation to
"high-school authorities, high-school studies, and also to religion."
During the recent summer vacation, these moods had not yet
existed.

The death of the father had suddenly destroyed the lulling flow
of life in a family whose well-being had seemed sure to go on
indefinitely. How can we avoid assuming that it was this blow
that imparted a new critical direction to Vladimir's thoughts?
The answers of the church catechism to questions of life and
death must have seemed to him wretched and humiliating, con-
fronted with the austere truth of nature. Whether in reality he
threw his cross into the garbage, or whether, as is more likely,
Krzhizhanovsky's memory converted a metaphorical expression
into a physical gesture, one thing is beyond doubt: Vladimir must
have broken with religion abruptly, without long hesitation,
without attempts at an eclectic reconciliation of truths with lies,
with that youthful courage which was here for the first time
spreading its wings.

Alexander was staying up nights engrossed in his work when the unexpected news came of his father's death. "For several days he dropped everything," relates a fellow student at the university, "pacing his room from corner to corner as though wounded." But wholly in the spirit of the family, in which strong feelings went hand in hand with discipline, Alexander did not leave the university, and did not hasten to Simbirsk. He pulled himself together and went back to work. After a few weeks his mother received a letter, brief as always: "I have received a gold medal for my zoological study of annelids." Maria Alexandrovna wept with joy for her son and with grief for her husband.

Henceforth the family would have to live on the mother's pension, pieced out perhaps with some small savings that the father had left. They crowded themselves a little and took in boarders. But the regimen of life remained the same. Maria Alexandrovna watched over the younger children, and waited for the elder to graduate from the university. They all worked hard. Vladimir delighted her with his successes, but alarmed her with his arrogance. So passed the year of mourning. Life was beginning to move again in its new, narrower channel, when a totally unexpected blow, and a double blow at that, descended upon the family: Both son and daughter were involved in a trial for an attempted assassination of the tsar. It was dreadful even to breathe those words!

Anna was arrested on March 1 in her brother's room, which she had entered while a search was in progress. Shrouded in dreadful uncertainty, the girl was locked up in prison in connection with a case in which she had no part. This, then, is what Sasha was busy with! They had grown up side by side, played together in their father's study with sealing wax and magnets, often fallen asleep together to their mother's music, studied together in Petersburg—and yet how little she knew him! The older Sasha grew, the more he withdrew from his sister. Anna remembered bitterly how, when she visited him, Alexander would tear himself from his books with evident regret. He did not share his thoughts with her. Each time he heard of some new vileness of the tsarist authorities his face would darken, and he would withdraw more deeply into himself. "A penetrating observer could have predicted even then his future course. . . ." But Anna was no penetrating observer. During the last year, Alexander had refused to share an apartment with her, explaining to his companions that he did not want to compromise his sister, who showed no desire for public activity. During that winter Anna saw Alexander with some strange objects in his hands. How far she was from the thought of bombs! Soon after that, she stumbled upon a meeting of conspirators in his apartment. But his friends were not her friends. She was not let in on anything. On one of the last days, February 26, when his spirit was grieving mortally, he came to her himself, unexpectedly, and sat thinking, waiting, as though expecting the miracle of intimacy. But she did not understand her brother's mood and tried to talk about everyday things. The miracle did not occur, and Alexander went away again, shut in, alien, doomed. And she was left with a feeling of frustration that they were concealing something from her. Only in her solitary cell did she understand that her brother had come to her for a last communion, and that she had not given him what he sought. From childhood she had been accustomed to seek in his eyes either approval or reproach. Now she felt clearly that she had not found approval, and that this was forever. She wrote to her brother from one prison cell to another: "There is no human being on earth better, more noble, than you." But her belated outcry of acknowledgment was never delivered.

A Petersburg relative of the Ulyanovs wrote of the arrest of Alexander and Anna to a former teacher of the children, asking her to prepare the mother cautiously. Narrowing his young brows, Vladimir stood silent a long time over the Petersburg letter. This lightning stroke revealed the figure of Alexander in a new light. "But this is a serious thing," he said. "It may end badly for Sasha." He evidently had no doubt of Anna's innocence. The task of preparing the mother fell to him. But she, sensing tragedy in the first words, demanded the letter, and immediately began to prepare for a journey.

There was still no railroad from Simbirsk; one had to travel by horse and wagon to Syzran. For the sake of economy and for safety on the journey, Vladimir sought a companion for his mother. But the news had already spread through the town. Everyone turned away fearfully. No one would travel with the mother of a terrorist. Vladimir never forgot this lesson. The

days that followed were to mean much in the forming of his character and its direction. The youth became austere and silent,
and frequently shut himself up in his room when not busy with
the younger children left in his charge. So that is what he was,
this tireless chemist and dissector of worms, this silent brother
so near and yet so unknown! When compelled to speak with
Kashkadamova of the catastrophe, he kept repeating: "It means
Alexander could not have acted otherwise." The mother came
back for a short time to see the children and told them of her
efforts and her dream of a life sentence to hard labor for Sasha.
"In that case I would go with him," she said. "The older children
are big enough and I will take the younger with me." Instead of a
chair at a university and scholarly glory, chains and stripes* now
became the chief object of the mother's hopes.

Maria Alexandrovna finally had her first meeting with her son
on March 30, a full month after his arrest. Sasha cried, embraced
her knees, asked her forgiveness, justified himself by saying that
besides his duty to his family he had a duty to the fatherland,
and tried to prepare his mother for the fate awaiting him. "You
must be resigned, Mama!" he said. But Mama would not be resigned. From her son she went to her daughter, and from her
daughter to the authorities and to men of influence. Her grief
was immeasurable, but her courage rose to the same heights. She
did not weaken. She knocked at every door. She tried to awaken
some hope in her son and to keep up the hopes of her daughter.
She was admitted to the sessions of the court. In his month and a
half of confinement, Alexander had grown more manly; even his
voice acquired an unfamiliar impressiveness. The youth had
become a man. "How well Sasha spoke—so convincingly, so elo-
quently." But the mother could not sit through the whole speech;
that eloquence would break her heart. On the eve of the execution, still hoping, she kept repeating to her son through the double
grating: "Have courage!" On May 5, on her way to an interview
with her daughter, she learned from a leaflet given out on the
street that Sasha was no more. The feelings that the bereaved
mother brought to the grating behind which her daughter stood

---

* The word *stripes* is a free translation; hard-labor convicts wore a red
diamond on their backs. (Trans.)

are not recorded. But Maria Alexandrovna did not bend, did not fall, did not betray the secret to her daughter. To Anna's questions about her brother, the mother answered: "Pray for Sasha." Anna did not detect the despair behind her mother's courage. How respectfully the prison authorities, who knew already of the execution of Alexander, admitted this severe woman in black! The daughter did not yet guess that the mourning for her father had become a mourning for her brother.

Simbirsk was fragrant with all the flowers of its orchards when news came from the capital of the hanging of Alexander Ulyanov. The family of a full state counselor, until then respected on every side, became overnight the family of an executed state criminal. Friends and acquaintances, without exception, avoided the house on Moscow Street. Even the aged schoolteacher who had so often dropped in for a game of chess with Ilya Nikolayevich no longer showed his face. Vladimir observed with a keen eye the neighbors around them, their cowardice and disloyalty. It was a precious lesson in political realism.

Anna was set free some days after the execution of her brother. Instead of sending her to Siberia, the authorities agreed to have her restricted, under police surveillance, to the village of Kokushkino, the home of her mother. A new life now began for Maria Alexandrovna. She had to reconstruct not only her relations with other people, but her inner self as well. The slow and stern movement of the Russian revolution over the bones of the young generation of the intelligentsia re-educated more than one conservative mother. Women of noble, bourgeois, or townsman origin would be torn away from their domestic rounds to spend long hours in the waiting rooms of the gendarmerie, in the offices of prosecutors, and in prison offices. They did not become revolutionaries, but in order to defend their children they waged their own battle with the tsarist regime in the rear guard of the revolution. They made the government hated solely by their complaints against its vengefulness and cruelty. The role of these mothers became a revolutionary role. Truly heroic figures arose among them, people of higher spiritual mold than the Christian *Mater Dolorosa,* who could only prostrate herself before the autocrat of heaven. For the remaining thirty years of her life, Maria

Alexandrovna belonged to the holy order of suffering and militant mothers.

During the very weeks when the elder brother's fate was being decided in the capital, the younger had to prepare himself for his high-school final examinations. Like Alexander after the death of his father, so Vladimir after the execution of his brother interrupted his intense labors for only a few days. The faculty council gave a most positive evaluation to the student of the eighth class, Ulyanov: "He studies all subjects, and especially the ancient languages, with love." In ten subjects Ulyanov received the grade "excellent," and only in logic "good." Could it be because Hegel, his future teacher, had called school logic *dies tote Gebein* and scornfully compared the game of syllogisms with the child's game of picture puzzles? Or had the logic of the future revolutionary already begun to diverge by one grade from official logic? Notwithstanding a still-fresh rebuke from Petersburg for graduating the future state criminal, Alexander Ulyanov, with a medal and the highest recommendations, the faculty council could not deny a gold medal to his younger brother. In his final examinations Vladimir's grades were straight "excellent." He graduated from high school at the age of seventeen years and two months.

In the *zemstvos*, in the press of those times a complaint was often voiced that the classical system of education was giving the country "weak-chested, nervous people, spineless and rather feeble-minded." And no wonder: the entire system was aimed at twisting people's minds and spines. Vladimir Ulyanov, however, emerged from high school unharmed. Although "Kubyshkin" had grown pretty thin, his chest was well developed and his nerves were in good shape. His brain, like his spine, was strong and straight. Handsome was the last thing you could call him, with his grayish-colored skin, Mongoloid eye-slits, protruding cheekbones, large and at the same time nondescript features, and reddish hair on a sturdy and big head. However, the small hazel eyes under the auburn brows glittered with verve and penetration, and the mobility of facial expressions spoke unmistakably of inner powers. Vladimir would not have stood out in any way in a group of high-school students frozen in front of a camera. But in lively conversation, at play, and still more at work, he was invariably first, and the second was far behind.

An official letter of recommendation given to Vladimir Ulyanov by his high-school principal, Fyodor Kerensky, deserves to
be quoted in full: "Quite talented, invariably diligent, prompt
and reliable, Ulyanov was first in all his classes, and upon graduation was awarded a gold medal as the most meritorious pupil in
achievement, growth and conduct. There is not a single instance
on record, either in school or outside of it, of Ulyanov's evoking
by word or deed any adverse opinion from the authorities and
teachers of this school. His parents always watched carefully
over the educational and moral progress of Ulyanov, and since
1886, i.e., after the death of his father, the mother alone has devoted all care and labor to the upbringing of her children. The
guiding principles of this upbringing were religion and rational
discipline. The goodly fruits of Ulyanov's upbringing were obvious in his excellent conduct. Upon closer examination of Ulyanov's home life and character, I could not but observe in him an
excessive introversion and lack of sociability even with acquaintances, and outside the school even with fellow students who
were the school's pride and joy, in short, an aversion to companionship. The mother of Ulyanov intends to remain with him
throughout his stay at the university." Fyodor Kerensky himself,
judging by his annual reports, directed his educational efforts
toward "the nurturing of religious sentiments, reverence for elders, obedience to authority, and respect for the property of
others." In the light of these irreproachable principles it is hard
to believe that this model reference described a future subverter
of religion, authority, and property. To be sure, the high-school
principal was at that time a friend of the family and, in the opinion of Anna Yelizarova, had hoped that his favorable report
would help Vladimir overcome those obstacles which the fate of
his older brother might put in his path. But whatever may have
been the oblique motives of Fyodor Kerensky, he would never
have dared, in full view of the entire faculty council, to give his
pupil such a favorable reference had he not been sure that it
corresponded to the facts. The respected principal acted with
all the greater confidence since his closeness to the Ulyanovs—
which had not, of course, grown up accidentally—had allowed
him to supplement observation of Vladimir at school with impressions of him in his home surroundings.

The statement in the recommendation that "religion and rational discipline" were the foundation of Vladimir's upbringing is supported by Anna Yelizarova: "Ilya Nikolayevich was . . . a sincerely and deeply devout man, and brought up his children in the same spirit," demanding of them, moreover, "conscientiousness to the point of pedantry." Vladimir retained his religious faith up to the age of sixteen. It follows from the conditions of development of Russian social thought, and from the distinguishing traits of his own character, with its absolute integrity, that so long as he clung to his religious beliefs, he could not possibly, at the same time, have entertained subversive political views. Hypocrites of the revolution notwithstanding, we must accept facts as they are. The kernel of Vladimir's personality, while filling with vital fluids, concealed itself for a time under the defensive shell of tradition. Vladimir had learned, especially since the unpleasant adventure with the "Frenchman," to put a muzzle, when necessary, upon his natural sarcasm. He did not seek adventures, and did not love excitement for its own sake. Without surrendering his natural inclinations, he was able to adjust smoothly to the high-school system, pitting against it his moral resilience, quick-wittedness, and buoyancy.

A year earlier, to be sure, Vladimir had turned his back upon religion, thereby adopting a starting point for a reconsideration of all traditional views. But this process still had a concealed character. Vladimir had only begun to become "a critically thinking personality." At the same time, what he had learned of the world in his seventeen years prompted him to conceal the change taking place within, even from a mentor who observed him closely. There is not a shred of evidence, therefore, for suspecting the esteemed principal of having betrayed, even if only for an instant, his loyal civil servant's principles for the sake of personal friendship.

Certain doubts are provoked not by the laudatory, but the critical part of this recommendation. A temporary state of depression caused by family tragedies certainly did not justify classifying this talkative and jolly youth with the loners and the antisocial types. One can only suppose that Kerensky the father was just as bad a psychologist as the son subsequently proved to be—unless, indeed, the very precise phrase "aversion to companionship" concealed some other trait the principal had noticed but could not understand and call by its true name. The problem was in truth not an easy one. Behind the self-restraint and discipline of Vladimir, some irreducible psychic element was to be felt. The same was true of his relations with his schoolmates. Everything seemed to go well, but nevertheless not quite as it should. Vladimir generously used his knowledge to help others. He successfully tutored his elder sister in Latin. For two years he gave free lessons to a Chuvash teacher, coaching him for his final examinations. He willingly wrote compositions for others, trying to phrase them in a style foreign to himself. But he brought nobody into his home. Vladimir Ulyanov was separated from his schoolmates, even from those who were "the school's pride and joy," by some invisible partition excluding both intimacy and familiarity. There were pleasant enough relations with many, but friendship with none. "Brother often made fun both of his companions and of certain teachers," writes Anna Yelizarova. His jokes, we may believe, were well aimed, and did not always spare the self-esteem of the victim. But what was more important, they made clear the distance between the victim and his mocker. "He had no great friends during the high-school years," acknowledges Anna Yelizarova. Bragging, self-importance, and putting on airs were completely alien to him both as a boy and as a young man; the very scope of his personality excluded such qualities. But the enormous personal superiority of this future fisher of men prevented those intimacies which demand, if not equality, at least commensurability. It was in spite of his sociability that Vladimir stood alone. In so far as he was capable of understanding it, the principal was noting this trait of his personality, which in the future was to cause so many reproaches and condemnations, until at last it compelled its own recognition. Maybe the best thing to do is to name this inconvenient trait "genius." The high-school student Vladimir Ulyanov was the larva of Lenin.

Fyodor Kerensky had a reason for writing about the mother's intention "to remain with" Vladimir. The director of the Police Department had "suggested" to Maria Alexandrovna, during her ceaseless efforts in behalf of Sasha, that she place her younger son far away from the source of infection, far away from the capital, in one of the more peaceful provincial universities. It was decided that Vladimir should study in Kazan. Maria Alexandrovna made up her mind to move there with her entire family. She wished to believe that under her protection Volodya would not be so easily drawn off onto the fatal road. Moreover, to remain in Simbirsk would be unbearable. There everything reminded her of the recent past, and what with the cowardly hostility of yesterday's friends, the family was pretty well forced to leave their home of many years. Maria Alexandrovna made haste to sell the house, and arrived with the other children in Kazan a few weeks after Vladimir. In its new location the family found itself again, as in the first Simbirsk period, isolated—and, moreover, under the black cloud of governmental disapproval.

The city of Kazan with its nearly 100,000 inhabitants, though called "the capital of the Volga" and possessing a university, had retained a completely provincial character. The ideas and hopes that had excited educated society two decades before, had now faded and decayed. "The boredom devouring the life of Kazan," writes a newspaper observer of that time, "has penetrated everywhere, and has introduced into its public institutions, its *duma* and its *zemstvos,* a deadening apathy."[1] Kazan university, founded at the beginning of the nineteenth century, had a dramatic history of its own. When the "Holy Alliance" spread its black wings over Europe, Russian universities, notwithstanding their humility, fell under the suspicion of the court hypocrites. Inspector General Magnitsky discovered to his horror that natural rights were deduced by the Kazan professors from reason and not from the Gospels, and proposed to close the university and raze its buildings to the ground. Alexander I found another way to accomplish the same goal; he appointed the inspector general the university's rector. Magnitsky instituted the strictest code of regulations for all the sciences—written by a corporal and supplemented by a drunken monk. From that time on, parabolas were described in the name of the Holy Trinity, and chemical reactions took place only with the consent of the Holy Ghost. Thus reduced for a long time to a state of complete abjection, the university experienced a certain revival during the twenty-year rectorship of the famous Lobachevsky, creator of a non-Euclidian, or "imaginary," geometry.[2] Ulyanov the father had been a pupil under Lobachevsky—but this at the time of a new decline in the Russian universities caused by the fright of Nicholas I at the revolutions of 1848. While teaching school in Penza, Ilya Nikolayevich had, on Lobachevsky's recommendation, worked hard and successfully for several years at the management of a meteorological station.

Vladimir entered Kazan University thirty-seven years after his father, choosing not physics and mathematics, but the Law School. The director of the Simbirsk High School regretted the choice; he had hoped his favorite pupil would study philology. But a teaching career had little attraction for Vladimir; he wanted to be a lawyer. The student body in Kazan was perhaps even more democratic than in other universities. But there was complete panic in the institutions of higher learning in those days. Only three months had passed since the execution of Alexander Ulyanov and his comrades. The government, with its all-powerful police system and its million soldiers, remained in constant fear of the students, who numbered fifteen thousand in all. The regulations of 1884 were now rigidly enforced. Liberal professors were dismissed, innocent home-town clubs dissolved, suspected students expelled and those remaining compelled to wear hated uniforms. The Minister of Education, Count Delyanov, a malicious nonentity, issued a special memorandum forbidding high schools to accept "the children of cooks" as students. Leonid Krasin, Lenin's contemporary and future associate, writes in his memoirs: "In the autumn of 1887 when I first came to Petersburg for the entrance examinations to the Technological Institute, Petersburg was going through a time of the very blackest reaction."[8] Things were certainly no better in Kazan.

Nevertheless the student body found enough strength to register a protest. The first notes of protest had sounded within the walls of Petersburg University in the spring, when Rector Andreyevsky in a speech devoted to the plot of Ulyanov and his comrades couched in the language of grandiloquent obsequiousness so characteristic of professorial heroes, said: "Why did these wretches use the door of our university? They crept into our delightful student family in order to disgrace it . . ." etc., etc. The next day a proclamation of the Union of Home-Town Clubs declared the university disgraced for having "followed its rector in slavishly crawling at the feet of despotism." The execution of the five students had stunned the university. The vacation months had somewhat relieved the mood of tension. But in the autumn the students again felt themselves caught in a vise. The atmosphere in the classrooms and corridors suddenly grew heavy. In November, a wave of "disorders" began to spread. Starting at Moscow, it reached the Volga in December.

The students of Kazan University held a meeting on their own initiative on December 4, demanded that the inspector appear before them, and noisily presented him with their demands, refusing to disperse. An inspector observed in the front row a young student who, as he went out, presented an identity card with the name of Ulyanov. On the same night, Ulyanov was arrested in his room. Had he really distinguished himself by his protesting conduct, or was he included in the list of forty arrestees because of his odious family name? It is not easy to decide. The role of leader was, in any case, more than this newcomer was up to. The organizers of these "disorders" were always more-experienced upperclassmen who had co-ordinated their own activities and also formed ties with other university centers. However, official documents of that time attempt to shed a different light on the conduct of the young student.

The superintendent of the district reported to the ministry, quoting the inspector, that during his short stay at the university Vladimir Ulyanov had distinguished himself by "secretiveness, inattention and even impoliteness." Only two days before the meeting, he had, it seemed, attracted the attention of the staff. He had been conversing in the smoking room with "the most suspicious of students" and kept going out and coming back with something in his hand. At the meeting of December 4, he had rushed into the auditorium with the first group, running through the corridor with a shout, "waving his arms as though desiring in this way to inspire others." From this colorful sketch at least one thing emerges clearly: from the first hour of his arrival at the university, Vladimir had been under close police surveillance. And this police surveillance had immediately discovered in him three vices: "secretiveness, inattention and even impoliteness." One may fully rely on the published testimony to the effect that Lenin, as he said in his own subsequent account, "played no significant role" in the disorders. On the other hand, the inspector,

with his spyglass trained on Ulyanov from the start, was probably not far off in claiming to have "discovered him in the first
group." Perhaps, too, the experienced eye of the policeman
caught a hot glimpse of hatred in the glances of this young man
with the inconvenient name. "In view of the exceptional circumstances affecting his family," adds the supervisor in his report,
"this attitude of Ulyanov toward the meeting moves the inspector
to consider him fully capable of various kinds of unlawful and
criminal demonstrations." The arrest, then, was preventive in
character.

In the fact that Ulyanov, when leaving the meeting, had
handed the inspector his student identity card, Anna Yelizarova
and others see yet another demonstrative act of protest. In reality
the meaning of the gesture remains unclear. It is possible that
the more-experienced students had managed to avoid presenting
their cards and that Ulyanov was caught unawares. But it is also
possible that in a state of excitement he drew out his card under
the nose of the inspector as though handing him a calling card.
While escorting Ulyanov to the precinct, the policeman tried to
reason with him: "Why are you causing trouble, young man?
You're breaking your head against a wall. . . ." "The wall is
rotten," answered the young man quickly. "One good shove
and it will collapse." This nimble answer was excessively opti-
mistic. More than one shove was required. But the rebel was only
seventeen years and eight months of age. A more realistic appraisal of the task would come with years. After some days in
prison Vladimir was expelled from the university, which he had
attended for only four months, and was banished from Kazan.
Thus within six months after the execution of Alexander a new
blow had fallen upon the family—not so tragic, but heavy enough.
The career of the second son was shattered.

It was only in the spring of that same year that the director of
the high school had solemnly testified that "not a single instance"
had been observed of Vladimir Ulyanov's "evoking by word or
deed any adverse opinion." But the streets of Kazan were hardly
covered with snow before Ulyanov had shown himself a subverter of society's foundations. He was hiding in the smoking
room hobnobbing with suspicious students, waving his arms to
inspire others. Is it true that the change was so abrupt? Or did

the testimonies of high-school and university authorities distort the young man's image in opposite directions? There was doubtless some distortion. But that was not the most important thing. In the intervening months, Vladimir had lived through a tremendous internal upheaval: the tsar had hanged his brother.

9

THE FATHER AND HIS TWO SONS

In Soviet sources it has become almost a rule to describe the revolutionary tendencies of the Ulyanov brothers as a result of the father's influence. The legend was created as follows: Everyone who ever came in contact with the family of the Simbirsk superintendent of public schools has deemed it his duty in recent years to express in print his retrospective understanding of the revolutionary character of the family. Just as in Christian hagiography not only the holy men themselves, but their ancestors, too, as far as possible, were endowed with the attributes of sublimest piety, so now the modern Muscovite-Byzantine evangelists consider it inadmissible to see in Lenin's father merely what he was, i.e., a government functionary devoted to the cause of education. This is pointless! Nobody demands poetic gifts from the father of a poet. And the father of a revolutionary need not be a conspirator. It is good if parents do not hinder their children in developing their gifts. But a biographer should not impose demands on his subject's parents. He ought to portray them as they were. What lessons can be learned from a life story if it is based on data that are not true? "Ilya Nikolayevich was very sympathetic to the revolutionary movement." The house of the Ulyanovs on Moscow Street was, it seems, something of a political club; in the debates on revolutionary questions, "Alexander set the pace." But Vladimir—could it be otherwise?—"often took part in the disputes, and with great success, too." Such an authoritative writer as the late Lunacharsky writes that Ilya Nikolayevich "sympathized with the revolutionaries and brought up his children in a revolutionary spirit."[1] Going even further, he reaches the conclusion that Lenin was "bound by blood ties through father and brother with the preceding revolution, that of the People's Will generation."

We learn with astonishment from the younger daughter Maria Ulyanova that Ilya Nikolayevich trained the rising cadre elements among his public-school teachers "in the spirit of the best ideas of the 1860s and 1870s." There is no doubt that his lectures were beneficial. But the phrase "best ideas of the 1860s and 1870s," in the history of Russian social thought, is understood to mean the ideas of the revolutionary Populists. These ideas meant: a break with the church, recognition of the doctrine of materialism, and implacable war with the exploiting class and with tsarism. There could have been no question of such instruction in official courses for schoolteachers even had their organizer himself shared in the "best ideas of the 1870s." But Ilya Nikolayevich did not share them at all. A reverent attitude toward education was characteristic of him. But it did not preclude a faith in the Holy Communion. This cannot be explained by mere references to "the times." Progressive people not only of the 1860s, but also of the 1840s, were both atheists and utopian socialists. Ilya Nikolayevich was not one of their number, either in the nature of his work or in his manner of thought. Suffice it to note that at the very beginning of his work as inspector he anxiously called the attention of his superiors to the sloppiness of the priests in their teaching of religion. Teachers educated by Ulyanov became, according to trustworthy reports, the best teachers of the *gubernia;* but at no point did they enter into the history of the revolutionary movement. The ideas of Ilya Nikolayevich and his pupils were not the revolutionary ideas of Chernyshevsky, Bakunin, Zhelyabov,[2] but those of moderate, liberal cultural pedagogues such as Pirogov,[3] Ushinsky,[4] Baron Korf.[5]

It so happened that many revolutionaries in those years were educators. Ilya Nikolayevich came into close contact with some, early in his career. But not one of them remained at his post; they were all expelled from the teaching profession. This happened to one of the teachers of the Noble Institute of Penza, who had the audacity to express dissenting views at the graduation ceremonies of 1860. Such an exploit, or such "madness," would never have occurred to Ilya Nikolayevich. As early as 1859 he received a prize of 150 rubles "for distinguished and zealous service." Soon thereafter a supervising senator singled him out for his "con-

scientious fulfillment of his duties." Three years later a new inspector general referred to Ulyanov with praise while making
adverse comments about a number of other teachers. The following year, in 1863, when in connection with the Polish uprising
Adjutant General Ogaryov was hunting for subversives among
teachers of the Volga and arrived at the conclusion that "the
spirit of disbelief and opposition" had its center at Kazan University, Ilya Nikolayevich, a graduate of the infected university,
remained, as before, in good standing. Three years later, one of
Ulyanov's colleagues and friends became embroiled in the affair
of Karakozov. Not even the slightest accidental or unfounded
suspicion fell upon him in this case either. His religious faith constituted in the eyes of the authorities—and they were quite right
—a sure barrier between him and the world of the revolutionaries.
Thus, even at the dawn of his activities, while still young and
unmarried, Ilya Nikolayevich kept strictly within the confines
of his functions as a teacher. Never in anything did he reveal
the slightest inclination to take the forbidden road.

The establishment of the office of inspector of public schools
was in itself an indication of bureaucratic reaction, directed
against the independence of the *zemstvos* in the realm of education. A pedagogue whose political "morality" was in the least
suspect could not possibly have been named to such a trusted
post. In his 1901 article tracing the history of the government's
struggle with the *zemstvos*, Lenin singles out two dates, 1869
and 1874, when the bureaucracy pushed aside local organs of self-
government and decisively took over supervision of public
education. Both dates are not only of historical but also of biographical interest. In 1869 Lenin's father was appointed inspector,
and in 1874 superintendent of public schools. Ilya Nikolayevich
was in the best possible standing with the ministry, rose steadily
up the hierarchical ladder, and received in due time the rank of
"Excellency" and the Order of St. Vladimir with the hereditary
nobility that it bestowed. No, this *curriculum vitae* in no way
resembles the life pattern of a revolutionary, or even of a peaceful citizen of dissenting views. We can place out trust in Ulyanov's
elder daughter when she states that "father was never a revolutionary." If the same daughter, Anna Yelizarova, compelled like
everyone else to pay homage to the official legend, writes in her

later essays that Ilya Nikolayevich was by conviction a "Populist," this label must be understood very broadly. Elements of Populism were to be found in the ideology not only of liberals, but also of independent conservatives. Under the influence of intensified revolutionary struggle in the latter half of the 1870s, Ilya Nikolayevich, like the majority of liberals, moved not to the left but to the right of his already moderate views. He once presented his older children with a collection of poems by Nekrasov, and Sasha drank in this plebeian poet's verses, which burned like nettles. But three or four years later, when Vladimir was growing up, the father not only did not spur on the young but began to pull back his older progeny. And soon thereafter he completely withdrew into his official shell. When a niece indignantly complained to him of the unjust dismissal of a public-school teacher whose activities were not in the least anti-governmental, Ilya Nikolayevich sat speechless, "withdrawn into himself, with his head down." He met the cross-questioning of his fourteen-year-old daughter with silence. This incident from real life sheds much light on the figure of the father and the general atmosphere in the family.

There can be no question of revolutionary debates in which "Alexander set the pace." "Father, who was never a revolutionary," continues Anna Yelizarova, "was by then forty years old. Burdened with a family, he wanted to save us, the younger generation." Those simple words should once and for all put an end to the legend of the father's revolutionary influence. But it is this irrefutable testimony of the elder daughter that is most often forgotten.

Yuli Tsederbaum, the future Martov, tells us that in 1887 some young lawyer secretly brought the indictment in the Lopatin case into his father's house and that he, Martov, then fourteen, listened with bated breath and with all the powers of his mind attuned to the nocturnal reading of the prosecutor's story of assassinations, escapes, and armed resistance. The Tsederbaums were a peaceful, liberal family, in no way linked with revolutionary circles. Nevertheless, such a reading of a secret document pertaining to a terrorist trial would have been unthinkable in the house of the state counselor Ulyanov. Although in the first years of his Simbirsk service Ilya Nikolayevich, as a stranger and a "liberal," found himself isolated in the little world of the provincial bigwigs, the general consensus was that he became, toward the end, "a very popular, beloved, and respected personality in Simbirsk"—that is, he moved closer to the bureaucratic milieu. It is no accident that the high-school principal, Fyodor Kerensky, a staunch conservative whose educational philosophy rested "on the Holy Gospels and Church services," found the Ulyanov family very congenial. As for the last years of Ilya Nikolayevich's life—those under the reign of Alexander III—perhaps the most realistic testimony is that of Delarov, a Simbirsk citizen and a deputy in the second State Duma: "I. N. Ulyanov was a man of conservative views, but he was no reactionary, not a conservative of the old type—he had certain aims in life . . . a desire to promote the welfare of the people."

If it is a question of Ilya Nikolayevich's direct influence upon his children's future, it was felt for a time only by the eldest daughter: her first conscious aspiration was to become a teacher. For about two years prior to going away to the university, she taught in public school. But it was this elder sister that Alexander found lacking in any revolutionary interests. As for the sons, during their high-school years, when they experienced their father's influence most directly, neither Alexander nor Vladimir belonged to any secret circle where future revolutionaries pored over tendentious books. It is very likely that no one even attempted to entice them into underground work, sons of an important government functionary as they were, invariably at the top of their classes and with irreproachable records in deportment. But there was another reason for this, one of a deeper kind. In a family of a serf-owning landlord, or a bribetaking functionary, or a greedy priest, a son and daughter, once they were caught up by the new influences, would be compelled to break with their parents abruptly at an early point and seek, so to speak, a new family. The Ulyanov children, on the contrary, long found satisfaction for their spiritual needs within the walls of their parental home. Moreover, inclined by nature to take everything seriously, they must even have regarded with some suspicion the rash solutions to serious problems proposed by certain schoolmates, often not very knowledgeable ones. In this family, too, however, the conflict between the two generations was preordained: the children thought through, and talked through, those conclusions which their parents hesitated to reach. Only an early death spared Ilya Nikolayevich the inevitable conflict with his children over politics.

"Who does not know," wrote Lenin eleven years after the death of his father, "how easy it is in Holy Mother Russia for a radical intellectual, a socialist intellectual, to be transformed into a functionary of the imperial government, a functionary who consoles himself with the thought that he is doing 'good' within the framework of office routine, a functionary who uses the 'good' he is doing to justify his political inertia, his kowtowing to the government's whiplash?" If an application of these stern words without qualification to Ilya Nikolayevich Ulyanov would constitute an injustice, it is only because he was in youth neither a socialist nor a radical in the true sense of the word. But there is no questioning the fact that he remained his entire life an obedient functionary of autocracy. Those immoderately zealous admirers who, for the sake of the son, are trying to paint up the political countenance of the father, reveal an excessive reverence for Lenin's blood ties and a lack of respect for his real ideas.

The now generally accepted thesis that Vladimir received his first revolutionary impulses from his terrorist brother appears so obvious from all circumstantial evidence as to require no proof. In reality, that hypothesis is also false. Alexander introduced no member of his family into his inner world, and least of all Vladimir. "These two," says Anna Yelizarova, "were undoubtedly brilliant, each in his own way, but they were totally different personalities." A comparison of the two brothers, even at the risk of running a little ahead of our story in regard to the younger, is required here by the course of our narrative.

The radical writer Vodovozov, who knew Alexander in Petersburg and afterward often visited the Ulyanovs in Samara, wrote many years later, when he was already an anti-Soviet émigré, that the "unusually attractive" Ulyanov family was divided "into two clearly expressed types." The first, best represented by Alexander, with a pale oval face and thoughtfully penetrating eyes, charmed everybody with its youthful freshness and spirituality. The second, a type hateful to Vodovozov, was most fully expressed in Vladimir, whose "whole face struck the observer with a combination of intellect and crudeness, I would almost say a kind of animalism. Most noticeable was the brow—brainy but slanting. A fleshy nose. Vladimir Ilyich was almost completely bald at 21 or 22." This contrast, obviously inspired by the images of the deities Ormazd and Ahriman, is not the exclusive property of Vodovozov. Alexander Kerensky, who, incidentally, was not personally acquainted with either of the brothers, being only six years old when Vladimir was about to graduate from high school, calls them "moral antipodeses." He contrasted the "charming and brilliant" Alexander with the "unsurpassed cynic" Vladimir. Approximately the same colors are employed by the Simbirsk litterateur Chirikov and others.[6] A sympathy for the older brother—sincere or feigned—adds weight to the hatred of the younger. Nevertheless, the contrast itself is not invented. It is easy to see in it a reflection of a natural contrast, though one distorted by hostility.

"The different characters of the two brothers," writes Anna Yelizarova, "were already evident in childhood; they were never close to each other." Volodya's attitude toward Sasha was one of "unlimited respect," but he obviously did not enjoy the sympathy of Sasha. (Yelizarova expresses this more cautiously: "Of the little ones, it was Olya who enjoyed Sasha's affection far more than the others.") On the basis of remote, badly remembered, and fragmentary stories of childhood recounted by her husband, Krupskaya attempts to describe in a few lines the relations between these brothers in their youth: "They had many tastes in common; both felt the need to be left alone for long periods of time. . . . They lived habitually together. . . . And when some of the innumerable young people came to see them . . . the boys had a favorite phrase: 'Delight us with your absence.'" This "favorite phrase" alone unmistakably demonstrates that Krupskaya had no clear notion of Alexander's personality or of the relationship between the two brothers. "Delight us with your absence"—it was quite possible for Vladimir to say that. But Alexander, who did not use sarcastic expressions, could only frown when hearing this from Vladimir.

Both in looks and personality, Alexander was more like his mother. The father's traits predominated both in the face and mentality of Vladimir. However, this contrast, although basically very important, is too simplistic to exhaust the question. Courage

—in Russian this word, *muzhestvo*, has been appropriated by the male (*muzhchina*)—constituted the most important trait of Maria Alexandrovna's personality.[7] But this was the courage of the mother who gives herself wholly to her family and children until the very end. The courage of Alexander, too, was, above all, the courage of self-sacrifice. Imperiousness, quick temper, humor, guttural r's, early baldness, and early death—all those features Vladimir derived from Ilya Nikolayevich. But if the elder brother was not a duplicate of the mother, still less was the younger an exact reproduction of the father. They received from their parents, and through them from more remote ancestors, certain "genes" which, combined, produced these two extraordinarily outstanding but dissimilar human beings.

The two brothers indubitably had certain traits in common: both were highly gifted (though not equally so), both loved work, both tended to devote themselves completely to a cause, both were careful and solicitous, astoundingly so at such a young age. And finally, last but not least,[8] both became revolutionaries. Reactionary writers never tired of portraying Russian revolutionaries as semieducated mediocrities. Even Turgenev and Goncharov were not, essentially, averse to this tendency. But it was not mediocrities who established the principal features generally shared by the revolutionary ranks. Not at all.

The Ulyanov brothers—both Alexander and Vladimir—as before them the leaders of the Decembrists, the men of the Enlightenment, the Populists, and the members of People's Will, were the genuine cream of the Russian intelligentsia.

"In all of my life—which, by now, means quite a span of time," writes Vodovozov, "I can count few people whom I found as charming, in the full sense of the term, as I did Alexander Ilyich Ulyanov." Those who knew the older brother unanimously report the disarming integrity of his character. There was not in him "the slightest pose or affectation." A sense of justice and a most meticulous thoughtfulness of others, even in trivial things, were part and parcel of his personality. We can easily believe that in personal relations Alexander was incomparably more winning than young Vladimir. To be sure, in freedom from falsehood and pose, and in hatred of cheap embellishments, Vladimir was in no way second to Alexander. The same was true of the integrity of his personality, except that his personality was wholly different, not designed by nature for personal relations. Each of the brothers was shaped out of a solid block of material, with nothing added, but the *kind* of material in each was different. And when Lunacharsky expressed his magnanimous conviction that Alexander "was not second to Vladimir Ilyich in genius," one cannot refrain from saying: These people measure genius with too short a yardstick. The application of this weighty epithet to Alexander is in reality a retrospective reflection from the historic figure of Vladimir.

Even in his high-school days the older brother was reading Dostoyevsky with emotional delight. The tortured psychology of the novelist was congenial to the spiritual universe of this thoughtful and sensitive boy who found his surroundings offensive. To Vladimir, the author of *Crime and Punishment* remained alien even in his mature years. Instead, he avidly read and re-read Turgenev, who was so hateful to Dostoyevsky, and then Tolstoy, the mightiest of Russian realists. The contrast between Tolstoy and Dostoyevsky was not accidentally a favorite theme of traditional Russian literary criticism, and had many different facets. Still, most important is the contrast between a tragic introspection and a joyous perception of the external world. It would be an oversimplification to project this contrast onto the two brothers in its entirety. But it is of considerable relevance to the understanding of their personalities.

Alexander was of melancholy temperament; Ilya Nikolayevich considered Vladimir's temperament choleric. Anna depicts her older brother as antisocial, often downright gloomy in his inexpressible sensitivity.

"I never saw him carelessly happy," writes one of the members of the conspiracy. "He was always meditative and sad." A complete contrast to Vladimir, whose most striking trait was an ever-overflowing joy in life, an expression of self-confident strength. Speaking of Alexander as a thoughtful organizer, another of the conspirators cautiously remarked: "He was perhaps a little slow-moving." In contrast, Vladimir (and not only in his youth, either) was distinguished above all by a vigorous assertiveness and a quick dexterity in work—qualities nourished by the richness, variety, and rapidity of subconscious associations. Are these not among the chief resources of genius?

"A very characteristic trait," writes Anna Yelizarova of Alexander, "was his inability to lie. If he did not want to say something he remained silent. This trait manifested itself so clearly at his trial." One wants to add: "Unfortunately." In irreconcilable social struggle such a psychic makeup means political defenselessness. Notwithstanding all the philosophizing of stern moralists (those liars by calling), a lie is an expression of social contradictions, and sometimes also a weapon in the struggle against them. It is impossible through individual moral effort to leap out of the framework of the social lie. As a type, Alexander was more like a knight than a politician. This created a psychic barrier between him and his younger brother, who was far more elastic, more opportunistic in questions of personal morals, better-armed for the struggle, but in no way less implacable toward social injustice.

Of Nikolai, the brother of Tolstoy, a subtle observer and psychologist, Turgenev said that he lacked only a few faults in order to become an admirable writer. Leo Tolstoy himself considered this paradoxical description "very true." Maybe obliquely he found in it a justification for those traits which made it difficult to communicate with him, even for members of his own family. Turgenev's words mean that, for the carrying out of some important public functions, certain supplementary attributes are necessary, attributes that by no means always serve to adorn one's personality. If this is true in regard to a writer, it is still more true of a statesman and—multiplied to the nth power—of a leader. But Turgenev's appraisal does not in any way imply that on the moral scale, if scales do exist for the weighing of imponderable substances, Leo Tolstoy weighed less than his brother Nikolai. The influence of Alexander on people close to him was great. But it could hardly have extended beyond them. Alexander had not the will to power, the ability to harness for a cause not only the virtues but the weaknesses of others and, should need arise, to proceed despite considerations of individual personality. He was too subjective, too much a prisoner of his own experiences, too much prone to consider a problem solved when he had solved it only for himself. He lacked the aggressive and tireless spirit of a missionary. And it was precisely the presence in his younger brother of the attributes of a future public figure, writer, speaker, agitator, tribune, that made him alien and perhaps even unattractive in Alexander's eyes.

In Vladimir one sees in all situations the instigator, the reformer, the leader of human masses. Alexander, under more civilized circumstances, could easily be pictured as a peaceful scientist and father of a family. Drawn into the revolution by the course of events, he took over the terrorist method sanctified by tradition, made bombs on the model of Kibalchich, and, shielding others with his own body, went to his death. The figure of Alexander was that of a saint; Vladimir was every inch a leader. One went down in the history of the revolution as the most tragic of her failures, the other as the greatest of her accomplishments.[9] Lev Kamenev, the original editor of the complete collection of Lenin's works, cautiously writes: "It is possible that it was from the lips of his elder brother that Lenin first heard about the teachings of Marx and about those ideas and aspirations which preoccupied the revolutionary intelligentsia of those years."[10] Another prominent Soviet writer, the former editor of *Izvestia* Steklov, speaks far more categorically: "Just a short time before his arrest the elder brother gave to the younger the first volume of [Marx's] *Das Kapital*. By this act Alexander Ulyanov created not only his own successor but also the successor and continuator of Karl Marx."[11] This story, though disseminated throughout the world, is in complete contradiction both with the facts and with circumstantial psychological evidence. "Sasha," says Anna, "never disputed or denied anything in front of the young." Even to his elder sister, who lived side by side with him in Petersburg, he did not confide that which was most important to him. The brothers lacked any secret sphere of interests and conversations—about God, about love, about the revolution—which in other families can bind together children of different ages. We have already learned from Anna: "The differing personalities of the two brothers became apparent from childhood on and they were never close to each other." In the summer of 1886, the last one the brothers spent together, they were farther apart than ever.

Recovering comparatively soon after the death of the father, Vladimir felt himself the man in the family. His recent emancipation from religion must have suddenly elevated his self-esteem.

As often happens with headstrong youths, the need for independence took a rough and tough form in him in that critical period—at the expense of others, and in particular, at the expense of his mother's authority. "Mockery was natural to Vladimir in general, and, at that transitional age, especially so." We can rely on these words the more surely since the elder sister, as she is portrayed in her own writing, would not easily have forgotten these mockeries. As for Alexander, he was painfully sensitive to jibes at the expense of others, and it would never occur to anyone to sneer at Alexander himself. He first came into contact with this in the summer spent with the fatherless family. His tender feeling toward his mother, made more acute by his previous absence and their common loss, was particularly intense. Besides the profound differences in their personalities, each brother was now tuned to a different key. The phase of childish worship, when Volodya wanted to do everything "like Sasha," had given way to a struggle for independence; the inevitable rejection of his elder brother had begun; his concentration, his attentiveness to other people, his fear of revealing his superiority, Vladimir offset with a noisy aggressiveness, sneering, jibes, and an organic desire to dominate. The summer passed in disharmony.

Let us listen to Anna Yelizarova. Volodya's abruptness and aggressiveness "became especially noticeable after the death of the father, whose presence had always had a restraining effect upon the boys." Vladimir began to "talk back to his mother, sometimes harshly, as he would never have dared while Father was with us." Perhaps this demonstrative impudence of Vladimir's was also, in a way, a retroactive protest against the father's authoritarianism. The mother subsequently remembered with emotion how Sasha had sometimes interceded on her behalf during that last summer. Once, while playing chess, Vladimir carelessly waved away his mother's reminder about some task, and when Maria Alexandrovna insisted with some irritation, he answered with a wisecrack. Then Alexander intervened: "Either you will do immediately what Mama tells you or I won't play with you any longer." The ultimatum was presented calmly, but so firmly that Vladimir immediately did as he was told. Anna herself, although she was annoyed at the "sneers, impertinence and arrogance" of Volodya, nevertheless fell under his influence, or at any rate willingly kept up a chatter with him full of jokes, digs, and laughter. Alexander not only did not join in these conversations, but found it difficult to tolerate them. He had his own moods, and Anna more than once brought upon herself his reproving looks. In the autumn, when they were in St. Petersburg, she summoned up the courage to put a question to Sasha: "How do you like our Volodya?" Sasha answered: "Undoubtedly a very able person, but we don't get along." Maybe he even said, ". . . don't get along at all," adds Anna. At any rate, her brother said this "decisively and firmly." "Why?" the surprised sister asked. But Alexander evaded the question, thus merely emphasizing the profundity of the differences. The elder brother did not call the other "an able boy" but "an able person," speaking as of an equal, and there is every reason to think that Anna's memory truthfully retained this nuance. At the same time, he surprised his sister by this special kind of moral dissociation from his brother. The absence of spiritual kinship was for Alexander more than enough to exclude the possibility of intimate conversation with Vladimir. There was, however, another and equally deep-seated reason. In the summer of 1886 Alexander had not yet decided anything for himself. He had read Marx, but had no clear idea what practical application he would make of the reading. Even in the autumn in Petersburg he was still trying to brush aside any revolutionary conclusion. Could he have confided these waverings and doubts to his younger brother, especially one with whom he was not getting along?

There can be no question, then, of Alexander's having any direct political influence upon Vladimir. But the moral influence had to find its political expression, though not necessarily at once. By his entire being, Alexander inculcated into his brother higher demands upon himself and others, and thus, regardless of his own intentions, speeded up the broadly speaking, inevitable conflict between Vladimir and his milieu. Anna recalls how Alexander, returning home on vacation, extended his hand "with friendly simplicity" to an old messenger in the employ of the father, which "attracted attention because it was not done." This interesting incident, which survived in the memory of the sister through no accident, sheds some reflected light on the social customs of the bourgeois bureaucratic circles of those times as they were practiced even in one of the best families. The atmosphere was still saturated to suffocation with the vapors of serfdom! There can be no doubt that Alexander's sincere "democratic" gestures had a more serious effect on the formation of Vladimir's personality than any haphazard conversations about People's Will or about Marx. Besides, there never were such conversations.

What ideas and moods captivated Vladimir in the summer of 1886, on the eve of his last year at high school? In the preceding winter, according to Anna Yelizarova, he had begun "rejecting authority in the period of his first, so to speak, negative formation of personality." But his criticisms, for all their boldness, still had limited scope. They were directed against high-school teachers, and to some extent against religion. "There was nothing definitely political in our conversations." On her return from the capital, Vladimir did not put any questions to his sister about revolutionary organizations, illegal books, or political groupings among the students. Anna adds: "I am convinced that with our relations being what they were at that time, Volodya would not have concealed such interests from me," had he had any. The tales about political debates in the home of the Ulyanovs, even during the father's lifetime, with Alexander playing the leading role and with apt replies from Vladimir, are pure invention from beginning to end. Notwithstanding the fact that among these Simbirsk high-school students (as shown by recent discoveries in the papers of the gendarmerie) there existed even in the dullest period of the 1880s certain secret circles and tendentious little library collections, half a year after the death of his father Vladimir remained completely untouched politically and did not show the slightest interest in those economics books that filled Alexander's shelf in their common room. The name of Marx meant nothing to this young man whose interests were almost exclusively in *belles lettres*. Moreover, he gave himself up to literature with passion. For whole days he drank in the novels of Turgenev, page by page, lying on his cot and carried away in his imagination into the realm of "superfluous people" and idealized maidens under the linden trees of aristocratic parks. Having read through to the end, he would begin all over again. His thirst was insatiable.

Thus, in spite of their proximity, each of the brothers lived his own life that summer. From dawn to dawn Alexander sat bent over a microscope. In this connection, Krupskaya places the following phrase on Lenin's lips: "No, my brother will never be a revolutionary, I thought then. A revolutionary cannot spend so much time investigating annelid worms." An obvious anachronism! The Vladimir of those times, remote from politics, could not have had such a thought about the brother to whom the whole family looked as a future scientist. Instead, after the arrest and execution of Alexander, Vladimir must have repeated to himself: Who could have thought that this brother would exchange his microscope for a bomb so quickly?

After her liberation from prison, Anna, sparing Vladimir, did not tell him what his dead brother had said of him. But Vladimir was neither deaf nor blind. In his relationship with Alexander he could not but detect an estrangement tinged with hidden irritation, if not distaste. Never mind, it is all temporary and subject to change—so he must have comforted himself—a closer association will surely ensue in the future; he, Volodya, will show what he is worth and Sasha will be compelled to recognize it. A whole life— that is, eternity—still lies ahead. As for today, we have Turgenev's wondrous world on the agenda. But instead, the agenda turned out to contain the Peter and Paul Fortress and Sasha's doom.

Some years later, the Social Democrat Lalayants questioned Lenin about the affair of March 1. Lenin answered: "Alexander's participation in a terrorist act was completely unexpected for all of us. Possibly my sister knew something—I knew nothing at all." As a matter of fact, the sister knew nothing either. The testimony of Lalayants fully corroborates Anna's story and coincides with what we know on this subject from Krupskaya's *Recollections*. In explaining this fact, Krupskaya refers to the difference in their ages, which wholly destroys her own account of the closeness of the brothers. But this reference, inadequate to say the least, does not alter the fact itself. Lenin's grief for his brother must have been colored with bitterness at the thought that Alexander had concealed from him what was deepest and most important. And with remorse over his own lack of attentiveness toward his brother and his arrogant assertions of his own independence. His childish worship of Sasha must have returned now with tenfold strength, sharpened by a feeling of guilt and a consciousness of the impossibility of making amends. His former teacher who handed him the fateful letter from Petersburg, says: "Before me sat no longer the carefree cheerful boy but a grown man buried in thought. . . ." Vladimir went through his final high-school experiences with his teeth clenched. There exists a photograph evidently made for the high-school diploma. On the still unformed but strongly concentrated features with the arrogantly pushed-out lower lip, lay the shadow of grief and of a first deep hatred. Two deaths stood at the beginning of the new period of Vladimir's life. The death of his father, convincing in its physiological naturalness, impelled him to a critical attitude toward the church and the religious myth. The execution of his brother awakened bitter hostility toward the hangmen. The future revolutionary had been planted in the personality of the youth and in the social conditions that formed him. But an initial impulse was needed. And this was provided by the unexpected death of his brother. The first political thoughts of Vladimir must inevitably have arisen out of a twofold need: to avenge Sasha and to refute by action Sasha's distrust.

Why, in that case, did Vladimir take the road of Marxism and not of terror, ask the official biographers. They answer with unanimous references to his "genius." In reality, not only the answer but the question itself is sheer invention. Vladimir, as will be seen, chose Marxism only after several years, after much intellectual labor; moreover, even after that, he continued for a long time to favor terror. Crude anachronisms are the disastrous price paid for the refusal to perceive a living man in his living development. Even Krupskaya was taken in by the notion of Lenin as a Marxist in 1887! In her attempts to explain why Alexander's execution did not inspire in Vladimir "a desire and a determination to follow in his brother's footsteps," she advances an unfounded hypothesis that Vladimir "at that time was already thinking independently of many things and had already decided for himself the question of the necessity of a revolutionary struggle." The youngest of the Ulyanovs, Maria, went still further along this road. At the memorial meeting for Lenin on February 7, 1924, she said that, upon receiving the news of his brother's execution, Vladimir cried out: "No, we will not follow that road. That is not the road to take." One might pass over the obvious incongruity of

Maria Ulyanova's story (at the time the event took place she was not quite nine years old), had not this phrase, carelessly tossed out by her, been, quite literally, canonized. It was said to demonstrate the profundity of political thought in the Simbirsk high-school boy—who, only the day before, had broken out of the shell of Eastern Orthodox faith, who did not yet know the name of Marx, had not read a single illegal book, knew nothing and could know nothing of the history of the Russian revolutionary movement, and had not yet even discovered in himself any interest in politics. In these conditions, what could the words attributed to him by the younger sister mean? In any case, not an opposition of the revolutionary struggle of the masses to the terror of the intellectuals. Even if one were to assume for a moment that a similar phrase was actually uttered, then it could not have expressed a program but only despair. Sasha should not have embarked on that path! Why did he not devote himself to science? Why did he doom himself?

Unlike coins, invented stories do not wear down with circulation, but on the contrary, grow bigger. The old Bolshevik Shelgunov tells this story: "When they read the telegram that Alexander was executed, Vladimir Ilyich wiped his brow and said, 'Well, then, we will seek a more effective road.'" All the laws of human psychology are here trampled on. Volodya is not thrown into despair upon receiving the dreadful news, does not grieve for the irredeemable loss, but wipes his brow and announces the need to find a "more effective road." To whom were these words addressed? The mother was in Petersburg, Anna was still in prison. Evidently Vladimir imparted his tactical discoveries to the thirteen-year-old Dimitri and the nine-year-old Maria. . . .

These loyal disciples step so lightly over facts and logic only because they are not satisfied with their teacher as he really was. They want a better Lenin. They embellish him in early youth with intellectual powers arrived at only as a result of Herculean labors. They endow him with supplementary qualities out of their own generosity. Thus they create for themselves a different, more perfect Lenin. We are satisfied with the one that really existed.

We have heard from Krupskaya that had young Vladimir not already possessed his own revolutionary views, he would have followed in his brother's steps after the execution. But Vladimir, in essence, did exactly that! He did not go into the countryside to the peasants, nor to the factories to the workers, but, just like Alexander, he entered a university. There he found the same circle of democratic youth who began with a struggle for the right to have their eating places and reading rooms and ended in terrorist conspiracies. Expelled from the university merely for a student protest, Vladimir was strengthened in his belief in terror. If he did not take the road of practical conspiracy it was not from considerations of principle but because, after the catastrophe of March 1, 1887, such attempts became for a long time psychologically and physically impossible. Revolutionary individuals without experience or perspectives were so alienated from their social milieux, even one composed of students, and so isolated from each other, that not a single hand was lifted in a practical effort. The old path of the intelligentsia was conclusively blocked by the tomb of the five students. New roads were not yet discovered. Calls to battle were nowhere to be heard. Vladimir knew not how to approach the task of revenge. The intensified reaction and the political decline of the intelligentsia provided the young man with a deferment. As we shall see, he made good use of it.

10

THE PREPARATIONS BEGIN

For reasons of "political hygiene," students expelled from universities were supposed to be banished "to their home towns." But in Simbirsk, where Vladimir had lived for over seventeen years, almost a third of his life, he had no relatives left. He was graciously permitted to go to the former estate of his grandfather Blank: his mother, Maria Alexandrovna, had inherited a fifth of that property. In December he departed for Kokushkino, some thirty miles from Kazan. He was to live there under unofficial surveillance until autumn of the following year. His elder sister was already there. At first she was to be exiled to Eastern Siberia —for the crime of being a sister of Alexander, there being no other grounds whatever—but through the fervent efforts of her mother, the sentence was commuted to exile in Kokushkino under official police surveillance. Maria Alexandrovna arrived from Kazan with the younger children a little later. The family lived in the cold and badly built wing belonging to one of the aunts. The neighbors could not have shown any great eagerness to make the acquaintance of the Ulyanovs. From time to time the police captain would drive up to make sure the criminal element was in its place. The alarmed aunts would entertain the captain, as was the custom, with tea and preserves, or perhaps even cherry brandy, and that would be all. At rare intervals an unremarkable cousin would also show up. Winter was peaceful in Kokushkino. The winds howled, the blizzard raged, the house was snowed in. The mother would heave a secret sigh, the aunts on occasion would shake their heads reproachfully: Why, after all, should Vladimir ruin his own life? Wasn't what happened with Sasha enough? They did, however, refrain from mentioning Sasha by name.

Vladimir grew to manhood, becoming quite attentive to his mother, who, as before, lavished an inexhaustible fountain of love and care upon her children. Anna, always distinguished by her uneven temperament, had grown more nervous since her prison experience. The family lived unhappily, not knowing what to expect from day to day. By good luck, there turned out to be an old bookcase in the wing, containing the books of a deceased uncle, considered in his time a well-read man. Such uncles, often of the type of Turgenev's "superfluous men," were to be found in many landowners' families. Departing for the cemetery they would bequeath to their nieces and nephews a couple of hundred stray volumes and some sets of old Russian journals. Vladimir fell upon his uncle's bookcase. This first spell of "serious" reading was thus of necessity chaotic. The choice of books was accidental; there was no guide. The young eyes roved thirstingly.

In making his acquaintance with progressive journals of previous years, Vladimir first came into contact with the struggle that surrounded the question of Russia's economic destiny. His knowledge of the journalism of the 1860s and 1870s—which he continued to expand in years to come—proved very useful to him subsequently in debates with the Populists and in his first efforts as a writer. But this village bookcase was not enough. He had to resort to the Kazan library. At the same time, the family subscribed to a newspaper, most likely Moscow's *Russkie vedomosti*, whose misty liberal gleam shone timidly in the twilight of the 1880s. It was evidently during these ten months in Kokushkino that Vladimir first learned to read a daily newspaper—a complicated art in which he subsequently became a virtuoso. For keeping in touch with the outside world, there were happy occasions all looked forward to: the arrival of a woven basket with books, newspapers, and letters was each time an event of importance. Vladimir, by the way, carried on no correspondence at this time. Only once did he attempt to inform a former high-school friend about his recent clash with the university authorities, honoring his foes with some verbal uppercuts; but the ever-cautious elder sister began to argue the folly of exposing himself and his correspondent to such a risk, and Vladimir, although he heartily disliked to give in to other people's arguments, refrained finally from sending off the letter which he had so enjoyed writing.

What with his uncle's bookshelf and the woven basket of mail from Kazan, he passed the days of his police-supervised life at

Kokushkino. The family wounds were gradually healing—quickly with the children, slowly with the mother. Vladimir tutored his younger brother Dimitri. He went sledding, and hunted rabbits and other game, gun in hand, although unsuccessfully. On the subject of Vladimir's unsuccessful hunting, Anna writes, "Like my two other brothers, he was never a hunter at heart." We can hardly agree. Lenin was in reality a passionate hunter, but too impatient. In this endeavor he yielded with difficulty to discipline. Later, too, that excessive impatience prevented him from becoming a good hunter, although in exile he did achieve a degree of prowess.

Spring came, Vladimir's first spring in the country. He was just turning eighteen, the springtime age. Now he must have better understood why Sasha so loved nature, and loved contemplating her in solitude. In summer his cousins came and the family continued to recover. Kokushkino came to life again; there were walks together, games of chess, songs, and hunting expeditions. Among the summer relatives there was no one with whom it would be worth while to exchange opinions upon troubled themes. Still, with cousins one could trade wisecracks with impunity. Even though they were older, they "were completely helpless before Volodya's well-aimed jibes and sly grin."

In May, five months after his expulsion, Vladimir made an attempt to regain entrance to the university. The head of the Kazan district schools sent a report to the minister in which it was made clear that the former student Ulyanov, "notwithstanding his distinguished abilities and excellent scholarship could not for the time being be considered a reliable person in either a moral or a political sense." The words "for the time being" implied that the director had not lost hope. The director of the department, without reading the report through, wrote in the margin: "Isn't this one a brother of that Ulyanov? Also from Simbirsk"—and then, having glanced at the latter part of the document, he saw that "the applicant is a brother of the executed Ulyanov," and he wrote beneath it: "Not to be accepted under any circumstances." The minister of education was Count Delyanov.[1] Witte described him as "a gentle and good man," and at the same time as "a shifty Armenian" who maneuvers in all directions.[2] With Ulyanov it was not necessary to maneuver; the minister simply turned down his petition.

Two months later, Maria Alexandrovna approached Delyanov in her own name. Before the certain refusal of the "gentle and good man" arrived, Vladimir sent a request to the Minister of Interior for permission to go abroad to continue his education. News of the refusal of the director of the police department to issue a foreign passport had already been sent through the Kazan police, since by then the authorities, as a result of the tireless efforts of the mother, had permitted Vladimir to take up his residence in Kazan once more. The family moved there in the autumn of 1888, all except Anna, who was permitted to leave Kokushkino only some time later.

Since the death of Ilya Nikolayevich Ulyanov, they had lived on a pension. The twelve hundred rubles a year issued by the treasury to the widow and children was a considerable sum of money in the provinces, but with so large a family it was still necessary to live frugally. The money received from the sale of the Simbrisk home constituted a reserve. Maria Alexandrovna took an apartment on the outskirts of town with a balcony and an orchard on the hill. In the lower story there were for some reason two kitchens. Vladimir occupied one of them and, enjoying comparative privacy, sat down to his books. For him the period of preparation had begun. From his expulsion from the university until his departure for Petersburg for revolutionary work, it lasted nearly six years. It was here, on the Volga, in Kokushkino, in Kazan, and later in the province of Samara, that the future Lenin was formed. For the biographer, those critical years 1888 to 1893 are of great interest, but at the same time they are the most difficult.

There are secret-police reports about each physical move of young Ulyanov. These reports, like little flags on the biographical chart, mark out his external course and ease the task of the researcher. But for Vladimir's inner course in that preparatory period, when he had not yet begun writing, there are no such flags. There are scattered bits of testimony, of some interest, but they are shapeless and some of them simply apocryphal. There was no politically mature person near him, no guide or even attentive observer, except for his elder sister, who has told us all she could of the growth of her brother. Only his schoolmates came in contact with Vladimir, but they were, in essence, his pupils. Moreover, the majority of them have retired from the scene without leaving behind any reminiscences. As an author, Vladimir did not appear on the stage until 1893. No documentary record of his evolution has been preserved, neither his ever so careful outlines of books nor even personal letters.

To the oft-repeated complaints about the paucity of material characterizing these critical years in Lenin's life, Yelizarova offers a rejoinder: "There wasn't much to say, anyway. He read, he studied, he debated." The note of irritation in these words makes it only more apparent that Yelizarova observed Vladimir's intellectual life only from the outside. For her, no question seems to arise about what he read, what he studied, what he debated. What was his attitude toward Populism, toward People's Will; how did his attitude change under the impact of his study of Marx, his personal observations, encounters, and influences? In short: How did the Simbirsk High-School boy, still remote from politics, barely emancipated from Eastern Orthodoxy, taking a carefree delight in Turgenev, become in those remote Volga provinces a full-fledged Marxist, an unbending revolutionary, a future leader? "I do not remember the names of his friends," writes Anna, who no more entered into Vladimir's inner life than she had earlier into the circle of Alexander's interests. Hence the meager content and the unreliability of this closest witness to the intellectual evolution of Vladimir.

The general direction of Vladimir's development was not, to be sure, exceptional. At the beginning of the 1890s, many of the young generation of the intelligentsia were turning abruptly to Marxism. The historic causes of this turn are no secret, either: the capitalist transformation of Russia; the awakening of the proletariat; the dead end in which the independent revolutionary course of the intelligentsia found itself. But a biography must not be overshadowed by history. We must show how the general historic forces and tendencies were refracted in a particular individual with all his personal traits and peculiarities. No small number of Russia's young men and women studied Marx in those years; some of them lived on the banks of the Volga. But only one of them succeeded in absorbing the doctrine into his flesh and blood, in subordinating to it his thoughts and his feelings, ultimately rising to tower above it, to feel himself the master, with the doctrine as his tool. This young man was Vladimir Ulyanov. Although the data for plotting the course of his preparatory development are scant, the position of the biographer is not altogether hopeless. Certain important signs exist with which to map his spiritual course. As for the gaps in the picture, we will have to resort to psychological speculation, while providing the reader with the data necessary for its evaluation.

The family continued in Kazan still quite isolated although probably not to the same degree as during the last months in Simbirsk. Maria Alexandrovna had broken with one milieu and not yet found another. Anna was living in her thoughts outside the family: she was about to marry Yelizarov. Vladimir was not new to Kazan. He sought out some of his old acquaintances and through them made new ones. Vladimir, as far as we know, brought nobody to the house. He had not brought any visitors even in his high-school years, and since his expulsion from the university he carefully protected his family from politically suspect visitors and any possible trouble they could bring. Besides, radically inclined young people must have avoided the family of Alexander Ulyanov to avoid attracting the attention of the police.

Among Vladimir's new acquaintances, we find the name of an old member of People's Will, Chetvergova, of whom, we are told, the young man was "very fond." Yelizarova writes that in general Lenin did not disavow the "heritage" of the old People's Will. Still, she obviously falls into one of her usual anachronisms in this case. In later years, when Lenin carefully appraised the constituent parts of the revolutionary past, he did in fact embrace some of the tenets of People's Will, such as centralism, conspiratorial tactics, and ruthlessness in the struggle against tsarism. But if in 1888 he "did not disavow" the heritage, then it was only because he had not yet approached it in a critical spirit. Ideas and tendencies were not yet marked off in his mind. To others, as to himself, he was still the younger brother of Alexander Ulyanov, a hero and martyr. He looked upon Chetvergova as a green recruit looks at a scar-covered veteran.

How and when did Vladimir first come into contact with his

future teacher, Karl Marx? Alexander read *Das Kapital* during his last vacation. In connection with his brother's fate, the name of Marx may well have emerged for Vladimir from that indifferent realm where so many names reside. One of his high-school friends states that after the death of Alexander, he and Vladimir, both in their last year of high school, attempted to translate *Das Kapital* from the German. If this recollection, on which the older sister casts doubt, is not a simple lapse of memory, the attempt at any rate could only have been of an episodic character and did not go beyond the first pages. As Yelizarova aptly comments, "How could two green high-school boys carry out such an undertaking?"

Another testimony, more reliable notwithstanding its factual errors, estimates Lenin's first acquaintance with Marx at approximately a year later. On the basis of conversations with Lenin in Western Europe during World War I, Radek says: "While still a high-school student, Vladimir Ilyich joined a circle of People's Will. There he first heard of Marx. The student Mandelshtam, a future Constitutional Democrat, read a paper developing the views of the Emancipation of Labor Group. . . . As though through a mist Ilyich caught sight of the mighty revolutionary theory. He got hold of the first volume of *Das Kapital* which revealed to him the external world."[3] All this happened not in Simbirsk but in Kazan; Vladimir was not a high-school student but a student expelled from the university. As for the rest of the story, although somewhat fictionalized, it evokes no great doubts. This is the first time we have encountered—in this particular connection—the name of Mandelshtam, a future liberal lawyer, who in his youth actually did go through the measles of Marxism. Such an interesting detail Radek could only have learned from Lenin himself. His mention of the People's Will circle confirms the fact that it was toward that milieu that the brother of the terrorist gravitated.

It would be a great mistake, however, to visualize the Kazan circle as a conspiratorial, let alone a terrorist, organization. It was merely a few young people gathered around someone under police surveillance—perhaps around that same Chetvergova. If we take literally Radek's statement that on that evening Lenin first heard the name of Marx, then we must not only regard the story about an attempt to translate *Das Kapital* in Simbirsk as apocryphal, but also concede that in the summer of 1886 Vladimir had absolutely no interest in the fat book that Alexander was poring over during the evening hours. There is nothing impossible in this. While busy with Turgenev or chess, the schoolboy might easily have glanced at the cover without even remembering the name of the author.

In the university city of Kazan, there were perhaps a dozen copies of the first Russian edition of Das Kapital; most of these were removed from public libraries or confiscated during searches of private apartments. The book had long since become a rarity. We have no way of knowing whether Vladimir succeeded in getting hold of the treasure from the secret shelf of some educated liberal, or through some exiled members of People's Will, or from local students. Perhaps it was the search for Das Kapital that brought him into contact with his first Marxist circles, either through Mandelshtam or in some other way.

However it may have come about, the student expelled from the Imperial University became a student in the secret university of Marx. And what a student! The biographer would pay a high price for an opportunity to take a peek at young Lenin reading the first chapter of Das Kapital in the extra kitchen of the Kazan apartment. When in the evening Anna would happen into his field of vision, he would immediately make her his audience. Vladimir could not shut his thoughts up inside himself as Alexander had. Ideas took hold of him, subjugated him to themselves, and demanded that he subjugate others to them. Seated on a cold kitchen range covered with old newspapers and gesticulating furiously, he would explain to his elder sister the mysteries of surplus value and exploitation.

Very little is known of the Kazan circle in which Vladimir took part. Anna Yelizarova, probably guessing, writes, "There was no authoritative leader in that circle." A few students read good books together and exchanged ideas about what they had read. Toward the spring of 1889 these studies assumed, it would seem, a more systematic character. Vladimir began to absent himself more often in the evenings. He had succeeded during these months in getting ahead with the study of Das Kapital and in maturing generally. We may assume with confidence that he had become first among equals in the circle and that he took his duties as unofficial leader seriously. But, for the time being, it was still only a search for roads.

In the university town there were several such circles. Most serious and important was Fedoseyev's group. The leader of this circle, who was born in 1869 and died tragically in 1929, was a truly remarkable figure. While still in the eighth grade in high school he was expelled for revolutionary agitation among his comrades. This lesson did not cure him; on the contrary, it impelled him to broaden the scope of his work. "Fedoseyev," a local gendarme officer reported, "enjoyed, in spite of his youth, considerable authority in revolutionary matters among local students." Fedoseyev's circle possessed a small illegal library and set up its own underground press. For those inert times this was a great and bold undertaking, although, to be sure, it did not get very far.

Vladimir, who did not belong to the inner circle, heard of these plans but took no part in them. He wanted to study. Alexander's fate not only beckoned to the revolutionary road but also warned him of its dangers. To throw himself in headlong, to become a martyr through sheer carelessness—such thoughts were alien to him even in those early years. A consciousness of his own significance had already awakened in him. He was getting ready without haste or feverish gestures. Not, to be sure, because of a lack of passion. But the ability to harness his passions was one of his most outstanding qualities, and it was this trait that made him a leader of others.

Without any concrete evidence, Anna Yelizarova places "the beginning of the formation of Vladimir Ilyich's Social Democratic convictions" in the winter of 1888–89. That circumspect formula, "the beginning of the formation," is almost meaningless. But we have at least moved quite a way from the assertion of the younger sister that the choice of the Social Democratic path had been made as early as 1887. However, the elder sister, too, is anticipating events. He was still only studying the economic theory of Marx, which was also recognized, after a fashion, by the Populists. Vladimir studied it more seriously than the others, but he was still far from drawing the necessary political conclusions from it. This is proven in part, although indirectly, by his relations with Fedoseyev. Anna Yelizarova thinks that "it is not necessary to as-

sume an influence of one upon the other," since it is a question
of "approximately equivalent magnitudes." For our purposes,
there is no need to compare the caliber of the two young men,
of whom Fedoseyev was the older by a year. It is a question of
the dates of development in the direction of Social Democracy.
All that is known about Fedoseyev implies that in this respect he
was well ahead of Ulyanov. According to Maxim Gorky, who lived
on the Volga in those years and moved in radical circles,
Fedoseyev had proclaimed his support of Plekhanov's *Our Disagreements* as early as 1887. True, when it comes to ideas or
dates, Gorky's memory is not particularly reliable, but his testimony is indirectly confirmed by other contemporaries. "By then
[1888] Fedoseyev was already maturing as a Marxist," writes the
former Kazan student Lalayants.[4] In answer to a question, Lenin
wrote a few years before his death: "N. E. Fedoseyev was one of
the first to declare his adherence to the Marxist tendency." Under
the influence of the old Social Democrat Skvortsov, Fedoseyev,
moreover, decisively condemned the terrorist tactics of People's
Will, a position that was by no means taken as a rule in Marxist
circles in those years.[5] It was precisely this point that must have
been the great stumbling block for the brother of Alexander
Ulyanov.

We may quite confidently assume that it was in connection with
Fedoseyev's propaganda activities that Vladimir first entered the
orbit of Marxist interests. It was probably from these same circles
that he received the precious volume of *Das Kapital.* Vladimir did
not make Fedoseyev's acquaintance, however, and never met him
even once during his entire stay in Kazan, although he did come
in close contact with less-committed members of his group. This
fact, to which the memoirists and biographers have paid no attention, requires some explanation. Lenin himself says: "I had
heard of Fedoseyev during my stay in Kazan but never met him
personally." We shall see further on that Lenin was always seeking closer acquaintance and connections with those who shared
his beliefs. Shortly thereafter, he was to enter into correspondence with this same Fedoseyev on theoretical questions of Marxism and was to make a special trip to the city of Vladimir in order
to try to meet him personally. Why, then, in Kazan, where making
his acquaintance would have been so simple, did he not seek out

Fedoseyev? One almost wants to say: Why did he avoid him? The idea that Fedoseyev himself, occupying a central position in the Marxist "underground" of the time, avoided making Lenin's acquaintance for conspiratorial reasons seems wholly improbable. Fedoseyev's name, as the citizen of Kazan Grigoryev relates, was widely spoken among the youth and "not entirely in secrecy." On the other hand, Vladimir, expelled from the university, was the brother of an executed terrorist. That was too strong a recommendation for Fedoseyev to disregard. It is far more probable that Vladimir himself shrank from the acquaintanceship. In taking up the study of *Das Kapital*, he did not intend at all to break with the traditions of People's Will. At the same time, he could not have felt sufficiently well grounded to defend that tradition from the criticism of a Social Democrat who rejected terror. If you add to this his distaste for surrendering to other people's arguments, especially people his own age, it becomes understandable why Vladimir might have preferred not to expose himself prematurely to an opponent's attacks. Through the other members of the circle, he found himself sufficiently *au courant* with the thoughts and arguments of Fedoseyev in order to take them into consideration as he studied. In later years Lenin resorted to such methods of cautious reconnoitering on more than one occasion. This testified first of all to his immense restraint and then to that quality which is best described as shrewdness. The psychological soundness of these conjectures permits us to put forth the hypothesis— and we shall soon find a number of corroborating factors—that for at least four years, from 1887 to 1891, Vladimir's revolutionary inclinations did not take on a Social Democratic coloring, and his study of Marxism did not imply, to him, a break with the cause of his elder brother.

Without knowing the works of Plekhanov, Vladimir could not even have seriously raised the question of a choice between Social Democracy and People's Will. To be sure, Kamenev, the first editor of Lenin's works, expresses his certainty that the writings of the Emancipation of Labor Group, then circulating in the radical circles of Kazan, were "undoubtedly read by Vladimir Ilyich." We are not at all certain of that. Vladimir spent only seven months in Kazan. The name of Plekhanov still meant nothing to him. The publications of the Emancipation of Labor Group, if they were circulating there, did so only in single copies. Vladimir was sufficiently engrossed in *Das Kapital*. Finally, even if Plekhanov's *Our Disagreements* also fell into his hands, he could hardly have gotten much out of a polemical book not addressed to beginners without some familiarity with the elements of political economy and the history of the Russian revolutionary movement.

As to the question of when Vladimir first came to read Russian Social Democratic literature, we have, aside from Kamenev's conjecture, one single affirmative indication: Lenin told Radek on a walk they took together that he had studied not only *Das Kapital* but also Engels' *Anti-Duehring* before he got hold of any publication of the Emancipation of Labor Group. We can consider it an established fact that Vladimir obtained *Anti-Duehring* in Petersburg not earlier than in the autumn of 1890. Therefore, his acquaintance with the works of Plekhanov, without which one could not have arrived at Social Democratic positions, must have taken place in 1891. Without setting aside rapturous anachronisms, one cannot establish the actual landmarks of Vladimir's development and demonstrate, if only approximately, how this young man, who began to study the social sciences at the age of nineteen, emerged four years later as a young warrior, armed to the teeth. The dates indicated above will gradually be filled in with some striking content. For the time being we will merely repeat: Lenin was no prodigy; his genius was organic, stubborn, at certain stages even slow, because it was profound. Must we not again advise the writers of memoirs, the biographers, worshipers, and sisters: Do not hurry Lenin along with childish whips; allow him to set his own pace. Rest assured; in good time he will come out on the road.

The winter spent in Kazan was a time of a burning passion for chess. Two considerations fed this passion: his youth, which required all kinds of exercise and disinterested expenditure of physical and mental energies, and the ambiguity of his position. Vladimir was an expelled student and did not know what to do with himself. For an amateur chess player he had attained considerable prowess even in high school, leaving his father far behind. During Alexander's last vacation, the brothers had played in the evenings—stubbornly, in silent concentration. In playing with Dimitri, the younger brother, and with weaker players in general, Vladimir did not show that weakening magnanimity which permits the opponent to take back a move, demoralizing them both. Observance of the rules of the game was for him an essential element of its very enjoyment. Lack of foresight and carelessness ought to be punished and not rewarded. A game is a dress rehearsal for a fight, and in a fight no moves are taken back. Vladimir regularly visited the Kazan chess club and at home tested his power to play without looking at the chessboard. During that winter, Anna Yelizarova arranged a match by correspondence for him with Khardin, a Samara lawyer and prominent amateur player. The duel, conducted on post cards, eventually reached a critical point: Vladimir thought that with his last move he had driven his opponent into a hopeless position. While awaiting an answer, he rearranged the pieces more than once and convinced himself again and again that nothing could save his opponent. Khardin answered with so unexpected a move that Vladimir gazed at it in bewilderment, which after careful analysis turned into a respectful exclamation: "Well, that is one hell of a fine player!" He always discovered real strength with an aesthetic satisfaction—even in an opponent. Three years later, the lawyer Khardin was to become the employer of the law clerk Vladimir Ulyanov.

Lenin's sister relates a curious incident from the Kazan period. Vladimir began to smoke, probably under the influence of his friends from the circle, where cloudy debates about capitalism were enveloped in the inevitable clouds of smoke. The mother was disturbed, as every mother should be. When her arguments about health proved to no avail, Maria Alexandrovna resorted to the claim that since he did not have any income of his own, he ought not to cause the family unnecessary expenses. Vladimir apparently felt keenly the reproach for unfulfilled hopes concealed in these words. He instantly gave up smoking and, moreover, conclusively—for the rest of his life.

A fear lest Vladimir should get into trouble impelled his mother, according to Anna, to acquire "a small farm in Samara *gubernia* and to secure permission to move there for the summer." Anna's story is incomplete. The "small farm"—as governor Sverbeyev immediately reported to the Police Department—

comprised a plot of nearly 225 acres of land and a mill: for a summer residence, that was far too much. In reality, Maria Alexandrovna was moved by economic considerations. One had to
think of means of subsistence for the family. Maria Alexandrovna's father, although a physician by training, busied himself with
agriculture in Kokushkino, and her mother was descended, in all
likelihood, from the German settlers of the Volga, who were
model farmers. Maria Alexandrovna herself had always assumed
the care of the family gardens and orchards. It is no wonder she
conceived the idea of buying a piece of land and settling there
for good. To convert Vladimir into a landowner and farmer offered an additional inducement: it was a means of protecting him
from political temptations and dangers.

Anna was then about to marry one of Alexander's university
friends, the former Petersburg student Yelizarov. To him fell the
task of buying the piece of land in his native Samara *gubernia*.
With the help of his brother, a prosperous peasant,[6] Yelizarov
successfully carried out the task, purchasing the farm at a bar-
gain price from an owner of gold mines named Sibiryakov. An
expansive extrovert and man of wealth, proponent of education
and left-wing liberal, Sibiryakov had earlier intended to establish streamlined business enterprises in Samara *gubernia*, experimental farms and model schools. Nothing had come of his plans,
and the gigantic property had had to be sold little by little.
Seventy-five hundred rubles was paid for the 223 acres with the
mill and buildings, some thirty miles from Samara. For those
times, this was a tidy sum of money. It included the cash received
from the sale of the Simbirsk house, as well as Maria Alexandrovna's share of the Kokushkino property. Thus the Ulyanovs became small landowners of the steppes.

Anna Yelizarova's silence about the economic side of the operation was evidently intended to protect the image of Vladimir
from associations with mundane problems of human existence.
In reality it only removed a very interesting link from his life's
chain. Fortunately, Krupskaya cites a very brief but highly en-
lightening observation on the subject by Lenin himself: "Mother
wanted me to run a farmstead. I had given it a try, but I saw that
it wouldn't work. My relations with the peasants were becoming
unnatural." We know nothing else about this incident. Only from

Vladimir's later letters to his mother is it evident that the business dealings and difficulties at Alakayevka were not entirely unknown to him. We are doubly grateful to Krupskaya for her two scanty lines. We know from them that Vladimir had tried to participate in the business plans of his mother, and even that he had become convinced through firsthand experience that "his relations with the peasants were becoming unnatural." This incident is more important than the ornate prose and verse about little Volodya and the peasants' children watching horses graze at night, and about the high-school boy's encounters with the peasants during his walks at Kokushkino.[7] The agricultural experiment occupied, it appears, only the first summer, because in the spring of 1890 Vladimir was permitted to take the examinations, and the agricultural plans, naturally, were laid aside. But they did leave an imprint on Vladimir's personality. During that short time he not only observed the peasants but also came into business contact with them. These two things are by no means the same!

The farm had no implements or hired hands. It could be cultivated only by contracts with peasants from neighboring Alakayevka, a poor and wretched little village. Out of thirty-four householders, nine had neither horses nor cows, four did not even have huts of their own; their plots of land were pitifully small; there were no schools, but there was a saloon. Out of a population of two hundred, only four boys learned something somewhere; the rest of the population could neither read nor write. Only a few prosperous *kulak* households rose above this poverty. They, too, were wretched enough, but they held the village in a tight grip. Profitable farming was possible only by working hand in glove with the *kulaks* and by ruthless exploitation of the poor. If in the future Lenin was to reveal an unusually penetrating ability to discern all forms of enslavement in agrarian relations, no small role in this was played by his own firsthand experiences with the peasants of Alakayevka.

It was necessary to give up the attempt at managing one's own farmstead and to rent the land, but the estate served the family as a haven for the four or five summer months. The expanse of the steppes and their silence, the old garden run to weeds, the precipice going down to the brook, the pond for swimming, the forest not far off where one could gather raspberries, all made for a splendid summer home. In the garden each one had his chosen corner for reading and work. The family was less isolated than in Kokushkino; the fear of contact with the Ulyanovs had lost its original acuteness. Still, at first, visitors were none too frequent. Maria remembers the shyness of her brothers and sisters, among them Vladimir, who, during visits by relative strangers, would hide in the garden, after going through the window. A distaste for strangers, and an inclination to enter and exit through windows, are characteristic of the young, and especially so in the country, where strangers are rare and windows are close to the ground. It is possible that the cover of shyness had not yet been shed by this self-confident youth. But in any case a desire not to waste himself on people who were not worth it was an increasingly prevalent element in this shyness.

In the district of Alakayevka the Populists had tried at the end of the 1870s to carry on propaganda, and in the 1880s they had established an agricultural commune on land acquired from that same Sibiryakov. From their anxiety to save the peasants through revolution, they had gone on to saving themselves through peasant work. The government viewed these schemes very suspiciously; but these communes and co-operatives of the intelligentsia springing up in various parts of the country led such a peaceful and sleepy life that for the most part they gave no reason for police action. A few of the more successful ones converted themselves in the course of events into capitalist enterprises, but the majority fell apart in short order. Such was the commune in the neighborhood of Alakayevka. Its members soon scattered in various directions, except for the stubborn organizer, Preobrazhensky. Vladimir became acquainted with him, and through him with certain other representatives of backwoods Populism. With Preobrazhensky he had long conversations, often lasting until the wee hours, walking back and forth on the road between the farm and the commune. Vladimir listened and observed. No, these subdued people who plowed the earth badly, partly for the sake of communism and partly for the salvation of their souls, could not win him over to their cause.

Alakayevka, it goes without saying, was not outside the field of vision of the police. The chief of the Samara gendarme administration reported to the department of police the arrival on the farm of the Ulyanov family, among them Anna, who was under official police surveillance, Vladimir, under unofficial surveillance, and Yelizarov, a former student "of doubtful political reliability." The Ministry of Public Education received, at regular intervals, detailed reports about the Ulyanov family from the head of the school district, Maslennikov. The high-school student Dimitri was also included in the round of observations, and the superintendent sent monthly reports about him as well. The matter was complicated by the fact that the Ulyanovs lived on one of the former farms of Sibiryakov, a friend of political exiles and patron of agricultural communes. "A series of coincidences have brought about a situation," reported Maslennikov to Petersburg, "in which the problem of the Samara farms and of the Ulyanov family have become closely intertwined." In short, there was no lack of observers and, in the language of the superintendent, the surveillance "was no secret to those under surveillance." The results, however, were modest. "Nothing suspicious," the Samara gendarme reported, "was observed." It was difficult to observe anything, for the suspicious processes were developing, for the time being, only in the most hidden convolutions of the brain. These were, however, dangerous processes.

Although it did not turn Vladimir into a gentleman farmer, the transfer to Alakayevka saved him from an untimely arrest along with his Kazan friends in July 1889, when not only the central circle of Fedoseyev was seized, but also the members of the auxiliary circle to which Vladimir belonged. He wrote many years later: "I think I might easily have been arrested as well, had I remained that summer in Kazan." In that particular respect his mother's calculations were justified, at least for the time being. The news of the arrests in Kazan made a deep impression on Vladimir. It must have strengthened him in the conviction that one must not fall into the hands of the enemy uselessly and on account of trifles; one must organize work properly so as to cause the enemy as much harm as possible. And that requires preparations.

In the garden, under the shade of the linden trees, Vladimir had his own permanent corner, with a table and a bench planted in the earth. Here he spent his working hours. "For five years, from 1889 to 1893," writes Dimitri Ulyanov, "that was a regular workroom" for Vladimir. Nearby, on two posts, was a horizontal bar for gymnastic exercises. The younger brother observed with astonishment what energy and passion Vladimir extended in order to lift himself to the bar, not facing it but with his back to it. It took him a long time to master this feat. Finally he summoned Mitya to witness his triumph: "I have balanced myself at last —look!" And, all in a glow, he was sitting on the bar. To overcome an obstacle, to discipline his own effort, to lift himself up and sit on that bar—"to balance himself"—there was nothing better than that! To show Mitya this new acrobatic feat was as necessary as to expound to Anna the mysteries of surplus value.

Vladimir swam much and skillfully in the Alakayevka pond, and went hunting in the neighboring forests for partridges, especially when this meant a good long walk. But he couldn't endure sitting still with a hooked line. At that time, sports were by no means fashionable among the democratic intelligentsia. But Vladimir had an untiring urge to keep his spiritual and physical powers in equilibrium. In exercises on the river, in swimming, in walking, in singing, he displayed an inexhaustible and at the same time disciplined enthusiasm. As in early childhood, life was, above all, motion. With this difference: now the motion of the mind was given priority.

Vladimir helped his younger sister Maria in her work, taught her to sew her notebook with white thread and not black, showed her how to draw parallels and meridians for a map. He revealed in these small tasks that conscientiousness which distinguished all of his work and which Maria remembered for the rest of her life. After dinner, in the same corner of the garden, Vladimir would read something light; sometimes it was fiction. He was often joined by Olga, who was preparing for the university in Petersburg, and they read together from Gleb Uspensky, the bard of Populism.

A roofed porch took the place of a terrace. Here they drank tea and read in the evening, in order not to attract mosquitoes into the house with the light. Here, too, they had supper in almost biblical simplicity. A big pitcher of milk was brought up from the cellar, and the children broke their whole-wheat bread into it. The evenings were often devoted to singing and music.

They sang in chorus, and Yelizarov, the husband of the elder sister, sang solos accompanied by Olga. Occasionally, Vladimir would be the soloist. A prominent place in his repertory was occupied by the romance "You Have Charming Little Eyes." And when he reached the grandiloquent stanza "I perish for the love of them," the singer's voice would invariably break on the high note. Vladimir would wave his hands in despair and shout out amid laughter: "Perished! Perished!"

We have noted that, immediately on his arrival in Alakayevka, Vladimir renewed his request for permission to go abroad, supposedly "for medical treatment" but in reality to enter one of the foreign universities. The department of police, however, preferred that the treatments take place in the Caucasus, and refused him a passport. The refusal was, of course, vexing, but still it was no great misfortune. Those two and a half years, which Fedoseyev spent in solitary confinement, Vladimir spent under his mother's wing in conditions favorable to his physical and intellectual health. Fate was obviously kind to this young man, as though he had been chosen in advance for some special purpose. But the young man knew how to make use of the indulgence of fate. They had concluded, it seemed, a secret treaty of mutual assistance.

11

UNDER THE COVER OF REACTION

THE regime of Alexander III was at its high point. The 1889
law on land captains had restored the administrative and judi-
cial powers of the local nobility over the peasants. Like landowners before the abolition of serfdom, the new land captains were
given the right not only to arrest peasants at will, but to flog them
as well. The *zemstvo* counterreform of 1890 transferred local
self-government, once and for all, into the hands of the nobility.
Of course the *zemstvo* decree of 1864, by means of a property
qualification specifying ownership of a minimum amount of
land, had sufficiently protected the dominance of the landowners over local administration. But since the land was slipping out
of the hands of the nobles, the property qualification had to be
reinforced with a qualification based on social class. The bureaucracy was acquiring a degree of power such as it had had only
in the days of Nicholas the Bludgeon.* Revolutionary propaganda, becoming more and more rare, was certainly punished
less severely now than under the "tsar/Liberator,"† usually with
a few years of prison or exile. Forced labor and hanging were
retained only for the terrorists. At the same time, as if to compensate for this, they began to select the most godforsaken places
for exile. Ferocious punishment of revolutionary prisoners for
any manifestations of protest received the personal endorsement
of the tsar. In March of 1889, thirty-five exiles who had locked
themselves up in one of the houses in Yakutsk were showered
with a hail of bullets.[1] Six were killed, nine wounded, three were
executed, the rest sent to forced labor. In November of the same
year a woman named Sigida, condemned to forced labor, was

* Refers to Nicholas I, who reigned from 1825 to 1855. (Ed.)
† Refers to Alexander II, who succeeded Nicholas I and reigned until his
assassination in 1881. (Ed.)

given one hundred lashes for insulting the prison superintendent, and died the next day. Thirty convicts retaliated by taking poison; of these, five died at once. But the revolutionary circles had become so scattered, drowning in an ocean of indifference, that these bloody punitive actions not only failed to arouse active protest, but even remained unknown for a long time. It is doubtful, for example, whether the news of the tragedies in Yakutsk and on the Kara[2] reached Vladimir Ulyanov in Samara until a year later.

After the assault on the universities, the morale of the students reached its lowest ebb. There was not a single attempt to answer the government's violence with terror. The affair of March 1, 1887, was the last convulsion of the period of People's Will. "The courage of people such as Ulyanov and his comrades," wrote the émigré Plekhanov, "reminds me of the courage of the ancient Stoics. . . . Their untimely death served only to emphasize the impotence and senility of the society around them. . . . Their courage is the courage of despair."

Eighteen eighty-eight was the blackest year of that gloomy period. "The attempt of 1887," writes the Petersburg student Brusnev, "extinguished the last glimmer of free thought among the students. . . . They all feared each other, and each one feared everybody in general." "Social reaction had reached its extreme limit," recalls the Moscow student Mitskevich. "Neither before nor after was there another year as dead. . . . In Moscow I did not see a single illegal publication." Informing, treachery, renunciations followed each other in vile succession. Lev Tikhomirov, the leader and theoretician of People's Will, who five years earlier had advocated the seizure of power for an immediate socialist revolution, proclaimed himself, early in 1888, a proponent of tsarist autocracy and published a pamphlet abroad entitled *Why I Have Ceased to Be a Revolutionary.* The mood of hopelessness impelled hundreds and thousands of turncoats to unite, no longer with the people, but with the propertied classes and the bureaucracy. The line written by the poet Nadson just before his death "No, I no longer believe in your ideals" sounded like the confession of an entire generation. Those less pliable shot or hanged themselves. Chekhov wrote to the author Grigorovich on the subject of suicide among young people: "On the one hand . . . a passionate thirst for life and truth, a dream of activity, broad as the steppes . . . ; on the other hand, an endless plain, a harsh climate, a gray austere people with its heavy chilling history, savagery, bureaucracy, poverty, and ignorance. . . . Russian life weighs upon a Russian like a thousand-ton stone."

At the very beginning of this mist-shrouded decade of reaction, however, a momentous political event took place: Russian Social Democracy was born. True, for the first years it vegetated almost exclusively in Geneva and Zurich and appeared to be a rootless émigré sect whose members could be counted on one's fingers. An acquaintance with its genealogy, however, demonstrates that Social Democracy was a natural outgrowth of Russia's evolution and that it was no accident that at the beginning of the 1890s Vladimir Ulyanov merged his own life with that of this party.

From Ippolit Myshkin, the chief defendant at the trial of the 193, we learn that the revolutionary activities of the intelligentsia were an expression—an oblique reflection would be a more accurate term—of peasant unrest. Indeed, were it not for old Russia's revolutionary peasant question, resulting in periodic famines, epidemics, and spontaneous revolts, there would never have arisen a revolutionary intelligentsia with its heroism and utopian programs. The land of the tsars was pregnant with a revolution whose social basis was the contradiction between the survivals of feudalism and the requirements of capitalist development. The conspiracies and terrorist attempts of the intelligentsia were merely the first labor pains of bourgeois revolution. But while the immediate task of this revolution was the liberation of the peasantry, the proletariat was to become its decisive motive force. In the revolutionary activities of the intelligentsia, a direct and evident dependence on the unrest among the industrial workers may be discerned even in the opening pages of Russia's revolutionary history.

The general turmoil in the country caused by the peasant reform of 1861 found expression in the cities in industrial strikes which confirmed the discontent of "the people" and encouraged the first revolutionary circles. The year of Lenin's birth was marked by the first large-scale strikes in Petersburg. We shall not seek any mystic significance in this coincidence. But what a unique coloration this imparts to the words of Marx in his address to members of the Russian section of the First International in that same year, 1870: "Your country is also beginning to participate in the general movement of our age!" By the second half of the 1870s, hundreds of workers had already been drawn into the revolutionary movement. It is true that, in accordance with prevailing views, they tried to see themselves as men temporarily separated from the communal plow. But in their energetic response to the peasant-loving gospel, to which the peasants themselves remained deaf, the advanced workers interpreted it in a way appropriate to their own social position, which often frightened their guardians among the intelligentsia. The prodigal sons of Populism established in the cities—both North and South—the first proletarian organizations; they raised demands for the right to strike and to unionize and called for freedom of assembly and the convocation of a representative assembly of the people. And their influence could be detected in the stormy disturbances among the industrial workers.

The Petersburg strikes of 1878 and 1879, which according to the testimony of an eyewitness and participant, Plekhanov, "came to be regarded as the foremost event of the period, capturing the attention of nearly all of the intelligentsia and thoughtful people of Petersburg generally," greatly increased the feverish mood among the revolutionary circles and indirectly heralded the move of the Populists to positions of terrorist struggle. Members of People's Will, in their turn, seeking combat reserves, occupied themselves, among other things, with propaganda among the workers. The revolutionary movements of the two social layers, the intelligentsia and the proletariat, although developing in close connection, each revealed a logic of its own. Even after People's Will had itself been completely shattered, workers' circles created by its members continued to exist, particularly in the provinces. But the ideas of Populism, although refracted by the workers in their own way, continued for a long time to hinder their search for the right path.

The Marxist struggle with exceptionalist views was made more difficult by the fact that the Populists themselves were by no means hostile to Marx. By virtue of a great theoretical misunderstanding, which had historic roots of its own, they sincerely counted him among their teachers. The Russian translation of *Das Kapital*, begun by Bakunin and continued by the Populist Danielson, was warmly received in radical circles when it appeared in 1872, and had an immediate circulation of three thousand copies.[3] The second edition was stopped by the censor. There was irony in the fact that the seeming success of the book was explained by an actual failure to grasp the doctrine. Its scientific analysis of the capitalist system was understood by the intelligentsia—the followers of Bakunin and Lavrov alike—as an exposé of the sins of Western Europe and as a warning against embarking on a false road.[4] The Executive Committee of People's Will wrote to Marx in 1880: "Citizen! The intellectual and progressive class in Russia . . . has reacted with enthusiasm to the publication of your scholarly works. They scientifically recognize the best principles of Russian life." Marx had no difficulty in guessing at the *quid pro quo:* the Russian revolutionaries had found in *Das Kapital* not what was there, i.e., a scientific analysis of the capitalist system, but a moral condemnation of exploitation, and hence scientific blessings bestowed on "the best principles of Russian life," that is, the communes and the cooperatives. Marx himself saw in the village communes not a socialist "principle," but a historic system of peasant enslavement and the economic foundation of tsarism. He did not spare his sarcasm at the expense of Herzen, whose eyes, like those of many others, had been opened to "Russian communism" by a Prussian traveler, a conservative baron by the name of Haxthausen. The baron's book appeared in Russian two years before *Das Kapital*, and the "intellectual and progressive class in Russia" stubbornly insisted on reconciling Marx with Haxthausen.[5] This is not surprising, for a combination of socialist aims with an idealization of the foundations of serfdom had indeed constituted the theoretical framework of Populism.

In 1879 the Land and Freedom group, as we remember, split into two organizations: the People's Will, which represented a democratic political tendency and comprised in its ranks the more militant elements of the former movement, and the Black Redistribution (*Chorny Peredel*), which tried to preserve the pure Populist principles of a peasant socialist upheaval. Opposing the political struggle that was indicated by the whole course of the movement, the Black Redistribution lost all power of attraction. "The organization had no luck from the first days of its creation," complains Deutsch, one of its founders, in his memoirs.[6] The best of the workers, such as Khalturin, went over to People's Will. The student youth also went that way. It was still worse among the peasants: "There we had absolutely nothing." The Black Redistribution played no revolutionary role whatsoever, but it was destined to become a bridge between Populism and Social Democracy.

The leaders of the organization—Plekhanov, Zasulich, Deutsch, Akselrod—were compelled during the years 1880 and 1881 to emigrate from Russia, one after another.[7] It was precisely these most stubborn Populists, who did not wish to lose themselves in the process of struggle for a liberal constitution, who sought with particular zeal for that part of the people to whom one might anchor. Their own experience, regardless of their intentions, had revealed with absolute certainty that only the industrial workers were receptive to socialist propaganda. At the same time, the Populist writings themselves, both literary and scholarly, in spite of their own bias had succeeded rather well in undermining a priori assumptions as to the harmoniousness of [cooperative] "manufacturing by the people," which upon scrutiny proved to be a barbaric stage of capitalism. It remained "only" to draw the necessary conclusions, but this amounted to an ideological revolution. The honor of re-examining the traditional notions and plotting out the new paths belongs unquestionably to the leader of the Black Redistribution, Georgi Valentinovich Plekhanov. We shall meet him again more than once—first as teacher, then as elder colleague, and finally as implacable opponent, of Lenin.

Russia was already on the road to capitalist development, and no intelligentsia was able to swerve her from that road. Bourgeois conditions would clash in ever more acute contradiction with autocracy, and at the same time create new forces for the struggle against it. Securing political freedom is a necessary precondition for the proletariat's further struggle for socialism. Russian workers would have to support liberal society and the intelligentsia in their demands for a constitution, and the peasantry in its revolt against the survivals of serfdom. In its turn, if it wanted to gain a mighty ally, the revolutionary intelligentsia would have to adopt Marxist theoretical positions and devote its efforts to propaganda among the workers.

Such were the main outlines of the new revolutionary conception. While it seems now a mere string of commonplaces, in 1883 it sounded like a bold challenge to the most sacred of prejudices. The situation of the innovators was complicated in the extreme by the fact that while appearing in the role of theoretical heralds of the proletariat, they were at first forced to appeal directly to the social stratum to which they themselves belonged. Between the pioneers of Marxism and the awakening workers stood the traditional barrier of the intelligentsia. The old views were still so firm in their minds that Plekhanov and his friends had even decided to avoid the very name of Social Democracy, styling themselves the Group for the Emancipation of Labor.

Thus, in little Switzerland arose the nucleus of the future great party, the Russian Social Democracy, which then begat Bolshevism, the creator of the Soviet Republic. The world is constructed so improvidently that the birth of great historic events is not heralded by the blowing of trumpets, and celestial bodies do not exude omens. For the first eight or ten years, the birth of Russian Marxism seemed hardly a noteworthy event.

Afraid of scaring off the not overly numerous left-wing intelligentsia, the Emancipation of Labor Group avoided dealing with the dogma of terror for several years. They saw as the sole mistake of the People's Will its failure to supplement terrorist activity with the "creation of the preconditions for a future workers' socialist party in Russia." Plekhanov tried, with good reason, to counterpose the terrorists as politicians with classical Populism, which rejected the notion of political struggle. "The People's Will," he wrote in 1883, "cannot find its justification, and ought not to seek it, outside of contemporary scientific socialism." But concessions to terrorism had no effect, and theoretical exhortations evoked no response.

The decline of the revolutionary movement in the second half of the 1880s affected all tendencies and created an intellectual stagnation that prevented any broad dissemination of Marxist ideas. The more the intelligentsia as a whole deserted the battlefield, the more stubbornly did individuals who remained loyal to the revolution stand by the traditions made holy by the heroic past. The adoption of Marxist ideas might have been facilitated by the example of revolutionary struggles on the part of the European proletariat. But in the West, too, the 1880s were years of reaction. In France the wounds of the Commune were not yet healed. Bismarck had driven the German workers underground. British trade unionism was saturated with conservative complacency. For reasons that were temporary in nature—they will be discussed later—the strike movement in Russia itself had also subsided. Little wonder that Plekhanov's group found itself compeletely isolated. He was accused of artificially fanning class antagonisms instead of effecting a necessary union of "all creative forces" against absolutism.

The program of the Terrorist Faction, drawn up in haste by Alexander Ulyanov between the preparation of nitric acid and the stuffing of bullets with strychnine, announced, to be sure, some "very marginal" differences with the Social Democrats. This said, it went on to express its hope for an "immediate transition of the national economy to a higher stage," by skipping the capitalist stage of development and recognizing "the great independent significance of the intelligentsia" and its ability "to wage immediate political struggle with the government." In practice, Alexander Ulyanov's group stood farther from the workers than had the terrorists of the preceding generation.

Communications between the émigré Emancipation of Labor Group and Russia were haphazard and unreliable. "We heard only confused rumors," Mitskevich recalls, "of the founding in 1883 of Plekhanov's Emancipation of Labor Group." In hostile émigré circles, stories were told with some glee about a group of radicals in Odessa who had solemnly burned Plekhanov's *Our Disagreements,* and these rumors were believed because they corresponded to the mood, if not to actual facts. The few adherents of the group among the Russian émigré youth were far inferior to the revolutionaries of the preceding decade both in their breadth of vision and in their personal courage. Some called themselves Marxists in the hope that this would free them from revolutionary obligations. Plekhanov, whose sharp tongue spared nobody, dubbed these questionable adherents "wounded veterans who have never seen action." By the beginning of the 1890s the leaders of the group were completely discouraged about any hope of winning over the intelligentsia. Akselrod explained its lack of receptivity to Marxist ideology by its bourgeois degeneration. Although correct on a broad historical scale and confirmed by the future course of events, this explanation was premature. The Russian intelligentsia was yet to pass through a phase of nearly universal enthusiasm for Marxism, and this phase was rapidly approaching.

In the meantime, without waiting for theoretical recognition, capitalism was carrying out, under the cover of reaction, its revolutionizing work. Government measures backing both serfdom and capitalism had consequences that refused to merge into a single harmonious pattern. Notwithstanding the generous financial aid of the government, the landed nobility went swiftly to ruin. During the three decades after the reform, the ruling social class let slip from its hands over 35 per cent of its land; thus, the reign of Alexander III, that period of aristocratic restoration, was pre-eminently the epoch of the nobility's ruin. It was chiefly, of course, the lower and middle levels of the gentry who lost their land. As for industry, whose profits, protected by high tariffs, went as high as 60 per cent, it was continually on the rise, especially toward the end of the decade. Thus, in spite of aristocratic counterreforms the capitalist transformation of the national economy was being accomplished. While pulling the knots of medievalism tighter and tighter, especially in the countryside, the government's policy promoted the growth of urban forces that were destined to cut these knots. The reactionary reign of Alexander III became the hotbed of the Russian revolution.

One must now introduce an important correction to the general picture of the 1880s given earlier. Political prostration characterized various strata of educated society—liberal *zemstvo* members, the radical intelligentsia, the revolutionary circles—but at the same time, under the cover of reaction, the awakening of the industrial workers was taking place in the depths of the nation: there were stormy strikes, sometimes the destruction of factories and shops, clashes with the police, as yet without clear revolutionary goals, but already producing revolutionary martyrs. Together with the rising level of workers' demands, came growing solidarity; personality ceased to slumber within the mass; here and there local leaders came to the fore. In the history of the Russian proletariat, the 1880s are recorded as the beginning of the upward turn.

The strike wave that had begun in the last years of the reign of Alexander II but reached its height between 1884 and 1886, compelled the press of all shades of opinion to recognize with alarm the birth in Russia of a special "labor problem." The tsarist administration, to do it justice, understood the revolutionary significance of the proletariat considerably earlier than did the left-wing intelligentsia. As early as the beginning of the 1870s, secret official documents began to single out the industrial workers as a very unreliable class—this at a time when Populist writers continued to regard the proletariat as part of the peasantry.

In addition to cruel repression against strikers, after 1882 new labor legislation was rapidly promulgated. There was prohibition of child labor, institution of factory inspection, some protective restrictions covering labor by women and adolescents. The law of June 3, 1886, immediately after a series of major strikes in the textile industry, made it mandatory for the bosses to pay wages at definite intervals and in general made the first breach in the wall of patriarchal arbitrariness. Thus, while complacently registering the surrender of all oppositional groupings among the educated classes, the tsarist government found itself compelled to surrender for the first time to the awakening working class. Without a correct appraisal of this fact, one cannot understand the subsequent history of Russia, up to and including the October Revolution.

Notwithstanding the continuation and even heightening of the agrarian crisis, the industrial depression, Populist theories to the contrary notwithstanding, was followed in the late 1880s by a boom. The number of workers grew rapidly. New factory laws and particularly the lower prices of consumer goods improved the condition of the workers, accustomed as they were to rural poverty. For the time being, the strikes subsided. During this interval the revolutionary movement declined to its lowest ebb in thirty years. Thus, a concrete study of the political zigzags of the Russian intelligentsia offers an extremely instructive chapter in sociology. Free "critical thought" proves to be dependent at every step upon economic causes unknown to it. If a thistledown, whisked this way or that by each passing breeze, were endowed with consciousness, it would consider itself the freest thing in the world!

In the strike movement of the early 1880s the guiding role was played by workers nurtured in the revolutionary movement of the preceding decade. The strikes, in their turn, stimulated the more responsive workers of the new generation. To be sure, the mystic searches of the time were noticeable also among the workers. But whereas for the intelligentsia Tolstoyanism meant a renunciation of active struggle, for the workers it was often a first, still confused protest against social injustice. Thus the same ideas frequently fulfill opposite functions in different strata of society. Among the advanced workers, echoes of Bakuninism, traditions of the People's Will, and the first Marxist slogans combined with their own strike experience and inevitably took on the coloration of class struggle. It was in 1887 that Leo Tolstoy gave himself up to grievous reflections on the results of revolutionary struggle over the course of the two preceding decades. "How much genuine goodwill and readiness for sacrifice has been expended by our young intelligentsia in order to arrive at the truth. . . . And what has been accomplished? Nothing. Worse than nothing." This time, too, the great artist was wrong about politics. The wasted spiritual energies of the intelligentsia sank deeper in the soil in order soon to grow up again as the first shoots of a mass consciousness.

Abandoned by their former leaders, the workers' circles continued to seek their roads independently. They read much and searched out in old and new magazines articles about the life of West European workers, trying to see whether these were applicable to themselves. One of the first Marxist workers, Shelgunov, recalls that in 1887–88, that is, the most terrible times, "workers' circles were growing more and more. . . . Progressive workers . . . were looking for books and buying them from secondhand dealers." These books had, undoubtedly, come into the hands of secondhand dealers from disenchanted members of the intelligentsia. Rare-book dealers charged forty to fifty rubles for a volume of *Das Kapital*. Still, Petersburg workers managed to get hold of that precious book. "I myself," writes Shelgunov, "had to tear up *Das Kapital* into parts, into chapters, so that it could be read simultaneously in three or four circles." Another worker, Moiseyenko, organizer of the biggest textile strike, studied with fellow exiles both *Das Kapital* and the works of Lassalle.[8] The seed did not fall on rocky ground.

In a salutation addressed to the old journalist Shelgunov (not to be confused with the above-mentioned worker of the same name) shortly prior to his death in 1891, a group of Petersburg workers thanked him especially for having shown the right path to Russian workers with his articles about the struggles of the proletariat of France and England.[9] Shelgunov's articles had been written for the intelligentsia. In workers' circles they served as a premise for conclusions going beyond the intentions of their author. Shaken by the visit of the workers' delegation, the old man carried with him to his grave a vision of newly awakening forces.

G. I. Uspensky, the most admirable of the Populist writers before the onset of mental illness, was able to learn that progressive workers valued and loved him, and he publicly congratulated Russian writers on the "new reader of the future." Worker orators at a secret Petersburg May Day celebration in 1891 remembered with gratitude the preceding struggle of the intelligentsia, and at the same time expressed unequivocally their intention to take its place. "The youth of today," said one of them, "does not think about the people. This youth is nothing but a parasitic element of society." The people will better understand propagandists who are workers, "because we stand closer to them than the intelligentsia."

On the dividing line between the two decades, however, new trends began to arise among the intelligentsia, although, to be sure, very slowly. Students came into contact with workers and were infected with their energy. Social Democrats began to appear most often among the very young, whose voices were just breaking—as was their respect for the old authorities. Grigoryev, then a young man in Kazan, recalls, "In 1888 an interest in Marx began to appear more and more insistently among the youth of Kazan." The young revolutionary Fedoseyev begins to stand out

in the center of the first Kazan Marxist circles. Beginning with
the winter of 1888–89 in Petersburg, according to Brusnev, "there
was a noticeable rise in interest in books on social and political
problems. There arose a demand for illegal publications." Newspapers began to be read differently. *Russkie vedomosti,* the
organ of *zemstvo* liberalism, in those days published lengthy dispatches from Berlin with generous excerpts from the speeches of
Bebel and other Social Democratic leaders.[10] In this manner
the liberal paper meant to tell the tsar and his advisers that freedom is not dangerous: the German emperor continued to sit
firmly on his throne, and property and order were firmly protected. But revolutionary students read something else in those
speeches. The propagandists dreamed of educating Russian
Bebels from among the workers. New ideas were brought in by
Polish students, the workers' movement having developed earlier in Poland than in Russia. According to Brusnev, who in the
coming months would assume a central position in the Social
Democrat groupings of St. Petersburg, a Marxist tendency prevailed among engineering students as early as 1889. Future engineers, trained for service to capitalism, found it particularly
difficult to keep up any faith in a special destiny for Russia. Engineering students conducted reasonably active propaganda
work in workers' circles. At the same time, there was renewed
lively activity in old and inactive groups. Members of People's
Will returning from exile attempted (for the time being, unsuccessfully) to resurrect the terrorist party.

Leonid Krasin with his brother German, who arrived in Petersburg from far-off Siberia, described their Marxist debuts somewhat jocularly: "Our lack of erudition was made up for by
youthful fervor and healthy voices. . . . By the end of 1889 the
combat qualities of our circle were considered firmly established."
Leonid was at that time nineteen years old. Mitskevich also observed a change of mood among Moscow students: gone was the
feeling of hopelessness; more circles for self-education sprang
up; an interest in the study of Marx had arisen. After a lull of
three years, large-scale student demonstrations erupted, in the
spring of 1890. As a result, the Krasin brothers, both of them engineering students, were exiled from Petersburg to Nizhni Novgorod. It was from their lips that Mitskevich, finding himself in

Nizhni, too, first heard the living gospel of Marxism, and threw himself upon Plekhanov's *Our Disagreements.* "A new world opened up before me; the key had been found to an understanding of surrounding reality." The *Communist Manifesto,* which he read soon thereafter, made an immense impression on Mitskevich: "I understood the bases of the great historical-philosophical theory of Marx. I became a Marxist—for life." During this time Leonid Krasin received permission to return to the capital and there began to propagandize among the weavers. Nevzorova, a university student in the early 1890s, tells what a revelation the first publications of the Emancipation of Labor Group were for the students: "I still remember the overwhelming impression made by the *Communist Manifesto* of Marx and Engels." Krasin, Mitskevich, Nevzorova, and their friends—these were the growing ranks of future Bolshevism.

The new moods among the Russian intelligentsia were also nourished by events in the West, where the workers' movement was emerging from a period of decline. The famous strike of English dockers under the leadership of the future renegade John Burns, led the way to a new militant unionism.[11] In France the workers were recovering from the catastrophe, and the Marxist teachings of Guesde[12] and Lafargue[13] were making themselves heard. In the autumn of 1889 the first congress of the new International was held in Paris. At the congress, Plekhanov made his prophetic announcement: "The Russian revolution will conquer only as a workers' revolution—there can be no other outcome." These words, passing in the hall of the congress almost unnoticed, reverberated in Russia in the hearts of several revolutionary generations. Finally, in the German elections of 1890 the illegal Social Democrats received almost one and a half million votes. Emergency laws directed against the Socialists that had remained in force for twelve years died an ignominious death.

How naïve is the faith in the spontaneous generation of ideas! A whole series of objective material conditions, linked together moreover in a definite sequence in a particular combination, were necessary in order for Marxism to gain access to the brains of Russian revolutionaries. Capitalism had to achieve significant successes; the intelligentsia had to exhaust completely all other alternatives—Bakuninism, Lavrovism, propaganda among the peasants, colonizing in the villages, terror, peaceful educational activities, and Tolstoyanism. The workers had to launch their waves of strikes. The Social Democratic movement in the West had to assume a more active character. Finally, the catastrophic famine of 1891 had to lay bare all the sores of Russia's national economy. Then, and only then, did the ideas of Marxism, which had received theoretical formulation almost half a century before and been disseminated in Russia by Plekhanov since 1883, begin finally to take root on Russian soil. Yet even that is not the entire story. The ideas, having gained wide currency among the intelligentsia, were immediately distorted to suit the character of this social stratum. Only with the appearance of a conscious proletarian vanguard did Russian Marxism finally stand firmly on its feet. Does this mean that ideas are unessential or impotent? No, this means only that ideas are socially conditioned; before becoming a cause of facts and events, an idea must first have been the result of them. Or, to put it more precisely: an idea does not tower above a fact like a court of higher appeal. The idea itself is a fact which can enter as a necessary link in a chain of other facts.

The personal evolution of Vladimir Ulyanov was closely linked with the evolution of the Russian intelligentsia and the formation of a thin layer of progressive workers. Here biography merges with history. The subjective sequence of his spiritual formation coincides with the objective sequence of the growth of a revolutionary crisis in Russia. Simultaneously with the appearance of the first Marxist cadres and the first Social Democratic circles, under the cover of reaction, the future leader of a revolutionary people was preparing himself and maturing.

12

IN SAMARA

In the autumn [of 1889] the family moved to Samara, where, together with the Yelizarovs, they occupied the upper half of a two-story wooden house with six or seven rooms. The city became the principal residence of the Ulyanovs for nearly four and a half years. In the life of Lenin these years form a special, Samara period. Later, in the middle of the 1890s, Samara became, not without Lenin's influence, the unofficial Marxist capital of the Volga region. We must, therefore, take a look, if only a brief one, at the profile of this city.

The administrative history of Samara differs little from the history of Simbirsk; the same struggle with the nomads, the same period of founding the "city"—or rather the building of wooden fortifications—the same struggle with Razin and Pugachev. But the social profile of Samara was nevertheless quite different. Simbirsk came into being as a secure nest for the gentlefolk. Samara, situated deeper on the steppes, became a center of the grain trade only after the abolition of serfdom. Although the main street of the city did bear the name Dvoryanskaya,* this was only a gesture designed to imitate other cities. In reality, serfdom barely touched the Samara steppes. The town had neither ancestry nor tradition. Unlike Kazan, it had no university and, consequently, it had neither academics nor students. Life in Samara was shaped by powerful cattlemen, wheat farmers, grain merchants, millers—sturdy pioneers of agrarian capitalism. Indifferent not only to aesthetics but also to personal comfort, they laid out no aristocratic gardens with mock-classic architecture, parks, and statues of nymphs. What they needed were docks, warehouses, mills, grain barns, bolted gates, and heavy locks. They did not keep hunting dogs, but watchdogs. Only

* "Of the Nobility." (Trans.)

upon amassing great wealth did they build themselves big stone houses.

Around the grain bourgeoisie of the Volga, with their docks and warehouses, there lurked a nomad and seminomad folk. At one time, the original free peasants of Samara had tried, following the example of the German Mennonites in Sarepta, to plant the lucrative crop of mustard. But the Russians lacked both know-how and perseverance. From the unsuccessful mustard plantations the Samara townsmen retained only the bitterness of disappointment and the ironical nickname "mustard-plasterers." When angry or, particularly, when drunk, the inhabitants of Samara villages, together with the barge haulers, caused the police much trouble. But their revolts were hopeless, as was all of their unhappy life.

In 1887 Shelgunov, the same old man to whom the Petersburg workers subsequently addressed a salutation, gave an interesting description of Samara, the city of frontiersmen: "Alongside palatial residences there are empty lots and fences or chimneys of houses that had burned down fifteen years earlier and would never be rebuilt, just as the reckless and ruined frontiersman would never stand on his feet again. Farther on, beyond the fences and the vacant lots and the smaller and smaller houses of the suburbs, stretch out the little villages of freemen where huts with two or three windows are crowded together. Here the village has abandoned the steppes and settled in the city in order to work for the frontiersmen. . . ."

Almost no industry, and therefore virtually no industrial workers, existed in Samara. And since the city was also free of the infection of a university, it appeared on the list of harmless cities in which the authorities permitted revolutionaries who had served their term of Siberian exile to settle for a time. It was also a city to which, from time to time, suspect individuals from the capital and from university towns were restricted, under police surveillance. This transient community, which up to the early 1890s was almost entirely Populist, served as a rallying center for the local leftist-oriented young people. Not only *zemstvo* members and merchants, but at times even government functionaries, permitted themselves to play the liberal with impunity in this province where there was neither aristocratic domination nor student or worker unrest. The obscure revolts of waterfront folk were never considered political. Among those under surveillance, one could always find sensible and honest *zemstvo* officials, administrators, secretaries, and tutors, although by law many of these professions required official clearance. According to the Samara police records for 1889, Vladimir Ulyanov, too, gave private lessons. The Samara administration closed its eyes to these petty transgressions by the unreliable elements.

The former exiles and persons under surveillance, acting as a center of gravity for circles of high-school students, seminarians, or teachers from the *zemstvo* nursing schools, with the addition of the students who came for the summer—all these constituted the vanguard, so to speak, of the *gubernia*. From this little world, threads led away to the liberals among *zemstvo* people, lawyers, merchants, and government functionaries. Both groups lived by the liberal Populist paper *Russkie vedomosti*. The more substantial of these citizens were chiefly interested in the moderate and ingratiating editorials and in the *zemstvo* news; the radical youth avidly read the foreign dispatches. Of the monthlies, the left wing avidly devoured each new volume of *Russkoye bogatstvo*, especially the articles of the talented Populist columnist Mikhailovsky, a tireless preacher of "subjective sociology."[1] More-solid citizens preferred *Vestnik Yevropy* and *Russkaya mysl*, mouthpieces of veiled constitutionalism. Propaganda in Samara did not reach beyond the bounds of the intelligentsia. The educational level of the few workers was extremely low. Individual railroad workers, to be sure, would join a Populist circle, not with the idea of propagandizing fellow workers, but rather to raise their own educational level.

Those under surveillance openly visited the Ulyanov family; the Ulyanov family, in turn, had lost any reason to avoid contact with those considered enemies of the tsar and the country. The widow of the state counselor came in contact with a world to which she had hardly given a thought during her husband's lifetime. Her circle of acquaintances no longer consisted of provincial functionaries and their wives, but of old Russian radicals, outcasts who had spent many years in prison and exile and reminisced about their friends who had died while engaging in terrorist activities or armed resistance, or at hard labor in prisons—in short, people of that world which Sasha had entered, never to return. They held unusual views about many things, their manners were not always the most impeccable, and some of them were distinguished by eccentricities acquired during long years of enforced solitude. Still, they were not bad people. On the contrary, Maria Alexandrovna must have become convinced that they were good people, selfless, faithful in friendship, and brave. It was impossible not to be friendly to them, and at the same time it was impossible not to fear them. Could they not draw another son off onto the fatal road?

Among the revolutionaries who lived in Samara under police surveillance, Dolgov stood out as a participant in the famous Nechayev affair. Then there was the Livanov couple. The husband had been involved in the case of the 193, while the wife had been a participant in the Odessa affair of Kovalsky, who had attempted armed resistance when arrested. Conversations with these people, especially the Livanovs, whom Anna Yelizarova describes as "typical members of People's Will, people of integrity and devotion to their cause," became for Vladimir a true practical academy of revolution. He eagerly listened to their tales and asked question after question, going into every last detail in order to reconstruct in his imagination the course of the past struggles. The great revolutionary epoch, which was still unstudied and almost unrecorded, and from which the new generation had, moreover, been separated by a stage of reaction, now arose before Vladimir in living human images. This young man possessed the rarest of gifts: he knew how to listen. Everything that touched upon the revolutionary struggle interested him: ideas, people, conspiratorial methods, underground techniques, forged passports, prison regulations, court trials, conditions of exile, and escape.

One of the centers for the radical *zemstvo* intelligentsia in Samara was the house of the magistrate Samoilov. Yelizarov often visited there, and he once had the good idea of bringing along his brother-in-law. Many years later, this visit enabled Samoilov's son to recontruct the image of young Ulyanov in a few very vivid strokes: "When I went out to shake hands with the guests, my attention was instantly caught by a newcomer. At the table, in a relaxed manner, sat a very slender young man. He had ruddy cheeks and a somewhat Kalmyk face, a sparse slightly reddish mustache and beard, evidently never touched by scissors, and a mocking expression in his lively dark eyes. He spoke little, but this was evidently not at all because he felt ill at ease in unfamiliar surroundings. It was perfectly clear that this circumstance did not bother him in the least. Quite the contrary, I definitely re-member noting that M. T. Yelizarov, usually quite at home among us, on this occasion seemed, if not exactly embarrassed by the new guest, then perhaps somewhat intimidated by him. The con-versation dealt with unimportant matters and touched, as I re-member, upon the student movement in Kazan as a result of which Vladimir Ilyich (for it was he) had been compelled to leave Kazan University. . . . He evidently was not inclined to regard his fate tragically. . . . In the middle of the conversation, while summing up some conclusion that evidently seemed to him particularly apt, he suddenly burst out laughing, with a gusty, short, distinctly Russian laugh. It was clear that some keen in-cisive idea that he had been groping for before had come to mind. That laugh, healthy but not without cunning, accentuated by crafty wrinkles in the corners of his eyes, remains in my memory. Everybody laughed, but he was already sitting quietly, again listening to the general conversation and fixing upon those present an attentive and slightly ironic look." When the guests left the house, the host, expansive by nature, summed up the impression with the excited words, "What a brain!" This exclama-tion of his father merged forever in the son's memory with the image of young Lenin—the ironic twinkle of his eyes and his short "Russian" laugh. "What a brain!" This portrait, caught by a keen memory, rewards us for laboring through the thousands of pages of pathetic impotence in which the majority of memoirs are drowned.

We are surprised only at the words "a very slender young man." Semyonov, another citizen of Samara, called Vladimir "skinny." In his childhood Volodya was called "little block." In his high-school pictures he looks stocky. Another Samara citizen, Klements, writes of him, "This was a young man of short stature but sturdy build with a fresh ruddy face." He is similarly described three years later by Lalayants, an intimate of his, as being "of short stature but very strong and sturdily built." This description cor-

responds more closely to what we know of Vladimir in those
years: that he was a great walker, a hunter, a fine swimmer and
skater, a gymnast, and, above all, a man who loved to make his
voice break on the high notes. Still it is possible that he arrived
in Samara a thin youth and filled out afterward in the fresh air of
the steppes.

It is absolutely certain that it was precisely during the Samara
period that Vladimir Ulyanov became a Marxist and Social Demo-
crat, but the Samara period lasted almost four and a half years.
How does the evolution of a youth fit into this spacious frame?
His official biographers have been spared any difficulties on this
point once and for all, thanks to the very convenient theory that
Lenin became a revolutionary through heredity and was a
Marxist at birth. But this is not quite true. We do not have, to be
sure, documentary proof that during the first years in Samara,
Vladimir adhered to the ideology of People's Will, but the data
of later years hardly leaves room for doubt. Later on, we shall
hear unimpeachable testimony from Lalayants, Krzhizhanovsky,
and others, to the effect that from 1893 to 1895, when Vladimir
was a confirmed Marxist on the question of terror, he professed
views unusual among Social Democrats, views that were regarded
by all as a survival from the preceding period of his evolution.
But even if this clear retroactive confirmation were lacking, we
should still be compelled to ask: How could there not be such
a period?

The political shadow of Alexander followed unrelentingly at
Vladimir's heels for a number of years. "Isn't this the brother of
that Ulyanov?" wrote a high-ranking bureaucrat on the margins
of an official document. Everybody saw him in this light. "Brother
of the Ulyanov who was hanged," the young radicals would
whisper with reverence. *Le mort saisit le vif!* Vladimir himself
never mentioned his brother unless forced by a direct question,
and never once named him in print, although there were many
opportunities to do so. This very restraint is the surest testimony
to the deep scar the death of Alexander left on his consciousness. In order to break with the People's Will traditions, then,
Vladimir needed motivation incomparably more convincing and
forceful than he would have for anything else.

The stubborn persistence of his terrorist sympathies, shedding a retrospective light upon that period in his evolution when he was under the influence of People's Will, had other than personal roots. Vladimir evolved with a whole generation, a whole epoch. Even the first works of the Emancipation of Labor Group (assuming that Vladimir had already become acquainted with them) did not confront him sharply with the question of a break with the traditions of his elder brother. In his discussion of the perspectives for capitalist development in Russia, Plekhanov had not yet contrasted the future Social Democrats to People's Will, but merely demanded that People's Will adopt Marxism. Shortly before, the Emancipation of Labor Group had made an attempt to unite with émigré representatives of People's Will. If such was the situation—though only at the beginning of the decade—among the émigrés, where militant theoreticians of both persuasions were at work, then in Russia itself the distinction between People's Will and the Social Democrats, even at the end of the 1880s, was still very blurred and uncertain. Akselrod, quite rightly, notes in his memoirs: "The watershed separating People's Will from the Social Democrats at the end of the 1880s did not follow the line of distinction between Marxism and Populism, but rather the line between direct political struggle, a phrase then synonymous with terror, and propaganda." In cases where Marxists approved of terror, the line of distinction disappeared completely. Thus, Alexander, who had read *Our Disagreements,* considered that in practice there were no differences between People's Will and the Social Democrats and that Plekhanov should not have adopted a polemical tone in his dispute with Tikhomirov. In the conspiracy of March 1, 1887, the representatives of both schools of thought acted in accordance with the principles of People's Will.

The rapprochement between the two ideologies, destined later to break into two irreconcilable camps, had in fact an illusory character that may be explained by their weakness and the general political fogginess of the period. But it was in the midst of this very fog that Vladimir embarked on a theoretical study of Marxism. At the same time, he became acquainted through the stories of the "old-timers" with the practical aspects of the recent struggle, of which Alexander's case had become the final constituent part. In Samara the workers' movement did not yet exist even in embryonic form; among the intelligentsia there were only some circles that arose belatedly and developed slowly. There were as yet no Social Democrats at all. Under these circumstances, Vladimir could make great progress in his study of Marxist classics without being forced to make a final choice between Social Democrats and People's Will. His striving for clarity and conclusiveness undoubtedly constituted a most important motivation for his will and his intellect. No less important was his feeling of responsibility. The fate of Alexander had immediately transferred his thoughts about the "struggle for freedom" from the realm of rosy, youthful dreams to that of stern reality. To make a choice under those circumstances meant to study, to understand, to verify, to become convinced. This required time.

Among Vladimir's first friends in Samara we find Sklyarenko, a young man of his own age. Expelled from high school while in the sixth grade, and arrested in 1887, he had spent a year in Petersburg's Kresty Prison. After his return to Samara he had resumed his propagandizing efforts among the youth. Primarily as a result of his efforts, a partly legal, partly clandestine little library for self-education was created. According to the instructions of a special guide for propagandists, the more-instructive articles were torn out of old monthly magazines, with the first and last pages often having to be copied by hand. Collections of such articles were bound; together with a hundred or so selected and, for the most part, banned books, they constituted The Library of Samara High-School Students, which Vladimir often used during his years in Samara. In collaboration with his friend Semyonov, Sklyarenko published mimeographed materials written in the spirit of People's Will, the point of view that generally prevailed then among their friends and acquaintances. Had Ulyanov considered himself a Social Democrat during the first two years of his stay in Samara, he would have had bitter debates with Sklyarenko, Semyonov, and their friends, which, if the opponents proved stubborn, would inevitably and very quickly have resulted in a break with them. But nothing of the kind happened, and personal ties were unaffected. On the other hand, his friendship with young members of People's Will did not result in Vladimir's participation in their clandestine activities. After what happened to Alexander, he could no longer be impressed by revolutionary schemes of inexperienced young men. He wanted first of all to study, and he soon won Sklyarenko and Semyonov over to the same course.

Vladimir was to spend four winters in Samara. He grew and changed during those years, gradually shifting to Social Democratic positions. Those who observed him and felt his influence changed, too. The boundaries between different stages have been erased in memory. The results of that evolution, which defined themselves by 1892, are now commonly credited to the entire Samara period. This is especially evident in the recollections of his elder sister. According to her, Vladimir debated "more and more bitterly" with the veterans of People's Will concerning their fundamental principles. This was undoubtedly true. But at what juncture did the disputes begin? And when did they take on a "bitter" character? It was just at the time of her move to Samara that Anna, who then had no particularly clear grasp of theoretical problems, married Yelizarov. Although the two families lived in the same house, the young couple naturally drifted apart from the rest. Vladimir's first two years in Samara have almost completely slipped from his elder sister's memory.

We can easily believe that the archaic views of Samara's "veterans" could not satisfy this young and deeply probing mind. Vladimir may, indeed must, have debated with the veterans even in the first years, not because he had found the truth but because he was looking for it. Only later, toward the end of the Samara period, did these disputes turn into a conflict between the two groups. It is remarkable that Anna Yelizarova, herself searching for a living illustration of these Samara disputes, names as an opponent Vodovozov, a man under police surveillance. The disputes with this hopeless eclectic who did not consider himself either a Populist or a Marxist, occurred in the winter of 1891–92, i.e., the end of Vladimir's third year of residence in Samara.

One of the Samarans, it is true, states that during a boating trip organized by a group of leftist youth (evidently in the summer or autumn of 1890) Ulyanov made mincemeat out of the idealistic theory of morality expounded by a certain Buchholtz, and advanced in its stead a class concept. This incident presents the pace of Vladimir's evolution as somewhat more rapid than other data would suggest. It is worth noting that Buchholtz, a German Social Democrat born in Russia, himself refutes the above story in the very respect that we find of interest: "At those meetings which we attended together," he writes, "V. I. Ulyanov, so far as I can remember, did not show any unusual activity and, in any case, did not expound Marxist views." The value of this testimony cannot be disputed. Can one suppose that Lenin would have hidden his light under a bushel if the light was already burning? If he did not expound Marxist views, it was because he had not yet arrived at them.

In October 1889, after his arrival in Samara, Vladimir sent to "his excellency, the honorable minister of public education," a new petition which was extremely impressive in tone. During the two years since his graduation from high school, he, Vladimir Ulyanov, had had "ample opportunity to convince himself of the immense difficulty, if not impossibility, of finding employment for a person without special education." Moreover the undersigned was in dire need of employment which would enable him "to support with his labor a family consisting of an aged mother, and of a brother and sister, both minors." This time it was not admission to the university he requested, but the right to take a final examination without attendance. Delyanov wrote in pencil on the request: "Ask the superintendent and the department of police about him. He's a rotten man." It is obvious that the department of police could not have had a more favorable opinion of the petitioner than the Minister of Education. Thus the "rotten man" received from the "kindly, charming man" yet another refusal.

The doors of formal learning, it seemed, were shut to Vladimir forever. In the long run it probably would not have altered his destiny very much, but in those days the question of a university diploma seemed very important both to Vladimir and, more especially, to his mother. Maria Alexandrovna traveled to Petersburg in May of 1890 to try to do something for Volodya's future, just as three years before she had done all she could to save the life of Sasha. "It is a grievous pain," she wrote, "to look at my son and see his best years being wasted away. . . ." In order to arouse the sympathy of the minister, the mother tried to alarm him with the idea that the aimless existence of her son "would almost inevitably drive him to the thought of suicide." In all conscience it must be said that Vladimir hardly resembled a candidate for suicide. But in war—and the mother was waging war for her son

—you cannot get along without military deceptions. Delyanov
was not, it seems, without sensitivity, for although he did not allow the "rotten man" to return to the university, he did this time
permit him to take final examinations in subjects taught by law
schools at one of the imperial universities. The Samara police administration officially informed Maria Ulyanova, widow of the
state counselor, of this gracious favor. A positive answer was also
received to Vladimir's request to take the examinations in Petersburg. The mother's efforts were undoubtedly assisted by the fact
that, for the two and a half years since his expulsion, Vladimir
had no record of any suspicious activity. Gradually, it seemed,
the family was emerging from official disfavor.

In a series of reports from the end of August, police clerks of
Samara and Kazan record a journey by Vladimir Ulyanov through
Kazan to Petersburg for the purpose of obtaining information re-
garding the taking of examinations. Vladimir spent six days in
Kazan. Which of his former friends did he seek out there? The
report of the Kazan police chief gives no information on this
point. Vladimir spent nearly two months in Petersburg. The
dates are established by the reports of the Samara precinct captain. But we know almost nothing else. It is certain, however, that
Vladimir did not waste his time. His chief concern was to make
sure he was thoroughly prepared for the examinations. He did
not intend to leave the test to chance, to flunk, or to withdraw.
He had to have all the elements of the problem before him clari-
fied fully beforehand: the scope of each subject, the textbooks,
the requirements of the professors. A considerable part of the
time in Petersburg was undoubtedly consumed by work at the
public library. In order to avoid buying expensive books it was
necessary to take notes and to draw outlines. Through his sister
Olga, who was studying in Petersburg, Vladimir got acquainted
with his future antagonist, Vodovozov, a classmate of Alexander's
at the university who had arrived from exile in order to take the
state examination. With his help, Vladimir succeeded in entering
the building where about four hundred students were taking
tests. He mingled with the crowd, and according to Vodovozov,
"sat there for several hours listening and observing." That preliminary reconnoitering of the arena and the conditions of the
coming examination was highly characteristic of young Lenin.

He never left to the caprice of chance anything that he might even to the slightest degree anticipate and prepare for in advance.

But Vladimir had one other important item of business in Petersburg. It was during this journey that, through his contacts, he finally obtained from Yavein, a teacher at the Technological Institute, the book by Engels *Herr Eugen Duehring's Revolution in Science*. If the fortunate owner, as we might assume, did not want to let the forbidden book travel to a far-off province, then Vladimir was forced to study this admirable scientific-philosophical tract with great concentration during his short stay in Petersburg. It is possible, however, that after a conversation with the insistent youth the young professor gave in and the *Anti-Duehring* made the journey from the Neva to the Volga. At any rate, Vladimir first had access to this book no earlier than the autumn of 1890. Radek, relating this incident, cited Lenin himself as the source, and added: "It would be a long time before he succeeded in getting at the works of Plekhanov published abroad." If the word "long" here means even a few months, then it seems that Vladimir got acquainted with the works of the Emancipation of Labor Group no earlier than the beginning of 1891. Let us keep these dates in mind. Although as a rule Radek's testimony is not overly accurate, in this case it is outwardly convincing, and it finds support in the general pattern of Vladimir's evolution.

At the beginning of November the Samara police precinct captain reported to his chief the return of Vladimir Ulyanov. This time, too, it appears, the precinct captain observed "nothing suspicious." However, this candidate in the field of transgressions returning from Petersburg did bring with him, if not in his skull, then in his suitcase, the explosive charge of materialist dialectics. But there was no reason to expect any explosions in the immediate future. For the time being, it was neither Marxism nor revolution that stood in the foreground. It was necessary to wrest a diploma from the hands of the Imperial University. A long period of "cramming" was at hand.

Ilya Nikolayevich's fears that his son Vladimir might fail to develop a capacity for work truly proved to be unfounded. One of the people under surveillance, the "Jacobin" Yasneva, who ar-

rived in Samara in the spring of 1891, remembers: "Such persistence, such stubborn self-discipline as Vladimir Ilyich revealed at
that time, I had never seen in anybody else." Vladimir came out
of his room only for tea and supper and spoke very little. Rarely
did any of the family enter his room. In his mode of living he now
must have reminded them of Alexander. His work area in the
country remained in the garden, in the depths of the linden avenue. Every morning at the same hour he would go out there with
his pile of law textbooks and would not return home until three
o'clock. "You would go out to call him for dinner," says a former
servant, "and there he would be with a book." That he did not
waste time is attested to by the level path he wore down alongside his bench while saying over what he had read or learned. By
way of rest after dinner he would read in German from Engels'
Condition of the Working Class in England or some other Marxist work. He studied German only incidentally, not for the sake of
the language but for the sake of Marxism, and for that reason the
more rapidly. A walk, a swim, and evening tea would precede
the latter part of the day's work, which was carried out on the
veranda by lamplight. Vladimir worked too intensely for any one
of the older or younger children even to think of disturbing him
during his working hours. Besides, there can be little doubt that,
as in his high-school days, he would have had no qualms about
telling anyone, "Delight us with your absence." To compensate
for this, during his hours of rest, at the dinner table or while
swimming, he was noisy, talkative, jocular, infectiously gay.
Every fiber of his brain and body strove to make up for the long
hours of Roman and canon law. This young man rested as intensely and passionately as he worked.

How much time did he spend in preparation? A year and a half,
says Anna Yelizarova. From her, too, we know that Vladimir
"set himself to cramming" only after permission was granted to
take the examinations. It would be difficult indeed to imagine that
he would have begun to study police law, canon law, or even
Roman law, either for his own pleasure or on a gamble that he
might receive permission. In that case, then, the preparation did
not take up a year and a half; from the ministerial amnesty to
the beginning of the examinations was less than eleven months,
to the end of the examinations, a year and a half. In another arti-

cle, Anna Yelizarova speaks of one year. Regular university students spent four years doing the same work!

The examinations had to be taken in two installments: in the spring, April and May; and in the autumn, September and November. Vladimir arrived in Petersburg in March, a week before the examinations, armed with a research paper on criminal law. It is very likely that the extra week was designed for getting acquainted with students' lecture notes available in printed form. In planning his own work, Ulyanov was a Taylorist before the Taylor system.[2] The examining commission was chaired by Sergeyevich, the then-popular professor of the history of Russian law, and it comprised the very best professors of the Law School. The examiners questioned the stranger whom they were seeing for the first time with distrust, but this distrust rapidly gave way to respect. The at-large student Ulyanov turned out to be excellently prepared.

The list of examination subjects reads like an ironical introduction to the subsequent activity of this defense counsel for the oppressed, of this prosecutor of the oppressors. In the history of Russian law Vladimir Ulyanov got a question about "the unfree," all the different categories of serfs; in public law, one about the institutions of social classes, which entailed specific data on the history of legislation affecting the gentry and the organization of peasant self-government. In giving the applicant the highest marks in these subjects, the Imperial University bore witness to the fact that before setting out to liquidate "unfree" conditions, serfdom, and the barbarism of social class, Vladimir Ulyanov had conscientiously prepared himself for his future profession.

In political economy, also in the spring, he had to answer questions on wages and their forms; in general jurisprudence and the history of the philosophy of law, he had one question on Plato's views on law. Unfortunately we do not know whether Ulyanov expounded to his examiners the labor theory of value and the materialist concept of law as constrasted with all forms of Platonic exploitation. In any case, if he did chide official learning, he did so very cautiously. The commission noted "very satisfactory," which meant the highest grade. The greater part of the examinations, however, was to be taken in the fall.

On the first Sunday of May a small band of Petersburg workers, about seventy in all, celebrated the proletarian holiday for the first time with a secret meeting outside the city; the speeches were soon mimeographed and later published abroad. A central role in Social Democratic propaganda work, which had already achieved significant results, was played by Brusnev, a young engineering student. Although in Petersburg at the time of the May Day celebration, Vladimir evidently knew nothing of this significant event. He had no revolutionary connections, and it is unlikely that he sought them. During the next two years he would still have time to catch up with the Petersburg Marxists, and would move quickly ahead of them thereafter.

At the height of the spring examinations a new blow fell upon the family. The victim was Olga, the sister who had grown up with Vladimir and accompanied him on the piano when he sang. Since the autumn of the previous year, Olga had been studying with great success at the Women's University in Petersburg. In memoirs this young girl is endowed with most-attractive features. Having graduated from high school at fifteen and a half, with a gold medal like those of her brothers, she read much and studied music, English, and Swedish. Z. Nevzorova, a friend of Olga's at the university and subsequently the wife of the engineer Krzhizhanovsky, the man responsible for the electrification of the USSR, writes in her memoirs: "Olga Ulyanov was not at all the usual type of woman university student of those times. At first glance she was no more impressive than a little black beetle, modest and very ordinary, but in fact she was intelligent and gifted, and worked with a kind of quiet concentration of will power and determination in achieving her aims. She was serious and penetrating in spite of her nineteen years, and was a marvelous companion." Anna Yelizarova writes, "In her, as in Sasha, the dominant trait was a sense of duty." Olga loved Sasha more than she loved the other brothers and sisters. With Vladimir, in spite of their closeness in age and conditions of their development, she did not feel any spiritual intimacy; but she did listen attentively to what he said and valued his opinion highly.

During Vladimir's stay in Petersburg that spring, Olga fell ill with typhoid fever. Between two examinations, Vladimir had to take his sister to the hospital—a very poor one, as it turned out. Summoned by a cable from her son, Maria Alexandrovna came immediately to Petersburg, but only to lose a second child there. Olga died on the eighth of May, the very same day on which four years earlier Alexander had been hanged. Just as in Simbirsk when Vladimir had been compelled to take his high-school final examinations immediately after the execution of his elder brother, so now he had to take university examinations during the fatal illness of his younger sister. Immediately after her funeral, Vladimir visited a university friend of Alexander's, Sergei Olden-burg, the future orientalist of the Academy of Sciences. In con-trast to all other memoirists, Oldenburg remembers his visitor as gloomy and silent, without a single smile. The first and most dif-ficult days, Vladimir remained with his mother in Petersburg; afterward they made the grief-stricken journey back to Samara together. Once again, all were astounded at the courage of the mother—her self-control and her selfless concern for the remaining children.

For three months and more, through the summer, Vladimir trod his path in the depths of the linden avenue. In September he arrived at the capital prepared for the battle. In criminal law he did very well on the questions about defense in criminal trials and about theft of documents. In Roman law he was questioned about impermissible activities and the influence of the statute of limitations on the creation and annulment of laws, two subjects of some interest to a man who was to engage in impermissible activities on rather a grand scale and to annul some rather im-portant laws. Vladimir did very well in "police science," which serves "to guarantee the people's condition of moral and mate-rial well-being." The candidate revealed a no less admirable familiarity with the subject of the organization of the Orthodox Church and the history of its laws. In international law he was questioned about neutrality and blockade. We must leave open the question whether this knowledge was useful to him twenty-eight years later, when Clemenceau and Lloyd George replied with a blockade to the attempts of the Soviets to withdraw from the war. For a diploma first class, one had to have top marks ("very satisfactory") in more than half the subjects; Vladimir received the highest mark in each of the thirteen. He could se-cretly congratulate himself and laugh his short "Russian" laugh.

Vladimir's third request for a passport to go abroad was denied in October 1891, a month before he finished the examinations. What may have been the aim of this journey? Vladimir had sought out and studied all the fundamental works of Marxism. Much was undoubtedly unavailable to him, especially the materials in the socialist periodicals. The idea of working freely in the libraries of Berlin after passing his examinations must have been particularly alluring to him. From Berlin it would not be difficult to take a trip to Zurich and Geneva, where he could get acquainted with the Emancipation of Labor Group, study all their publications, and clarify points of disagreement. These motives were reason enough, by far, but the police department thought otherwise. Having expressed some strong opinions about the higher authorities, Vladimir did not wait in the capital for the decision of the examinations commission; there was no reason to doubt the result. Indeed, on the fifteenth of November, the very day when the Samara precinct captain secretly reported to his chief the return to Samara of Vladimir Ulyanov, a man under unofficial surveillance, the examinations commission of the Law School at St. Petersburg's Imperial University awarded this same person a diploma first class. In a year and a half, in the Samara back country, without any help from professors or older comrades, Vladimir not only accomplished the tasks to which others had to devote four years of their lives, but accomplished them better than others: he stood first in a class of one hundred thirty-four students and at-large candidates. His sister notes that "many were amazed" at this result. And no wonder! In this admirable deed one is attracted, among other things, by an element of intellectual athleticism. He had "balanced" himself well, as well as could be!

13

A YEAR OF FAMINE. LAW PRACTICE

THE summer of 1891 was hot and dry; the sun burned out the harvest and the grass in twenty *gubernias,* together having a population of thirty million. When Vladimir came home after his fall examinations, Samara *gubernia,* which had suffered more than others, was writhing in the pangs of famine. True, the entire history of peasant Russia is one of periodic poor harvests and mass epidemics, but the famine of 1891–92 stands out not only because of its dimensions, but also because of its influence on the political evolution of society. Later, looking back, the reactionaries would recall nostalgically how stable the order had been under Alexander III, who could break a horseshoe with his bare hands, and they would blame on the weak Nicholas II the cataclysms that came later. In actual fact, the last three years of the reign of the "unforgettable progenitor" already heralded the beginning of a new era, a direct preparation for the revolution of 1905.

The danger crept up from where the source of power really resided: the villages. During the thirty years that had elapsed since the abolition of serfdom, the condition of the mass of peasants had greatly deteriorated. In land-rich Samara *gubernia,* more than 40 per cent of the peasants held only starvation allotments of land. Their parcels, depleted and poorly cultivated, were continually exposed to the adversities of nature. A feverish industrialization accompanied by the reintroduction of semi-serfdom in the villages, along with the rapid growth of the *kulak* class, resulted in a frightening impoverishment of the peasant masses. Outwardly, the might of the state appeared unshakable: factories and railroads were built, the budget was balanced, and gold reserves piled up in the cellars of the state bank. And suddenly, against the background of these successes, the peasant fell

to the ground and let out the agonized howl of one who is
starving.

The government, taken by surprise, at first tried to deny that
there was a famine, calling it merely a poor harvest, but then it
lost its head and, for the first time since 1881, slightly loosened its
hold on the reins. The dark aura of unshakable power that had
surrounded Alexander III's regime began to evaporate. The
calamity stirred public opinion, so long inert. A fresh wind
swept through the country. A part of the wealthy classes and
broad sectors of the intelligentsia were caught up in a sudden
desire to help the peasants: to give bread to the hungry and
medicine to those sick with typhoid. The *zemstvos* and the liberal
press sounded the alarm. Donations were collected on all sides.
Leo Tolstoy began to open up canteens for famine relief. Once
more, hundreds of intellectuals went to the people, this time with
more-modest objectives than in the 1870s. The authorities believed, with some justification, that the philanthropic movement
concealed subversive tendencies: this peaceful form of aid was
the line of least resistance for those forces of opposition which
had been forming during the years of the new reign.

The revolutionaries could not take that road. For them, the
problem was not merely to mitigate the consequences of a social calamity, but to remove its causes. Ten or fifteen years
earlier, the Populist intelligentsia, in contrast to the liberals and
the philanthropists, viewed things in exactly this way. But the
revolutionary spirit had deserted the Populists; now, coming out
of their long hibernation, they were glad to merge with the liberals in a common "service to the people." But a sharp struggle
had already erupted among the intelligentsia on the question of
the prospects of the country's further development, even prior
to the catastrophe. The Marxists, who were few in number, had
found themselves opposed to the broad circles of educated "society" on the burning question, What is to be done right now?
Some thirty years later, Vodovozov, to whom we have already
referred, wrote in the émigré press: ". . . the greatest and most
profound conflict of views I had with Vladimir Ulyanov was over
the question of attitude toward the famine of 1891–92." At a time
when Samara society as a whole responded to the appeal for aid,
"only Vladimir Ulyanov with his family and the small circle of

people who echoed his views took a different position." Ulyanov, it seems, welcomed the famine as a progressive factor: "In destroying peasant economy . . . the famine creates a proletariat and promotes the industrialization of the region." Vodovozov's reminiscences on the subject represent not so much Ulyanov's views as their distorted reflection in the minds of liberals and Populists. The idea that the ruination and decimation of the peasants could promote the industrialization of the country is too absurd in itself. The ruined peasants became paupers, not proletarians; the famine fed the parasitic, not the progressive, trends of the economy. The very tendentiousness of Vodovozov's story, however, gives a fair idea of the heated atmosphere of those old controversies.

The accusation commonly leveled in those days against Marxists, to the effect that they viewed the national calamity through the spectacles of their doctrine, was indicative only of the low theoretical level of the debates. In point of fact, all forces and groupings took political positions: the government, which in the interest of its prestige, denied or underestimated the famine; the liberals, who while disclosing the existence of the famine, were at the same time eager to prove by their "positive work" that they would be the best of the collaborators for the tsar if he would only give them a crumb of power; the Populists, who by rushing to the canteens and typhoid wards, hoped to find a peaceful and legal way of enlisting the sympathies of the people. The Marxists, of course, opposed not aid to the starving, but the illusion that a sea of need could be emptied with the teaspoon of philanthropy. If, in a lawful committee or canteen, a revolutionary takes up a place that rightfully belongs to a *zemstvo* member or an official, then who will take the revolutionary's place in the movement? It is clear beyond dispute from ministry memoranda and directives made public later that the government was increasing allocations for the starving only because it feared revolutionary agitation, so that from the point of view of actual aid the revolutionary policy proved to be far more effective than neutral philanthropy.

The Marxist Akselrod, then an émigré, was not alone in championing the view that "for the socialist . . . a genuine struggle against hunger is possible only within the framework of the struggle against the autocracy." Even the old moralist of the rev-

olution, Lavrov, proclaimed in print: "Yes, the only 'good cause'
we can possibly embrace is not the philanthropic but the revolutionary cause."[1] However, in the center of a starving province,
in an atmosphere of general enthusiasm for canteens, it was far
harder to demonstrate revolutionary steadfastness than in the
emigration, which in those years was isolated from Russia.
Ulyanov was obliged for the first time, and quite independently
at that, to take a stand on a burning political question. He did not
join the local aid committee. More than that: "At the meetings
and gatherings . . . he conducted a systematic and outspoken
propaganda against the committee." It should be added: not
against the committee's practical activities, but against its illusions. He was opposed by Vodovozov. Ulyanov was backed by
"a very small minority, but this minority stuck to its positions."
Vodovozov did not win away a single one of them; on the other
hand, there were cases when Ulyanov was able to win over an
opponent: "They were few in number, but they existed."

It was precisely at that time that the skirmishes with the
Populists were to take on the character of a struggle between two
divergent tendencies. It is not by accident that the image of
Vodovozov floats up in Yelizarova's memory when, without giving dates, she speaks of the Samara disputes: they began,
precisely, late in 1891. Thus, the disastrous famine became an
important landmark in Vladimir's political evolution. By this time
he must certainly have familiarized himself with Plekhanov's
writings; toward the end of that year or the beginning of the next
he, as Vodovozov reports, spoke with great respect of Plekhanov's
Our Differences of Opinion. If he still had any lingering doubts
as to Russia's economic development and the revolutionary path,
they must have been entirely dissipated in the light of that
disaster. In other words, from a theoretical Marxist, Vladimir
Ulyanov definitely was on the way to becoming a revolutionary
Social Democrat.

According to Vodovozov, on the question of aid to the hungry
the entire family shared Vladimir's position. Yet we learn from
the younger sister that in 1892, when the famine had brought
cholera in its wake, Anna "expended considerable efforts in help-
ing the sick with medicine and advice." And surely Vladimir
would have been the last to oppose her. Yasneva's story, too, does

not entirely coincide with Vodovozov's. "Of all the Samara exiles," she writes, "only Vladimir Ilyich and I did not take part in the work of these canteens." It appears, then, that at this time Vladimir did not as yet have any circle of adherents who shared his views. This is not hard to believe. Social Democratic propaganda had not yet begun for him. The only way to undertake it was to break with those who represented the old faith and the stagnant elements. "Peaceful at first," says Vodovozov, "our disputes gradually became very acrimonious."

The political test of the divergent views was not long in coming. The liberals did not, in the end, succeed in worming their way into the government's confidence; on the contrary, quite soon, and with some reason, the government accused the Samara *zemstvo* of having purchased rotten grain for the starving. The Populists failed to bring about a rapprochement with the people. The peasants mistrusted city folk. They had never seen anything but evil come from the educated. If the hungry are being fed, that must be on the tsar's orders, and the gentry are surely lining their pockets. When a cholera epidemic came in the wake of the famine and patients died *en masse* in the barracks where they were devotedly cared for by doctors and university students, the peasants decided that the landlords were poisoning the people in order to clear as much land for themselves as they could. There ensued a wave of cholera riots, when doctors, university students, and nurses were murdered. The authorities then "came to the defense" of the intelligentsia by armed force. The year of famine thus showed up the net results of educational work in the villages. In Simbirsk *gubernia*, which Ilya Nikolayevich Ulyanov had tirelessly sought to educate for sixteen years, the cholera riots were particularly widespread; the consequence was that entire villages were flogged—every tenth man—and there were cases of death from flogging. It was only when their brother, the worker, who held an allotment of land in the village, would come to them from the city and begin to explain who was in the right, that the Russian peasants would begin to listen to the socialists with a little more trust. But before that could happen, the city worker himself had to be won over to socialism.

During that year of famine and cholera, one other conflict of principle contributed to the parting of political groupings.

Vodovozov proposed that an expression of sympathy be sent to the governor of one of the Volga *gubernias*, a certain Kosich, who had been dismissed because of "liberalism." Vladimir sharply opposed such philistine sentimentality, always ready to shed a tear at the least manifestation of "humaneness" on the part of a representative of the ruling classes. This episode, incidentally, shows once again how absurd it is to try to draw a line of direct succession between the director of public schools Ilya Nikolaye-vich Ulyanov, who unlike Kosich was never even dismissed for liberalism, and his all-out intransigent son, whose heart was not touched even by the most humane of governors. Vodovozov seems to have been defeated; his message was never sent.

As he himself reports, Vodovozov began to call his young antagonist Marat—behind his back, naturally.[2] The nickname shows a certain insight—unless it was really invented later. According to his older sister, present opponents, only recently his friends, considered Vladimir "a very gifted but excessively self-assured young man." The man who only the other day seemed to be merely "Alexander Ulyanov's brother" was now becoming a person in his own right and was showing his claws. Vladimir not only would not adjust his position to the political attitudes of his opponents, but on the contrary, made it as extreme, uncompromising, cutting, and thorny as possible. In so doing, he experienced a double joy, caused by his own inner self-assurance and also by the expression of indignation on his opponents' faces. According to Vodovozov's admission, "A profound faith in his being right could be discerned in all his speeches." This made him seem doubly intolerable. "All this more-respectable public," as Yeliza-rova says, were "quite shocked by the great arrogance of this young man during disputes, but often bowed to him." What was particularly held against him was the derogatory tone in which he now spoke of the greatest authorities of Populism. However, these were only the first blossoms; the fruit was yet to come.

"It is hard to say," Vodovozov says modestly in summing up his debates with Ulyanov, "which side carried off the victory." In reality, there was no need even to wait for the October Revolution to guess the answer to this. When famine recurred seven years later, there were immeasurably fewer political illusions, and the intelligentsia, having in the meantime found another course, did not go to the villages. *Russkaya mysl,* a very moderate liberal journal, wrote at that time that all those who returned from the famine-stricken areas were extremely dissatisfied with their own work, seeing it as a "pitiful palliative," whereas "general measures" were needed. After a little political experience, even the meek constitutionalists were forced to translate into liberal lingo, bits and pieces of those ideas which a few years earlier had sounded blasphemous.

But Vladimir had to think of his own lot, his own future. He had won his diploma. He had to make use of it. Vladimir joined the bar, with the intention of making the law his profession. "After all," as Yelizarova reminds us, "Vladimir Ilyich had no means except his mother's pension and the farm in Alakayevka, which was gradually being mortgaged." As his sponsor he chose the same lawyer with whom he had played chess by correspondence when he was still living in Kazan. Khardin was a prominent figure, not only as a lawyer and chess strategist of whom the then king of Russian chess players, Chigorin, spoke with respect, but also as a man active in provincial affairs. Having become, at the age of twenty-eight, chairman of the province *zemstvo* administration, he was shortly dismissed "by His Majesty's order" as politically untrustworthy, the order becoming effective within twenty-four hours. Not many were found worthy of such an honor! According to N. Samoilov, who has given so colorful a description of his first encounter with Vladimir, Khardin in his mature years still retained his sympathies with the radicals and managed to avoid taking a hostile stand toward Marxist ideology. According to Yelizarova, Vladimir respected Khardin as a very intelligent man. As a chess player, he had appreciated his "devilish" ability back in Kazan, and he became a regular participant in the weekly contests at his sponsor's home.

Admission to the bar, however, was not entirely smooth. The Samara District Court required a certificate of Ulyanov's political trustworthiness; St. Petersburg University, which had issued the diploma, was unable to provide the required certificate, since it had not known Ulyanov as a student. In the end, the court, at Vladimir's insistence, went straight to the Police Department, which generously replied that it had "no objections." After the matter had dragged on for five months, Vladimir at last, in July 1892, received a certificate entitling him to appear in court.

He appeared as counsel for the defense in a total of only ten criminal cases, by appointment in seven and by agreement in three. These were all petty cases involving petty people, hopeless cases, and he lost them all. He had to defend peasants, village workers, semi-paupers, mainly for minor thefts prompted by extreme poverty. Some of the defendants were: a few peasants who together had stolen three hundred rubles from a rich peasant of the same village; several hired hands who tried to steal grain from a barn but were caught red-handed; a peasant who had been reduced to utter misery and who had committed four petty thefts; another of the same type; and, again, a few village hired hands who, "after breaking and entering," stole effects valued at one hundred sixty rubles. All these crimes were so uncomplicated that in each case the hearing lasted from one and a half to two hours, and the secretary did not even bother to take minutes but merely made the perfunctory note: After the charge was made by the assistant prosecutor, counsel Ulyanov spoke for the defense. Only two thirteen-year-old boys, who had been accessories to thefts committed by their elders, were acquitted—on the ground of age and not through the defense counsel's arguments. All the other defendants were found guilty and sentenced. Ulyanov also took on the case of Gusev, a Samara townsman who had severely beaten his wife with a whip. After a short hearing in court in which the victim testified, defense counsel Ulyanov refused to appeal the sentence as overly severe. In this case, as in all such cases throughout his life, he was a merciless prosecutor.

In three cases, also run-of-the-mill, Ulyanov appeared as counsel for the defense at the request of the accused. A group of peasants and townspeople were tried for stealing rails and a cast-iron wheel from a Samara woman merchant. All were found guilty. A young peasant was accused of disobeying and insulting his father. The case, postponed on a plea from the defense, did not come to trial: the son gave his father a written promise to obey him unquestionably and the two sides settled on that. Lastly, Ulyanov appeared as defense counsel for a station master accused of negligence, as a result of which empty freight cars had collided. The defense counsel was of no help here either, and the accused was found guilty. These are the court cases of assistant attorney Ulyanov. They were gray and hopeless cases, just as the life of the classes from which the accused came was gray and hopeless. The young defense lawyer—can we possibly doubt this? —gave keen attention to each case and each accused. But they could not be helped singly. They could be helped only en masse. For this, however, another forum was needed, not the forum of the Samara District Court.

Ulyanov won only one court case; but here—as though by the hand of fate—he acted not as counsel for the defense, but as prosecutor. In the summer of 1892 Vladimir and Yelizarov were going from Syzran, on the left bank of the Volga, to the village of Bestuzhevka, where Yelizarov's brother had a farm. The merchant Arefyev, who ran a ferry on the Volga, regarded the river as his fief: every time a boatman took on passengers, he would be overtaken by Arefyev's little steamboat, which would take them all back by force. That happened in this case as well. Threats of court action for arbitrary behavior did not help. They had to bow to force. Vladimir wrote down the names of the participants and witnesses. The case was heard by the *zemstvo* chief near Syzran, some seventy miles from Samara. At Arefyev's request, the chief postponed the hearing. This was repeated once again. The merchant apparently decided to fight his accuser by attrition. The third date of the hearing came much later, in winter. Vladimir had to face a sleepless night on the train and tiring periods of waiting at railway stations and in the *zemstvo* chief's chambers. Maria Alexandrovna tried to persuade her son not to go. But Vladimir would not be moved: the case had been begun and must be finished. On this third occasion the *zemstvo* chief was unable to continue his evasive tactics: under the young lawyer's pressure he found himself obliged to sentence a well-known merchant to one month in prison. It can be imagined what music was in the victor's soul as he returned to Samara!

The experiment with law practice was unsuccessful, as earlier the experiment with agriculture had been. Certainly not because Vladimir did not have the necessary qualities for these professions. He had persistence, a practical eye, attention to detail, a capacity to evaluate people and put them in their right place, and finally a love of nature. He would have been a first-class farmer. His ability to analyze a complicated situation, to find its main threads, to appraise the strengths and weaknesses of the opponent, and to marshal the best arguments in defense of his thesis made itself apparent even in his youth. Khardin had no doubt that his assistant could become "an outstanding civil lawyer." But it was precisely in 1892, when Vladimir entered law practice, that his theoretical and revolutionary interests, heightened by the disastrous famine and political turmoil in the country, were becoming more intense and demanding from day to day.

It is true that, despite the young lawyer's conscientiousness, the preparation of petty court cases barely distracted him from his study of Marxism. But surely his law career could not continue to be limited in the future to cases concerning the theft of a cast-iron wheel by a criminal band of three townsmen and two peasants! It was written in the book of fate that Vladimir Ulyanov could not serve two gods. A choice had to be made. And he made his choice without difficulty. Having begun in March, his brief series of court appearances came to an end in December. True, he obtained a court certificate of his right to practice law for the year 1893, but by now he needed this document solely as legal cover for an activity directed against the fundamental laws of the Russian Empire.

14

LANDMARKS OF GROWTH

LET us set down here against the background of the country's political development young Lenin's most important biographical landmarks. The backward and remote shores of the Volga. The generation of yesterday's slaveowners and slaves is still alive. The People's Will's attack has been fought off. The political impasse of the 1880s. In a patriarchal and close-knit official's family, Vladimir grows, studies, and gains in intelligence without cares or upheavals. The critical faculty awakens in him only toward the end of his studies in high school, after his father's death, and is at first directed against the school administration and the church. His elder brother's unexpected death opens Vladimir's eyes to politics. Participation in a student demonstration as his first response to Alexander's execution. The temptation to avenge his brother by the brother's own methods must have been especially acute in those days. But the most hopeless times had come: the year 1888, when it was impossible even to think of terror. The reaction not only saved Vladimir physically, but it also prompted him to give deeper attention to theory.

Years of revolutionary apprenticeship. In Kazan Vladimir begins to read *Das Kapital*. Understanding of the theory of labor value does not mean to him that he must break with the Populist tradition: Sasha, too, was an adherent of Marx. At first in Kazan and later in Samara, Vladimir comes into contact with revolutionaries of the older generation, mainly members of People's Will; he is an attentive student, one inclined, certainly, to examine things critically, but not an opponent. The fact that, despite his revolutionary attitudes, amply manifested both in his choice of acquaintances and in the direction taken by his intellectual interests, he did not join any political group in those years shows unmistakably that he did not yet have a political credo, not even a youthful credo, but was still only searching for one. Nevertheless, the search began on the basis of the Populist tradition, a fact that left a marked imprint on the course of his future development. Even after he had become a militant Marxist, Vladimir continued for several years to sympathize with individual terrorism, an attitude that set him distinctly apart from other young Social Democrats and was unquestionably a vestigial remnant from the period when Marxist ideas were still intermingled in his mind with Populist sympathies.

From the spring of 1890 to the autumn of 1891 Vladimir was almost wholly absorbed in studying for his examinations. Intensive study of law seemed to be an external interruption to the gradual formation of his over-all view of life. There was, of course, no complete break. In his hours of leisure Vladimir read Marxist classics, met friends, exchanged views. Besides, he used legal scholasticism, by the inverse method, to check and strengthen his materialist views. But this critical work was done only on the side. Unresolved problems and doubts had to be put off until there was more free time. Vladimir was in no hurry to define his position. An indirect but interesting confirmation of this is furnished by the fact that early in 1891 two Samara "Jacobin" women had still not lost hope of enlisting Ulyanov in their ranks: obviously they did not regard him as a fixed quantity politically.

Late in 1891 Vladimir got his diploma and thus found himself at a crossroads. The courtroom arena could not but attract him. According to his sister, he was seriously considering the legal profession at that time, as one "that in the future could provide a means of livelihood." However, the political excitement in the country and the course of his own development placed him face to face with other problems, which demanded all of him. His hesitation did not last long. Law had to give way to politics and at the same time become a temporary cover for it.

The year and a half of legal fever relegated the first stage of his revolutionary apprenticeship to the background and made his thinking more independent of the recent past, which had been overshadowed by Sasha's influence: this created the conditions for a bold termination of the transitional period. The winter of the famine year must have been a time for drawing the final balance.

Gradual spiritual development does not exclude sudden jumps, provided they have been prepared for by an accumulation of ideas.

The shaping of Vladimir's revolutionary personality in part reflected, and in part anticipated, a shift in theoretical sympathies among the provincial leftist intelligentsia. Marxist doctrine began to arouse keen interest among Samara youth beginning with 1891, the year of the famine. A lot of people then became eager to master the first volume of *Das Kapital,* but the majority, to quote Semyonov, "broke their teeth" on the first chapter. There began discussions on the mysteries of dialectics. The Hegelian triad was hotly debated on a special "Marxist" bench in the city park on the bank of the Volga.

The older generation of the Samara intelligentsia became agitated. Both its groups, the moderate and the radical, which had been living peacefully together surrounded by familiar ideas, paid respectful lip service to Marx, of whose works, incidentally, they remained blissfully ignorant. They reacted to the first Russian Social Democrats as if there had been an unfortunate misunderstanding. Most sincerely indignant were the former exiles, who had brought with them to the Volga traditional views that had remained well preserved in the harsh Siberian climate.

A political crack may easily widen into an unbridgeable gap. Vladimir now spared no sarcasm in regard to the Populist complaints that the Marxists, allegedly, "do not love the peasant," "welcome the ruination of the village," etc. He soon learned to despise the substitution of moralizing and sentimental laments for realistic analysis. Literary tears, which were of no benefit to the peasants, blurred the intelligentsia's eyes and prevented it from seeing the road that was opening up. Increasingly embittered clashes with the Populists and the "educators" gradually split Samara's radical intelligentsia into two warring camps and greatly strained personal relations. Little wonder, then, that that last year and a half, when Vladimir emerged from the shadows into the light, has decisively colored the reminiscences of contemporaries about the Samara period as a whole. The young Lenin as he arrived in Alakayevka in May of 1889 a prospective farmer, and as he left Samara in the autumn of 1893, is portrayed identically as a revolutionary Marxist, thus excluding from his life that which has been its main element—motion and change.

P. Lepeshinsky, for once coming close to the truth, writes of Lenin's preparatory period in Samara: "There are reasons to think that even in 1891 he had already worked out his Marxist philosophy in general outline." This view is seconded by Vodovozov: "In questions of political economy and history, his knowledge was surprising in its scope and depth, especially for a man of his age. He read German, French, and English fluently, was already familiar with *Das Kapital* and a large amount of Marxist literature (German). . . . He declared that he was a confirmed Marxist. . . ." Such intellectual equipment might have sufficed for a dozen others; but this young man, so strict with himself, did not consider himself prepared for revolutionary work, and with good reason. In the chain that ties doctrine to action he still lacked a number of important links. Here, too, the facts speak for themselves: if Vladimir had thought himself fully armed in 1891, he could not have remained two more years in Samara.

True, his elder sister maintains that Vladimir stayed with the family out of concern for his mother, who, after Olga's death, had once again won her children's devotion by the combination of courage and tenderness she displayed. But this explanation is clearly inadequate. Olga died in May 1891, but it was not until August 1893, more than two years later, that Vladimir tore himself away from his family. Out of consideration for his mother, he might have postponed his revolutionary duties for some weeks or months, while the new wound was still too fresh, but not for years. In his attitude toward people, and his mother was no exception, there was no passive sentimentality. His living in Samara brought practically nothing to his family. If Vladimir had the self-control to remain so long away from the great battlefield, it was only because his years of training were not yet over.

From now on, side by side with the basic works of Marx and Engels and the German Social Democratic publications, more and more room would be taken up on his desk by Russian statistical compilations. He began his first independent monographs aimed at shedding some light on the contemporary Russian scene. Once the subject of study, historical materialism and the labor theory of value now became for Vladimir tools of political orientation. He studied Russia as a battlefield and noted the disposition on it of the main contending forces.

To help us determine a most important landmark in Vladimir Ulyanov's evolution, we have one absolutely invaluable piece of testimony which official biographers generally ignore because it contradicts the myth. In a 1921 Party questionnaire, Lenin himself indicated as the beginning of his revolutionary activity: "1892–93. Samara. Illegal groups of Social Democrats." This information, supplied by a witness whose accuracy cannot be questioned, leads to two conclusions: Vladimir did not take part in the political work of the People's Will, or he would have so indicated in the questionnaire. Vladimir did not definitely become a Social Democrat until 1892; otherwise he would have engaged in Social Democratic propaganda earlier. Disputes and doubts are thus resolved once and for all. In the interest of impartiality we should point out that a Soviet scholar who is, by virtue of his office, head of mausoleum historiography—we are referring to Adoratsky, the present director of the Marx-Engels-Lenin Institute—arrives at roughly the same conclusion on the question.[1] "During his last years in Samara, 1892–93," he writes with all due caution, "Lenin was already a Marxist, although he still retained traits associated with People's Will (e.g., a special attitude toward terror)." We can now bid farewell forever to the amusing legend according to which Vladimir, "after rubbing his forehead," condemned terrorism in May 1887, on the same day he received the news of Alexander's execution.

The stages of young Lenin's political formation as outlined above find a possibly somewhat unexpected but very lively confirmation in his history as a chess player. According to his younger brother, during the winter of 1889–90 Vladimir "became interested in chess more than ever." An expelled student who could not gain admission to any university, a potential revolutionary without program or guidance, he sought in chess a release for his inner turmoil. The one and a half years that followed were taken up with studying for examinations, and chess was temporarily relegated to the background. It came again to the fore when, after obtaining his diploma, Vladimir, hesitant about choosing a career, did not take on many court cases, but found his sponsor a first-class chess partner. Another year or year and a half of preparation, and the young Marxist began to feel that he was armed for the struggle. "From 1893 on, Vladimir Ilyich began to play chess less and less frequently." Dimitri's testimony on this matter can be accepted without question; himself a keen devotee of the game, he followed closely his elder brother's passion for chess.

While in Kazan, Vladimir, in search of an audience, tried to share the first ideas he had borrowed from Marx with his elder sister. He did not get very far, however, and Anna soon lost track of her brother's studies. We do not know when he mastered the first volume of *Das Kapital*. In any event, it was not during his short stay in Kazan. In later years, Lenin used to astound people with his ability to read quickly and grasp the essence of what he read at a glance. But he had developed this faculty by learning, when necessary, to read very slowly. Beginning in each new field by laying down a solid foundation, he worked like a conscientious mason. He retained to the end of his life the capacity to reread a necessary and important book or chapter several times. Indeed, he truly valued only those books which have to be reread.

No one, unfortunately, has told us how Lenin passed through the school of Marx. Only a few superficial impressions, and very sketchy ones at that, have been preserved. Yasneva writes: "He spent entire days poring over his Marx, making abstracts, copying excerpts, and jotting down notes. At times like that, it was difficult to get him away from his work." His abstracts of *Das Kapital* were not preserved. It is only on the basis of his notebooks of later years that one can partly reconstruct the young athlete's labors over Marx. Even back in high school, Vladimir always began his compositions with a complete outline, which he then gradually clothed with arguments and quotations. This creative method reflected that quality which Ferdinand Lassalle had aptly defined as the physical strength of the intellect. Study, when it is not mere rote memorizing, is also a creative act, but of a reverse variety. To summarize another person's book is to lay bare its logical skeleton by removing arguments, illustrations, and digressions. Vladimir took this difficult course as a fierce but joyful effort: he made a summary of each chapter and sometimes each page, analyzing and verifying the logical structure, dialectical transitions, and terminology. In mastering the result, he assimilated the method. He proceeded from one step to the next in the other person's system as if he were erecting it anew. Everything remained solidly lodged in that remarkably shaped head with the powerful dome of its skull. For the rest of his life Lenin never departed from the Russian political-economic terminology he had acquired or worked out during his Samara period. This was not merely from stubbornness—although intellectual stubbornness was a salient characteristic of his—but because even in those early years he made his selection after weighing and thinking through each term from every angle until it merged in his mind with an entire series of concepts. The first and second volumes of *Das Kapital* were Vladimir's main textbooks in Alakayevka and Samara; the third volume, at that time, had not yet been published: old Engels was still putting Marx's drafts in order. Vladimir studied *Das Kapital* so thoroughly that every time he looked at it again he was able to discover new ideas in it. Even during his Samara period he learned, as he himself said later, to "confer" with Marx.

Before the master's books, impertinence and mockery automatically left that questioning mind, which was in the highest degree capable of the emotion of gratitude. To follow the evolution of Marx's thought, to experience its irresistible force upon oneself, to discover under introductory sentences or notes lateral galleries of conclusions, to become convinced over and over of the aptness and depth of his sarcasm, and to bow in gratitude before a genius who has been merciless to himself became for Vladimir not only a necessity, but a delight. Marx has never had a better reader, one more penetrating or more grateful, nor a more attentive, congenial, or capable student.

"To him, Marxism was not a conviction, but a religion," says Vodovozov. "In him . . . one sensed that degree of certainty which . . . is incompatible with truly scientific knowledge." Only that sociology is scientific which allows the philistine to retain his inalienable right to hesitate. It is true that Ulyanov, as Vodovozov admits, "was greatly interested in objections to Marxism, studied them and thought about them," but he did so "not for the purpose of seeking out the truth," but only in order to find in those objections error "of whose existence he was convinced *a priori.*" One thing is correct in this description: Ulyanov mastered Marxism as the summation of the previous development of human thought; from this highest level yet attained, he did not wish to descend to a lower one; he fiercely defended what he had thought through to the end and had tested out day after day; and he mistrusted in advance the attempts of self-satisfied ignoramuses and well-read mediocrities to replace Marxism with some other, more-portable theory.

In the fields of technology or medicine, backwardness, dilettantism, and obscurantism meet with the contempt they deserve; in the field of sociology, they invariably claim to embody freedom of scientific inquiry. Those for whom theory is merely an intellectual pastime easily move from one revelation to another or, what is more common, content themselves with a hash made of bits and pieces of all revelations. Immeasurably more exacting, disciplined, and stable is he for whom theory is a guide to action. The drawing-room skeptic may with impunity make fun of medicine. The surgeon, however, cannot function in an atmosphere of scientific hesitation. The more a revolutionary needs a theoretical basis for his action, the more stubbornly he will defend it. Vladimir Ulyanov despised dilettantism and hated obscurantism. He admired in Marxism, above all, the method's power of discipline.

The last books of V. Vorontsov and N. Danielson (published, respectively, under the pseudonyms "V. V." and "Nikolai-on") came out in 1893.[2] Both of these Populist economists proved with enviable obstinacy the impossibility of bourgeois development in Russia at the very time when Russian capitalism was on the verge of a particularly rapid expansion. One doubts whether the faded Populists of that day read the belated revelations of their theoreticians with the same attention as did the young Samara Marxist. Ulyanov had to be familiar with his opponents not just for the purpose of refuting them in print; he sought, above all, to be sure of his own correctness in order to struggle more effectively. It is true that he studied facts polemically, and directed all his arguments against Populism, which he believed to be a living anachronism; but to no one was pure polemics more

foreign than to the future author of twenty-seven volumes of
polemic writings. He had to know life as it was.

The more attention Vladimir paid to the problems of the Russian revolution, the more he learned from Plekhanov and the
more respect he felt for the latter's critical work. The latter-day
falsifiers of the history of Bolshevism speak of "the spontaneous
birth of Marxism on Russian soil without any direct influence
from the émigré group and Plekhanov." (Presnyakov)[3] They
might as well have eliminated Marx himself, that émigré par
excellence, and made Lenin the founder of that home-grown,
truly Russian "Marxism" out of which the theory and practice of
"socialism in one country" were later to grow.[4]

The doctrine of the spontaneous birth of Marxism as a direct
"reflection" of Russia's capitalist development is in itself a malicious caricature of Marxism. Economic processes are reflected
not in "pure" consciousness, with all its natural ignorance, but
in historical consciousness, enriched by all the achievements of
the history of mankind. The class struggle of capitalist society
was able to lead to Marxism in the mid-nineteenth century only
because it had already found a fully prepared dialectical method:
the culmination of classical philosophy in Germany, the political
economy of Adam Smith and David Ricardo in England, and
the revolutionary and socialist doctrines in France, all raised
by the yeast of the great revolution. Thus, the international character of Marxism was inherent in its very sources. The rise of the
kulak class on the Volga and the development of metallurgy in
the Urals were completely insufficient for these same scientific
conclusions to be reached independently. It was not accidental
that the Emancipation of Labor Group was formed abroad:
Russian Marxism came into the world not as an inevitable consequence of Russian capitalism (along with beet sugar and cal-
ico, which, incidentally, required imported machinery). But
rather, it was a complex merger of the entire preceding experience of Russian revolutionary struggle with the theory of scientific socialism which had arisen in the West. The Marxist
generation of the 1890s stood on the foundations laid down by
Plekhanov.

To appreciate fully Lenin's historic contribution, there is certainly no need to make it seem that from his youth he had had

to plow only virgin soil. Yelizarova, following Kamenev and others, writes, "Comprehensive theoretical works were almost nonexistent; it was necessary to study primary sources and base one's conclusions on them. It was in Samara that Vladimir Ulyanov undertook this giant task never before attempted." There could be no greater insult to Lenin's scholarly conscientiousness than to ignore the work of his teachers and predecessors. It is not true that Russian Marxism possessed no comprehensive theoretical works in the early 1890s. The publications of the Emancipation of Labor Group were in themselves a concise encyclopedia of the new trend. After six years of brilliant and heroic struggle against the prejudices of the Russian intelligentsia, Plekhanov proclaimed in 1889 at the International Socialist Congress in Paris: "The revolutionary movement in Russia can triumph only as a revolutionary movement of the workers. We have no other way out, nor can we possibly have one." These words contained the most important generalization of the entire preceding epoch, and it was on the basis of this "émigré" generalization that Vladimir Ulyanov completed his training on the banks of Volga.

Vodovozov recalls that "Lenin spoke of Plekhanov with great sympathy, particularly of *Our Disagreements.*" The sympathy must have been expressed very vividly if Vodovozov was able to remember it for thirty years. The main strength of *Our Disagreements* lies in the fact that it treats questions of revolutionary policy without ever losing sight of the materialist conception of history and the analysis of Russia's economic development. Ulyanov's first Samara attacks on the Populists are thus closely linked with his glowing praise of the work of the founder of the Russian Social Democratic Party. Next to Marx and Engels, Vladimir owed the most to Plekhanov.

Late in 1922, writing on another subject, Lenin said of the early nineties: "Marxism as a trend began to broaden, moving in the direction of the Social Democratic trend which had been proclaimed much earlier in Western Europe by the Emancipation of Labor Group." These lines, which sum up the development of an entire generation, incorporate a particle of Lenin's own biography: he began by using Marxism as an economic and historical doctrine, and then, under the influence of the ideas of the Emancipation of Labor Group (which was far ahead of the Russian intelligentsia's development), he became a Social Democrat. Only the poor in spirit can imagine that they add to Lenin's stature by ascribing to his natural father, the civil counselor Ulyanov, revolutionary views he never held, while minimizing the revolutionary influence of Plekhanov, the émigré whom Lenin himself considered his spiritual father.

In Kazan, in Samara, and in Alakayevka, Vladimir thought of himself primarily as a disciple. But even as great painters in their youth show an independent style even while copying the canvases of old masters, so Vladimir Ulyanov brought to his apprenticeship such a power of intellectual curiosity and initiative that it is difficult to draw a line between the mastering of other people's work and his own independent elaborations. During the last year of the Samara training, this line was completely erased: the pupil had become a scholar.

The dispute with the Populists quite naturally took up the assessment of specific processes: Is capitalism continuing to develop in Russia or is it not? Tables listing factory smokestacks and industrial workers acquired a tendentious meaning, as did tables on the class stratification of the peasantry. In order to ascertain dynamic movements, today's figures had to be compared with yesterday's. Thus, economic statistics became the science of sciences. Columns of figures concealed the answer to the fate of Russia, of her intelligentsia, and of her revolution. The registration of horses, carried out periodically by the Ministry of War, was called upon to provide an answer to the question of who was stronger, Marx or the Russian peasant commune.

The statistical data in Plekhanov's early works could not help but be sparse: *Zemstvo* statistics, which alone were of value in studying the economy of the village, began to be compiled systematically only in the 1880s. Moreover, such materials were not readily accessible to an émigré who in those years was almost completely cut off from Russia. Nevertheless, the general orientation toward scientific processing of statistical data was quite correctly indicated by Plekhanov. The course he charted was to be followed by the first statisticians of the new school. The American professor I. A. Gurvich, himself a native of Russia, published in 1888 and 1892 two monographs on the Russian village, which Vladimir Ulyanov studied and held in high esteem. He himself never failed to note with gratitude the work of his predecessors.

During the last year or so of his life in Samara, statistical compilations occupied a place of honor on Vladimir's desk. Although his major work on the growth of Russian capitalism did not appear until 1889, it was preceded by a considerable number of preliminary theoretical and statistical studies on which he had begun to work back in Samara. From the records of the Samara library just for 1893, a year for which they were accidentally preserved, it may be seen that Vladimir did not miss any publications relevant to his subject, be they official statistical compilations or economic studies by the Populists. He summarized most of these books and articles, and he reported to his closest associates on the most important of them.

Vladimir Ulyanov's oldest surviving study dates back to the last months of his stay in Samara. It is a digest of a recently published book on peasant economy in the south of Russia by a former government official, Postnikov. This article dealt with statistics on the class stratification of the peasantry and the proletarianization of its weakest layers—developments that were particularly noticeable in the South. It reveals the young author's remarkable ability to handle statistical data and to make the details disclose a picture of the whole. The legally published journal for which this carefully and dryly worded article was intended rejected it, most probably because of its Marxist bias—this in spite of the fact that the author had refrained from entering into open polemics with Populism. A copy of the article, given to the student Mitskevich, was confiscated by the police during a search. It was preserved in the archives of the gendarmerie, where it was discovered in 1923 and published thirty years after its writing. This article is the first item in the present edition of Lenin's *Collected Works*.

Was he planning to become a writer, once he had given up the idea of practicing law? It is unlikely that he considered writing as such a goal in life. True, he was a confirmed "doctrinaire": ever since his youth he had understood that even as heavenly bodies cannot be observed without a telescope or bacteria without a microscope, so public affairs must be viewed through the lens of doctrine. But he also knew how to work the other way around and look at doctrine through the isolated fragments of reality; he knew how to observe, question, listen to, and watch life and living people. And he performed these complicated functions as naturally as he breathed. It may well have been that, if only unwittingly, he was preparing to become not a theoretician, not a writer, but a leader.

Back in Kazan, he had served an apprenticeship with revolutionaries of the older generation, people under police surveillance and former deportees. Among them there were many simple-minded people whose development had been arrested and who had no intellectual pretensions. But they had seen, heard, and lived through things the new generation knew nothing of, and this made them significant in their way. Yasneva, the Jacobin, who was nine years older than Vladimir, wrote, "I remember I was surprised to see Vladimir Ilyich listen so attentively and seriously to the simple-minded and sometimes rather quaint reminiscences of V. Yu. Vitten," Livanov's wife and herself an old member of People's Will. Others, gazing at the surface, might notice only what was quaint, whereas Vladimir would sweep away the chaff and select the grain. He seemed to be conducting two conversations simultaneously: the first, an overt one, which depended not only on himself but on his interlocutor as well and contained of necessity much that was superfluous; and the other, an internal and far more significant conversation, which he alone directed. And his slanting eyes would flash, reflecting the one and the other.

In seeming contradiction with Yasneva, Semyonov reports: "Vladimir Ilyich was acquainted with the Livanovs but did not attend their gatherings; instead, he listened very attentively to our tales of the old folks' grumblings." The explanation is that Semyonov's story relates to a later period, perhaps a year later. Vladimir visited the old people as long as they had something to teach him, but to argue to no purpose, continuing the same arguments and losing one's temper, was not in his nature. Once he felt that the chapter of personal relations was closed, he firmly put an end to it. To act in such a way required a great deal of self-control, a quality Vladimir never lacked. Although he stopped seeing the Livanovs, he continued to take an interest in

what was going on in the enemy camp: war requires military intelligence, and Vladimir was already at war with the Populists.
He listened with great attention to the tales told, or rather the
reports made, by those cothinkers of his who were less economi-
cal in their use of time. Here, in this young man of twenty-two,
we observe already a capacity for maneuvering flexibly in the
sphere of personal relations—a trait that is to be observed
throughout his political life. No less remarkable in young Lenin's
intellectual makeup is the wide scope of his observations. The
overwhelming majority of radical intellectuals lived the life of
their little circles, beyond which existed an alien world. Vladimir's vision was not limited by blinders. His interests were unusually wide-ranging, but at the same time he was capable of
the greatest concentration. He studied reality wherever he found
it, and now he transferred his attention from the Populists to the
people. Samara *gubernia* was populated almost entirely by
peasants. The Ulyanovs spent five summers in Alakayevka. Vladimir would never have started by propagandizing the peasants—
even if he had not been paralyzed by his position as a man
under police surveillance in the remote steppe. Therefore, he
observed the village all the more attentively, verifying theoretical assumptions on living material.

It is true that after his brief experience with farming, his personal contact with the peasants was sporadic and distant, but he
knew how to turn his friends' attention in a desired direction and
make use of other men's observations. Sklyarenko, who was close
to him, worked as a clerk for the village judge Samoilov, who,
before the appointment of *zemstvo* chiefs, was totally involved
in peasant litigations. Yelizarov was of Samara peasant stock and
had retained contacts in his native village. To subject Sklyarenko
to an interrogation, to question the village judge himself, to go
with his brother-in-law to the latter's native Bestuzhevka, to talk
for hours with a cunning and self-satisfied *kulak* (Yelizarov's
elder brother)—what an inexhaustible textbook of political
economy and social psychology this was! Vladimir would seize
on a casual but indiscreet remark and slyly urge on the speaker:
he would listen closely, pierce his captive with a glance, chuckle,
or sometimes lean back and laugh, as his father did. The *kulak*
found it flattering to converse with an educated person, a young

lawyer, His Excellency's son, although perhaps it was not always clear to him why his merry interlocutor was laughing as he drank his hot tea.

Vladimir obviously inherited from his father the knack of talking easily to people of different social levels and backgrounds. Without boredom or having to force himself, often without any definite purpose, but simply prompted by his untamable intellectual curiosity and nearly perfect intuition, he was able to extract what he needed from every casual conversationalist. That is why he listened so contentedly when others were bored. None of those around him could guess that his guttural chatter concealed a vast amount of subliminal activity: he was collecting and sorting out impressions, filling the storehouse of his memory with invaluable factual material, using petty facts to verify vast generalizations. The partitions between books and life were thus removed: even at this time, Vladimir had begun to use Marxism as a carpenter uses his saw and ax.

15

·THE YOUNG LENIN

THE innumerable insults that Lenin meted out to opponents, both
to individuals and, later, to entire social classes, have prompted
a number of writers, both journalists and novelists, to portray
him, even in childhood, as a redheaded monster, full of cruelty,
conceit, and vindictiveness. Yevgeni Chirikov, who had been
expelled from Kazan University together with Ulyanov, in a novel
written after the October Revolution, when he was already a member of the White emigration, endowed Vladimir with "pathological vanity and readiness to take offense." Vodovozov relates that
"Vladimir's crude behavior, coarse gestures, acrimonious remarks, etc.—and there were many—greatly shocked Maria Alexandrovna. Often she couldn't help saying, 'Oh, Volodya, Volodya,
how *can* you!' " In actual fact, however, Vladimir was too aware
of his own importance to fall prey to pathological vanity. Further,
he really had no occasion to take offense, because there were all
too few who dared give offense. But there can be no doubt that
Vladimir's rough-edged ruthlessness did not always spare the
vanity of others. According to Yasneva, some opponents "felt
hostile toward him from the very first encounter," and their hostility was intense enough to last through their lifetimes.

The late Vodovozov must be counted among those who had
been insulted once and forever. When he had first arrived in Samara, Vladimir had treated him in a friendly way and helped
him to get settled, but he very soon saw through Vodovozov,
that sterile eclectic who could neither be won over as a partisan
nor taken seriously as an opponent. Their clashes in connection
with aid to victims of the famine and the message to the governor
left their imprint: Vodovozov's irritation with young Ulyanov
has given us several pages of reminiscences in which the author,
to the reader's profit, tells more than he had intended.

In describing Vladimir's appearance, Vodovozov says, "His face as a whole startled one by its odd mixture of intelligence and crudeness. I would say it showed a sort of animality. One's attention was drawn to his forehead—intelligent but sloping. A fleshy nose . . . something stubborn and cruel in these features was combined with undoubted intelligence." In his slanderous novel, Chirikov has some young people of Simbirsk speak as follows about Valdimir Ulyanov: "His hands are always damp! And yesterday he shot a kitten . . . then grabbed it by the tail and threw it over the fence! . . ." Another fairly well-known Russian writer, Kuprin, discovered, although in later years, that Lenin had green eyes "like a monkey."[1] Thus even physical appearance —what one would take to be the aspect least open to question— was subject to tendentious transformation by memory and imagination.

A photograph of 1890 shows a fresh young face in whose calm one senses reserve. The stubborn forehead has not yet been accented by baldness. The small eyes look sharply forth out of Asiatic slits. The cheekbones, too, hint slightly at Asia. Below a broad nose, fleshy lips and a strong chin are lightly covered with a sparse growth that has not yet known scissors or razor. The face is certainly not handsome. But behind these primitive, unpolished features, one is all too clearly aware of the disciplined intellect to admit any suggestion of animality. Vladimir's hands were dry, plebeian in shape, with short fingers—warm and manly hands. For kittens, as for everything weak and defenseless, he displayed the lenient affection of the strong. The literary gentlemen have slandered him!

"In the moral makeup of Vladimir Ilyich," Vodovozov continues, "one was at once struck by a certain amoralism. In my opinion, it was an inborn trait of his character." This amoralism, it turns out, consisted in recognizing that any means was admissible if it led to the desired end. Yes, Ulyanov was no admirer of clerical or Kantian morals, which are allegedly supposed to regulate our lives from celestial heights. His purposes were so great and so far above personal considerations that he openly subordinated his moral criteria to them. He regarded with an ironic indifference, if not with disgust, those cowards and hypocrites who concealed the pettiness of their goals or the shabbiness of their methods behind high principles, which though absolute in theory are quite flexible in practice.

And then Vodovozov suddenly qualifies his statement: "I do not know of any specific facts that prove Lenin's amoralism." However, after digging in his memory, he does recall that his sensitive conscience "was struck by the fact that Lenin was inclined to encourage gossip." Let us bend down and listen to the accuser. Once, in a small group, Vodovozov said that Ulyanov did not hesitate to use arguments he knew to be false, "so long as they lead . . . to success with poorly informed audiences." It turns out, however, that Vodovozov himself "attached no importance" to his own accusation, and soon went to visit the Ulyanovs as though nothing were wrong. However, Vladimir, having heard about the insulting remark from one of his friends, demanded that his guest explain himself. In replying, Vodovozov "tried to tone down his language." The conversation led to a formal reconciliation, but by the spring of 1892 their relations had deteriorated so far that they almost stopped seeing each other.

Banal as it is, this incident is truly remarkable. The moralist accuses the amoralist, behind the latter's back, of deliberately using false arguments. After that, "attaching no importance" to his own insinuation, he goes to pay a friendly visit to the man he has slandered. The amoralist, who is in the habit of attaching importance to what he says, openly demands an explanation. The moralist, with his back to the wall, tries to evade the issue, retreats, and then retracts his own words. On the basis of Vodovozov's own report, one cannot but reach the conclusion that the moralist's actions make him look very much like a none-too-courageous gossip, whereas the amoralist's conduct demonstrates in him precisely the absence of any inclination "to encourage gossip." Let us also add that Vodovozov himself refuted the substance of his accusation that Ulyanov used arguments he knew to be false: writing about Ulyanov in another connection, he stated that "a deep conviction that he was right was felt in all his speeches." Let us remember this entire incident: it will serve us well as the key to the many conflicts in which hypocrites accused the revolutionary of lack of moral scruples.

No letters by or about Vladimir, nor any other human-interest stories, have been preserved from the Samara period. The opinions of both friends and foes are all stated in retrospect and have inevitably been colored by the powerful influence of the Soviet period. Nevertheless, whether taken together or juxtaposed, they often allow us to restore Lenin at least partly as he was at the dawn of his revolutionary career.

First of all, it should be noted that Vladimir Ulyanov bore no resemblance at all to the classic type of Russian nihilist encountered not only in reactionary novels but occasionally in real life as well—with a wild shock of unkempt hair, untidy clothes, and a gnarled walking stick. "His hairline had already begun to recede quite a bit," as Semyonov recalls. There was nothing startling or defiant either in his clothing or in his manners. Sergievsky, who belongs to roughly the same Marxist generation, gives an interesting description of Vladimir at the end of the Samara period: ". . . a modest man, neatly and, as they say, properly but unpretentiously dressed, with nothing about him to attract the attention of the man in the street. This protective coloration appealed to me. . . . I did not notice at the time the sly expression which later, after deportation, attracted my attention. . . . He seemed careful, looking around keenly, observant, calm, restrained, despite the temperamental nature I was already familiar with from his letters. . . ."

In passing, Semyonov offers a vignette of the mores of Samara's radical youth. Upon arriving in Sklyarenko's apartment, Ulyanov would stretch out on the bed, "first putting a newspaper under his feet," and start listening to the conversations around the samovar. Someone's opinion would make him raise his voice. "Nonsense," came the voice from the bed, and then a systematic refutation would ensue. The unpraiseworthy habit of sitting or lying down on someone else's bed was common among young people and stemmed both from simplicity of manners and from the shortage of chairs. If anything distinguished Vladimir from the others it was the fact that he put a newspaper under his feet. The abruptness of his remarks reflected the irreconcilability of his opposition, and served as a means of forcing his opponent to show his true colors.

In these talks around the samovar or in a rowboat on the Volga, Ulyanov, after having thoroughly studied Engels' *Anti-Duehring,* that polemical encyclopedia of Marxism, tirelessly cleansed meta-physical values out of young minds. Justice? A myth to conceal that might is right. Absolute principles? Morality is the servant of material interests. State power? The executive committee of the exploiters. Revolution? Be kind enough to specify, bour-geois revolution. It is in these and similar pronouncements, which shattered the fine porcelain of idealism, that we must, apparently, seek the key to Ulyanov's early reputation as an "amoralist." The listeners, who had been taught otherwise at school, were amazed and tried to protest. That was all the young athlete needed. "Sophistry?" "Paradoxes?" Friendly blows rained right and left. The opponent, taken by surprise, might grow si-lent, occasionally even forgetting to shut his mouth, then look for the books cited by Ulyanov, and later still he might even de-clare himself to be a Marxist.

In his debates with the Jacobins and members of People's Will, Vladimir, a star in the growing Marxist clan, used the Socratic method. "All right, you have seized power, and what comes then?" he would ask his opponent. "Decrees!" "And who would be your support?" "The people!" "And who are the 'people'?" This would be followed by an analysis of class contradictions. By the end of the Samara period, a manuscript by Ulyanov was circulating among the young. It was entitled A *Dispute Between a Social Democrat and a Populist,* and most likely was a summary of Samara disputes presented in dialogue form. Unfortunately, the paper has been lost.

Vladimir argued passionately—he did everything with pas-sion—but not indiscriminately and not without forethought. He was in no hurry to enter the fray, did not interrupt, did not try to outshout the others, but allowed his opponent to have his say even when he was shaking with indignation, noted carefully the weaknesses in his opponent's arguments, and then rushed mag-nificently into a headlong attack. But even in the fiercest blows dealt out by the young polemicist, there was nothing personal. He attacked ideas or the unscrupulous use of ideas; he hit the person only indirectly. It was now the opponent's turn to be si-lent. While not interrupting others, Vladimir did not allow them to interrupt him. As in a game of chess, he never retracted any moves or allowed others to do so.

Maria Ulyanova's remark that Vladimir's shyness was a family trait seems strange. This lack of psychological insight, which is apparent in much of the younger sister's testimony, calls for caution, the more so since it was natural for her to try to find in Lenin as many "family" traits as possible. True, the photograph of 1890, with which we are already familiar, does seem to hint at a conflict between shyness and a self-assurance as yet not fully developed. It looks as though the young man felt awkward in the presence of a photographer or had unwillingly given in to him, just as thirty years later Lenin was to feel shy about dictating his letters and articles to a stenographer. If this is "shyness," it certainly does not imply either a sense of weakness or excessive sensitivity; it conceals strength. Its purpose is to protect his inner world from overly close contacts and unwanted intimacy.

A trait that is called by the same name may, in different members of the family, not only vary greatly but become its own opposite. The shyness of Alexander, noted by all those close to him, is quite in line with his generally self-contained and reticent personality. Alexander was certainly embarrassed by his superiority when he was aware of it. But this is the very trait that separated him from his younger brother, who without hesitation, let it become apparent that he was bigger than others. It could even be said that Vladimir's aggressive turn of mind, being fully subordinated to ideas and free of any personal vanity, in a sense freed him from the restraints of shyness. In any event, even if he did sometimes, particularly in his youth, feel the constraint of embarrassment, it was not for himself but for others—because of their banal interests, their vulgar jokes, and sometimes because of their stupidity. Samoilov has shown us Vladimir surrounded by strangers: "He spoke little, but this apparently was not at all because he felt ill at ease in unfamiliar surroundings." On the contrary, his presence put others on their guard; people inclined to take too many liberties began to behave with a degree of caution, if not timidity.

The elder sister told us earlier that Alexander's comrades restrained themselves in his presence, and that they "were embarrassed to talk nonsense in front of him, looked to him, and awaited his verdict." Different as the brothers' personalities were, in this respect Vladimir acted toward others "like Sasha": he forced them to rise above themselves. Semyonov writes that "even in his youth, Vladimir Ilyich was alien to any kind of bohemianism . . . and in his presence all of us, who comprised Sklyarenko's group, seemed to pull ourselves together . . . ; idle chatter and coarse joking were out of the question in his presence." What invaluable testimony! Vladimir was capable of using a down-to-earth expression in the heat of debate or in a description of an enemy, but he did not tolerate in himself the vulgar hints, trivial jokes, or dirty stories that are so common among young men. This was not because he adhered to any rules of asceticism—this "amoralist" did not need the threat of the transcendent whip—nor was it because by nature he was indifferent to other than the political side of life. No, nothing human was alien to him. True, we have no stories whatsoever about young Ulyanov's attitude toward women. There probably were courtships and infatuations: otherwise he would hardly have sung of beautiful eyes, even if his emotion was masked by irony. But even without knowing the details, one can say with assurance that young Vladimir's pure attitude toward women remained unchanged for the rest of his life. It was not because of a cold disposition that his spiritual makeup had an almost Spartan tinge. On the contrary, passion was the basis of his nature. But it was supplemented by—I find it difficult to think of another word—chastity.[2] The natural merger or these two elements, passion and chastity, precludes any idea of immorality or impropriety. Vladimir had no need of any moral shackles in order to rise above others: his inborn revulsion from vulgarity and triviality sufficed.

It is also Vodovozov who attests that in the Samara Marxist group Vladimir was "an unquestioned authority—they almost idolized him, just as his family did," even though some were older than he. "His authority in the group was beyond question," Semyonov agrees. Lalayants wrote that Ulyanov, whom he met a year after the incident with Vodovozov, won him over at once. "This man of twenty-three was a most remarkable combination of simplicity, sensitivity, love of life, and enthusiasm on the one hand, and of firm and profound knowledge and merciless logical consistency . . . on the other." After their very first meeting, Lalayants was glad that he had chosen Samara as his place of residence while under police surveillance.

To elicit such contradictory impressions is a privilege of the elect. It is unlikely that even in his youth Ulyanov was inclined to complain of other people's partiality. The emotions he aroused were too much like inductive currents flowing from his own partiality. To him, a person was not an end in himself, but a tool. "In his dealings with people," Semyonov writes, "sharp differences were readily discerned. With comrades whom he believed shared his views he argued gently, with good-natured joking . . . , but if he decided that his opponent represented another ideology . . . his polemical fire was merciless. He hit the opponent where it hurt most and was very free in his choice of expressions." This observation by a companion of his youth is of paramount importance for the understanding of Lenin.

His "partial," since utilitarian, approach to people flowed from the deepest sources of his nature, which were wholly directed toward a transformation of the external world. Even if there was some calculation in this—and there certainly was, and, as time went on, it became more farsighted and sophisticated—it could not be separated from true feeling. Lenin very easily "fell in love" with people when they showed him their valuable and important features. But he was not to be won over by any personal qualities in the case of an enemy. His attitude toward the same people changed radically, depending on whether at a given moment they were on his side or against him. In such "falling in love" and in the period of hostility that succeeded it, there was not a trace of superficiality, whim, or vanity. His code of justice was the laws of struggle. It is for that reason that one often finds startling contradictions even in his published comments on different people, and yet in all these contradictions Lenin remained true to himself.

Individualist gentlemen proclaim that personality is an end in itself, but this does not prevent them in practice from being guided by their tastes in their attitudes toward people, if not indeed by the state of their liver. The great historical task to which our "amoralist" dedicated himself ennobled his attitude toward people; in practice, he applied to them the same yardstick he applied to himself. Partiality dictated by the interests of the cause became, in the last analysis, the highest kind of impartiality, and this rare quality—truly an attribute of a leader—imparted to Lenin an extraordinary authoritativeness even during his youth.

Semyonov, who was perhaps three years older than Vladimir, once remarked in a general talk about himself and his friends that they had little understanding of Marxism, because they were not sufficiently familiar with history and bourgeois economy. Vladimir replied briefly and sternly: "If you are poor at *that,* you are poor at *everything*—you must study. . . ." When it came to major questions, this simple and cheerful youth spoke as one who wielded power. And the others fell silent, anxiously searching their souls.

This same Semyonov reports with what assurance and firmness Vladimir refuted unconvincing arguments advanced by his brother-in-law Yelizarov, who tried to lend his support in a dispute with Vodovozov. No, he was not shy! It should be borne in mind, moreover, that both Yelizarov, who idolized Vladimir, and Vodovozov, who took a dislike to him, were six years older than he, if not more. When it came to revolutionary ideas, Vladimir did not recognize friendship or kinship, let alone respect for age.

According to Vodovozov, at the age of twenty-two Ulyanov gave the impression of a "politically fully formed and mature person." Semyonov, for his part, writes: "Even then Vladimir Ilyich already seemed a man whose views were completely formed, and who conducted himself at group gatherings . . . with assurance and complete independence." The future economist of the Menshevik Party, P. P. Maslov, then a university student, heard from visitors who came to see him in a village of Ufa *gubernia,* where he was being held under police surveillance, that there lived in Samara a certain Vladimir Ulyanov, who "also takes an interest" in economic questions and who is, moreover, "a person of outstanding intelligence and erudition." On reading a manuscript sent to him by Ulyanov—in those days Russian Marxism did not yet have access to a printing press—Maslov was particularly struck by "the categorical and definite formulation of his basic ideas, indicative of a man with fully formed views."[3]

Even during the Samara period, the term "old man," which in the future was to become Lenin's nickname, begins in some strange way to be associated with the figure of the young Vladimir. And yet neither in his youth nor until the end of his life was there anything about him that smacked of old age, except, perhaps, his baldness. What was impressive about the young man was the maturity of his thought, the balance of his intellectual forces, the sureness of his attack. "Of course," says Vodovozov, "I did not foresee the part he was destined to play, but even then I was convinced, and said so openly, that Ulyanov's role would be a major one."

The heretical doctrine had in the meantime succeeded in winning over adherents in the groups of Samara youth and received something approaching official recognition in radical circles. Populism, which continued as the dominant political tendency, had to give it a little room. Social Democratic propaganda among students was conducted chiefly by Sklyarenko, a gifted but rather restless youth. In March of 1893, Lalayants, a Kazan University student and former comrade of Fedoseyev, arrived in Samara. He was sent there to reside under police surveillance. Almost immediately, Lalayants struck up a close friendship with Ulyanov and Sklyarenko. The three comprised—true, only for a few months—Samara's Marxist general staff. Vladimir took no part in propaganda work. Lalayants states outright: "In Samara, at least during my stay there, he did not join any circles and did not conduct any courses in them." The general direction, on the other hand, was decidedly in his hands. The *troika* met frequently: now in Sklyarenko's apartment, now in one of the Samara beer halls, of which Sklyarenko was overly fond. Ulyanov told his friends about his writings and learned from them about the latest events in the Samara circles. Theoretical disputes frequently broke out among them, but even then it was turning out that Ulyanov had the last word. In the summer, Sklyarenko would pay visits to Alakayevka, where everyone liked him because of his gregariousness and cheerful disposition, and where he would gather a supply of new ideas to take back to seminary students and girls in the Nursing School. Both Sklyarenko and Lalayants subsequently became prominent Bolsheviks.[4]

By this time Vladimir had also definitely succeeded in winning over Preobrazhensky, the onetime organizer of a farming commune, with whom he frequently, while engrossed in impassioned debate, paced off the nearly mile-long distance between their two villages. Preobrazhensky was later active in Samara's Social Democratic organization, and many years later, under the Soviet regime, he was in charge of Gorki—that same estate where the leader of Soviet Russia rested, became ill, and died. In general, contacts formed in his youth occupied an important place in Lenin's life.

From provincial life on the Volga, Vladimir extracted everything it had to offer. Toward the end of the winter of 1892–93, according to Yelizarova, "he was sometimes quite bored, eager to go to some livelier city. . . ." But since it made little sense to leave Alakayevka during the summer, his departure was postponed until the autumn. At this time, his younger brother was about to graduate from high school and was planning to enter Moscow University. Maria Alexandrovna intended to follow Dimitri and move to Moscow, just as she had moved to Kazan six years earlier to follow Vladimir. The time had come to leave his family. St. Petersburg, the most European of Russian cities, attracted Vladimir far more than did Moscow, which was then "a big village." Moreover, by living apart from his family he ran less risk of having his revolutionary work cast a shadow over his brother and sisters.

The last months in Samara and Alakayevka were filled with active preparations for the departure. Vladimir summarized books and articles, grouped together his most important conclusions, drafted polemical studies. He checked, polished, and sharpened the weapons he would soon have to put to active use. The critical movement in the minds of the intelligentsia, like the more profound movement in the industrial areas, required a doctrine, a program, an instructor. The wheel of Russian history began to turn faster. The time had come to say good-by to Samara, to Alakayevka, and to the avenue of linden trees. Vladimir Ulyanov left his provincial hide-out to find himself standing head and shoulders above his generation as soon as he appeared in the arena of the capital.

It is thus, between his brother's execution and the move to St. Petersburg, in these simultaneously short and long six years of stubborn work, that the future Lenin was formed. He was still to make great strides forward, not only externally but internally; several clearly delineated stages can be seen in his later development. But all the fundamental features of his personality, his outlook on life, and his mode of action were already formed during the interval between the seventeenth and twenty-third years of his life.

NOTES

CHAPTER 1

1. Trotsky is mistaken. The division of Russia into eight administrative units (*gubernii*), each of them headed by a governor, was accomplished in 1708, i.e. during the reign of Peter the Great. (Ed.)

2. After Lenin's death in 1924 the city was renamed Ulyanovsk. (Ed.)

3. Subsequently renamed Stalingrad, and more recently Volgograd. (Ed.)

4. Subsequently renamed Kuibyshev. (Ed.)

5. Pronounced Pugachov. (Trans.)

6. Trotsky is imprecise. The Table of Ranks, promulgated in 1722 by Peter the Great, established the hierarchy of fourteen ranks in three parallel branches of government service, i.e. military, civil, and court. Upon promotion to the eighth rank (in military service the rank of major), a commoner would achieve the status of a nobleman. Thus, in the words of the great Russian historian V. O. Kliuchevsky, ". . . government service opened the ranks of the nobility to everybody"—at least in theory. (Ed.)

7. Until the abolition of serfdom in 1861, peasants could be disposed of like any other property. Fraudulent commerce in serfs inspired a great Russian novel, Nikolai Gogol's *Dead Souls* (1837). (Ed.)

8. Institutions of local government established in 1864. Elected on a restricted franchise, the *zemstvos* enjoyed a measure of authority in such fields as education and public health. (Ed.)

9. Following the bloody suppression of the 1863 Polish uprising, numerous Poles were exiled to Siberia as well as to the Russian provinces. (Ed.)

CHAPTER 2

1. Lenin's ethnic background has long been a matter of dispute among non-Soviet biographers. Robert Payne in his massive *Lenin* (New York, 1964) maintains that Lenin's father was not of Slavic, but of Chuvash ancestry, i.e., descended from a Turkic-speaking minority in the North of European Russia. As for Lenin's mother, she is said to be of Northern European stock. Payne concludes: "He [Lenin] was German, Swedish, and Chuvash, and there was not a drop of Russian blood in him." Other biographers suggest that the mystery surrounding the origins of Lenin's maternal grandfather has its source in the "embarrassing" fact that he was of Jewish descent. (Ed.)

CHAPTER 3

1. Nikolai Chernyshevsky (1828–89), author of *What Is to Be Done,* the famous programatic novel, is one of the foremost figures in the history of Russian radical thought. (Ed.)

2. Sergei Nechayev (1847–82), an anarchist revolutionary, proponent of ruthless terror and absolute conspiracy. His famous *Catechism of a Revolutionary* advanced the idea that for the sake of the cause a true revolutionary should disregard all rules of elementary human decency. Some of Nechayev's ideas are reflected in Dostoyevsky's *The Possessed.* (Ed.)

3. Situated less than 30 miles from St. Petersburg, Gatchina was a favorite residence of Russia's emperors during the nineteenth century. (Ed.)

CHAPTER 4

1. Nikolai Nekrasov (1821–77) described his poetry as inspired by the muse of "sadness and vengeance." His verse, most of it describing the ordeal of Russia's peasantry, was held in high esteem by the revolutionary intelligentsia. (Ed.)

2. Alexander Herzen (1812–70), editor of *Kolokol* (The Bell), the first émigré Russian newspaper, and author of *My Past and Thoughts,* is sometimes described as the founder of Russia's liberal socialist tradition. (Ed.)

3. The earlier reference was to Dimitri Minayev (1835–89), not to Polezhayev. Alexander Poleshayev (1804–38) was a romantic poet, whose irreverent and playful poem *Sashka* enjoyed great popularity with Russian students. Trotsky obviously meant Minayev. (Ed.)

4. Semyon Nadson (1862–87) wrote impassioned "civic" verse. (Ed.)

5. Mikhail Saltykov-Shchedrin (1826–89), Russia's foremost social satirist. (Ed.)

6. Yevgeni Chirikov (1864–1932), a radical novelist. (Ed.)

7. Dimitri Mendeleyev (1834–1907), a chemist, creator of the periodic table of the elements. (Ed.)

CHAPTER 5

1. Konstantin Pobedonostsev (1827–1907), the reactionary statesman, is sometimes credited with inspiring Alexander III's repressive policies. (Ed.)

2. Presumably for the abolition of serfdom. (Ed.)

3. Mikhail Katkov (1818–87), conservative writer and editor. (Ed.)

4. Konstantin Kavelin (1818–85), historian and philosopher, was a rather "radical" liberal for his time, advocating emancipation of peasants with land allotments, full equality of women, and strong local government. (Ed.)

5. Pyotr Yakubovich (1860–1911), a minor poet and prose writer and a member of the radical terrorist wing of the Populists. (Ed.)

6. Gleb Uspensky (1843–1902) was a journalist and novelist best remembered for his portrayals of peasants and the city poor. (Ed.)

7. Isaak Levitan (1860–1900), the foremost painter of Russian landscape. (Ed.)

8. Vladimir Solovyov (1853–1900), a poet and liberal theologian, one of the early proponents of ecumenical reconciliation of Christendom. (Ed.)

CHAPTER 6

1. Nikolai Dobrolyubov (1836–61), a radical literary critic. (Ed.)

2. Jozef Pilsudski (1867–1935), once active in the Russian revolutionary movement and then in the Polish Socialist Party, led the struggle for Polish independence and subsequently became the Head of the Polish State. During his tenure of office Poland fought a victorious war against the Soviet Republic, whose War Commissar was Trotsky. (Ed.)

CHAPTER 7

1. See Editor's note 1 to Chapter 2.

2. Mikhail Bakunin (1814–76), a leader and theoretician of anarchism. (Ed.)

3. Vissarion Belinsky (1811–48), a radical critic, founder of sociopolitical literary criticism in Russia. (Ed.)

4. Yuli Martov (pseudonym of Tsederbaum, 1873–1923), a Social Democrat, broke with Lenin in 1903. In 1920 Martov left Soviet Russia, never to return. *A Blue Notebook*, a novel published in 1961 by the Soviet writer Emmanuel Kazakevich, was severely criticized for suggesting that Martov's departure was arranged with the approval of Lenin, who, in spite of disagreements, retained a fondness for his former associate. Such "sentimentality," Soviet critics maintained, was completely alien to Lenin. (Ed.)

5. Nadezhda Krupskaya (1869–1939), Lenin's wife and an important figure in the Communist movement in her own right. (Ed.)

6. Fyodor Kerensky, the father of Alexander Kerensky (1881–1970), the future prime minister of the democratic provisional government who was deposed as a result of Lenin's *coup d'état* of November 7, 1917. (Ed.)

7. Gleb Krzhizhanovsky (1872–1959), revolutionary and promulgator of plans for a huge expansion in the Soviet output of electric power. (Ed.)

8. Panteleimon Lepeshinsky (1868–1944), a historian of the Soviet Communist Party, was himself a son of a priest. (Ed.)

CHAPTER 8

1. *Duma* was the city council. (Ed.)
2. Nikolai Lobachevsky (1793–1856), a mathematician, was Kazan University's rector from 1827 to 1846. (Ed.)
3. Leonid Krasin (1870–1926) was subsequently active in Soviet diplomatic service and in economic management. (Ed.)

CHAPTER 9

1. Anatoli Lunacharsky (1873–1933), the first Soviet Commissar for Education. (Ed.)
2. Andrei Zhelyabov (1851–81), one of the leaders of the People's Will, executed for participation in the assassination of Alexander II. (Ed.)
3. Nikolai Pirogov (1810–81), surgeon and liberal educator, probably the most famous figure in the history of Russian medicine. (Ed.)
4. Konstantin Ushinsky (1824–70), an educational theoretician and one of the founders of universal primary schooling in Russia. (Ed.)
5. Modest Korf (1800–76), a historian and jurist, for a time director of the Imperial Public Library. (Ed.)
6. Yevgeni Chirikov (1864–1932), a radical novelist, left Russia after 1917. (Ed.)
7. The word's literal meaning is, roughly, "manliness." (Ed.)
8. English in the original. (Ed.)
9. The Russian terms used were *neudachnik* and *svershitel*. (Ed.)
10. Lev Kamenev (real name Rozenfeld, 1883–1936), a Bolshevik leader and close associate of Lenin. Though allied with Stalin against Trotsky after Lenin's death, he was ultimately sentenced to death, thus joining in the fate of most of the old Bolsheviks.

The publication of Lenin's complete writings represents one of the most impressive chapters in the history of world publishing. Between 1920 and 1965, there were *five* different Russian-language editions of Lenin's works, the latest in fifty-five volumes. In addition, over the years, thirty-six *Lenin Almanacs* were brought out.

The various editions of Lenin's collected works (each claiming to be "complete"), not unexpectedly reflected the political exigencies of different periods in Soviet history. This resulted in a number of "suppressed works," the most notorious of these being Lenin's "testament," which warned the Party not to allow Stalin to become its secretary general. The "testament," though widely known as an "apocryphal" work, was admitted into the "canonical" body of Lenin's writings only after Stalin's death. (Ed.)
11. Yuri Steklov (pseudonym of Nakhamkes, 1873–1941) was also the

author of a four-volume monograph on Mikhail Bakunin, the anarchist leader and theoretician. Arrested in the mid-1930s, Steklov died in a Soviet prison. (Ed.)

CHAPTER 10

1. Ivan Delyanov (1818–97), Minister of Education from 1882 to 1897, known for a number of reactionary reforms (closing down the Women's University, restricting admission of "children of coachmen, laundresses, small shopkeepers, etc.," and establishing discriminatory admission quotas for the Jews). (Ed.)

2. Sergei Witte (1849–1915), Minister of Finance (1892–1903) and Prime Minister (1903–6). A moderate, he was suspect by both right-wing conservatives and liberals, as well as by Nicholas II, who ultimately dismissed him. (Ed.)

3. Karl Radek (pseudonym of Sobelsohn, 1885–1939), a Communist journalist and a leading figure in the Communist International, died in a Stalinist prison. (Ed.)

4. Isaak Lalayants (Party nickname "Izorov," 1870–1933) was a member of N. E. Fedoseyev's circle. Imprisoned for his revolutionary activities, after 1917 he occupied minor posts in the Soviet Ministry of Education. Lalayants wrote two volumes of reminiscences, entitled *At the Sources of Bolshevism* (*U istokov bol'shevizma*, 1930–32). (Ed.)

5. Ivan Skvortsov-Stepanov (1870–1928), an active Social Democrat, after 1917 occupied a number of important posts. An economist and historian of the revolutionary movement, he is the author of a monograph on the Paris Commune of 1871, and translated *Das Kapital* into Russian. (Ed.)

6. Trotsky uses the derogatory term *kulak*. (Ed.)

7. Trotsky's sarcasm is directed at the idealized portrayals of young Lenin in Soviet literature and politically inspired "folklore." Though already numerous in the 1930s, examples of such art have multiplied in the decades following, particularly in connection with the centennial of Lenin's birth in 1970. (Ed.)

CHAPTER 11

1. Yakutsk is a city in Eastern Siberia. (Ed.)

2. The Kara Sea is part of the Arctic Ocean, off the shores of Western Siberia. (Ed.)

3. Paradoxically, Nikolai Danielson (1844–1918), an economist by training, never became a "true" Marxist. (Ed.)

4. Pyotr Lavrov (1823–1900), the leader of Populism. (Ed.)

5. August Haxthausen (1792–1866), author of *Studien über die inneren Zustände, das Volksleben und insbesondere die ländliche Einrichtungen*

Russlands (1847–52); the book's Russian translation appeared in 1870. Haxthausen's study emphasized Russia's lack of preparedness for an economic system based on free hired labor, and advocated a gradual abolition of serfdom, which, it claimed, would also avert the creation of an impoverished urban proletariat. Haxthausen viewed serfdom as a system of peasant communes headed by landowners. (Ed.)

6. Lev Deutsch (1855–1943) was later a founder, together with Akselrod and Plekhanov, of the first Russian Marxist group, the Emancipation of Labor, and ultimately became a Menshevik. (Ed.)

7. Pavel Akselrod (1850–1928), later a cofounder together with Deutsch and Plekhanov of the first Russian Marxist group, the Emancipation of Labor, ultimately became a right-wing Menshevik and advocated abandonment of illegal political activities and concentration on trade-union activity. Vera Zasulich (1849–1919), a revolutionary and terrorist, was later a leader in the Emancipation of Labor group, and toward the end of her life a Menshevik. Zasulich was a Russian translator of Marx and Engels. (Ed.)

8. Ferdinand Lassalle (1825–64), German Socialist, founder, in 1863, of Germany's first workers' party. (Ed.)

9. Nikolai Shelgunov (1824–91), liberal writer and journalist, advocate of general education, emancipation of women, etc. (Ed.)

10. August Bebel (1840–1913), a German Socialist, best known for his 1883 treatise *Women and Socialism.* (Ed.)

11. John Burns (1858–1943), a British Socialist, ultimately became a member of the Cabinet (1903–14). (Ed.)

12. Jules Guesde (pseudonym of Basile, 1845–1922), French Socialist. Though a Marxist, he served in the Cabinet during World War I. (Ed.)

13. Paul Lafargue (1842–1911), French Socialist theoretician, author of *The Religion of Capital* (1887) and *The Evolution of Property from Savagery to Civilization* (1891), and son-in-law of Karl Marx. (Ed.)

CHAPTER 12

1. Nikolai Mikhailovsky (1842–1904), sociologist and literary critic, foremost theoretician of Populism. (Ed.)

2. Presumably refers to Frederick Winslow Taylor (1856–1915), an American industrial engineer and efficiency expert sometimes called the father of "scientific management." (Ed.)

CHAPTER 13

1. Pyotr Lavrov (1823–1900), a leader of the Populists, also had a serious scholarly interest in ethics and published widely on the subject. (Ed.)

2. Jean Paul Marat (1743–93), one of the most radical leaders in the French Revolution of 1789. (Ed.)

CHAPTER 14

1. Vladimir Adoratsky (1878–1945) directed the Institute from 1931 to 1939. He was editor of the 15-volume Russian edition of the collected works of Marx and Engels, and a member of the editorial board of Lenin's collected works. (Ed.)

2. Vasili Vorontsov (1847–1918), a liberal Populist economist, held that, unlike in Western Europe, in Russia capitalism was neither desirable nor possible, and therefore Marxism, which ignored such specifically Russian institutions as the peasant commune, is unsuitable for Russia. Nikolai Danielson (1844–1918), the Russian translator of *Das Kapital*, arrived at similar conclusions, although his opposition to capitalism in Russia was based largely on the belief that foreign markets are necessary for successful capitalist development, and that these were already captured by the industrial countries of Western Europe. It should be emphasized that both Vorontsov and Danielson found Marxism a useful doctrine—but, unfortunately, inapplicable to Russia. (Ed.)

3. Alexander Presnyakov (1870–1929), Soviet historian. Primarily a medievalist, he also wrote about the Russian revolutionary movement. (Ed.)

4. The slogans of "socialism in one country" and of the "permanent revolution" came to symbolize the struggle between Stalin and Trotsky. (Ed.)

CHAPTER 15

1. Alexander Kuprin (1870–1938), a leading Russian novelist and short-story writer, ultimately returned to the USSR, where he died a year later. Needless to say, his uncomplimentary reference to Lenin is not to be found in any Soviet source, including the nine-volume set of Kuprin's writings brought out in 1964. (Ed.)

2. Trotsky's term, *tselomudrie*, is defined in Dal's standard dictionary of Russian as "purity of the flesh" and "the virtue of retaining virginal or marital purity, of being immaculate." (Ed.)

3. Pyotr Maslov (1867–1946), though a Menshevik before 1917, remained in the USSR, where he continued his scholarly career. In 1929 he was elected a member of the USSR Academy of Sciences. Since Maslov's memoirs were almost certainly written after 1917, Trotsky's characterization of him as a Menshevik is misleading. (Ed.)

4. Aleksei Sklyarenko (1870–1916) was active in Party journalism. He died before the Revolution. (Ed.)

INDEX

Aborigines, non-Russian peasants in Simbirsk *gubernia*, 3

Adoratsky, Vladimir, 185, 214

Agrarian crisis (1880s), 48–49. *See also* Famine

Akselrod, Pavel, 144, 147, 160, 173, 213

Alakayevka (village), 134–38, 177, 183–86, 187, 191, 194, 205, 206

Alexander I, Tsar, 97

Alexander II, Tsar, 40, 139, 148; assassination of, 26, 27, 32, 35–36, 41, 51, 58, 79

Alexander III, Tsar, 36, 47–48, 49, 50, 58, 139, 147, 171, 209; Alexander Ulyanov and attempt on life of, 61–69, 116, 140; described, 50, 65; famine of 1891–92 and, 171, 172; reactionary reign of, 139–53; statue by Trubetskoy of, 51

Ananyina (student), and Alexander Ulyanov and attempt on life of Alexander III, 64

Anarchism (anarchists), 35. *See also* Bakunin, Mikhail, and Bakuninism; Terrorism (terrorists); specific aspects, individuals

Andreyevsky (rector, St. Petersburg University), 98

Andreyushkin, and Alexander Ulyanov and attempt on life of Alexander III, 62–63, 68

Anti-Duehring (Engels), 131, 165, 199–200

Arefyev, Lenin's legal victory over, 179

Aristocracy (nobility), 2, 3–4, 6–8, 9, 10, 11, 13, 18, 24, 47–56, 139, 147; Table of Ranks, 6, 208

Arson, 11–12

Art (1880s), 53–55

Assassination(s), 26, 27, 31–32, 33, 35–36, 47–48, 58, 60–69. *See also* Terrorism (terrorists); specific individuals

Astrakhan, 13, 14, 21, 70

Bakunin, Mikhail, and Bakuninism, 9, 28–29, 30, 72, 103, 143, 149, 152, 212

Bebel, August, 151, 213

Belinsky, Vissarion, 76

Beloriztsy (religious sect), 5

Berlin: Congress of (1879), 32; Lenin in, 170

Bestuzhevka (village), 179, 194

Bismarck, Otto, Prince von, 146

Black Redistribution (*Chorny Peredel*), 33, 42, 143–44

Blank family, and Lenin's ancestry, 19, 71, 120. *See also* specific individuals

Blank, Maria Alexandrovna. *See* Ulyanov, Maria Alexandrovna Blank

Bogolyubov, and Trepov shooting, 31

Bolshevism, 145, 152. *See also* Communism

Bourgeoisie, 15, 24, 49, 54, 56, 114–15, 141, 144 ff., 147, 155, 188, 204

Boyars, 2, 3

Brusnev, and students in revolutionary movement, 140, 151, 168

Buchholtz, and debates with Lenin, 162–63

Buckle, Henry Thomas, 52

Bureaucracy, 6–8, 13, 20, 24, 26, 104, 106, 114–15, 139. *See also* Zemstvos

Burns, John, 152, 213

N